DATE			

Counseling
and
Social Support

To my kith and kin
whose support (recognized and unrecognized)
sustains me. Most especially, to Ann.

Counseling
and
Social Support
Perspectives and Practice

Richard E. Pearson

Foreword by George M. Gazda

SAGE PUBLICATIONS
The International Professional Publishers
Newbury Park   London   New Delhi

847 29880

For information address:

SAGE Publications, Inc.
2111 West Hillcrest Drive
Newbury Park, California 91320

SAGE Publications Ltd.
28 Banner Street
London EC1Y 8QE
England

SAGE Publications Pvt. Ltd.
M-32 Market
Greater Kailash I
New Delhi 110 048 India

Printed in the United States of America

Library of Congress Cataloging-in-Publication Data

Pearson, Richard E., 1937–
 Counseling and social suport : perspectives and practice /
Richard E. Pearson.
  p. cm.
 Includes bibliographical references.
 ISBN 0-8039-3210-3. — ISBN 0-8039-3211-1 (pbk.)
 1. Counseling. 2. Social networks. I. Title.
BF637.C6P327 1990
361.3'23 — dc20

                                        89-27911
                                        CIP

FIRST PRINTING, 1990

Contents

Foreword   7

1. Introductory Perspectives   9
2. When Are Social Support Issues Important?   24
3. Assessment of Social Support Resources   44
4. Client-Based Barriers   72
5. Client-Focused Interventions   95
6. Other- and Context-Based Barriers   122
7. Externally Focused Support Interventions   143
8. Ansel: A Case Study   177
9. Other Directions   201

Appendix A: Personal Support System
    Survey Form   223

Appendix B: Rose's Personal Support System
    Survey Protocol   234

Appendix C: Ansel's Personal Support System
    Survey Protocol   245

References   256

Index   266

About the Author   271

Foreword

In Pearson's conclusion of this text, he asks himself, "So what's new about all this?" This is an appropriate question because, as he answers his own question, social support is not a new phenomenon. What is new is the wide ranging renewed interest in the interactive effects of social conditions on the human condition. Illustrative of this interest is the rapid expansion of self-help groups — probably the most rapidly expanding movement related to the health professions. No less important is the current phenomenal growth of the social skills training movement which is rapidly replacing the traditional *interview* group counseling/therapy interventions. Also, the popularity of the family systems approach to family therapy illustrates Pearson's expression of our need to work with natural systems. It is, therefore, timely that Pearson redirects our attention to the fundamental relationship between the functioning of the individual and his or her natural and social support systems. My speculation is that counselors have recognized, but turned away from, accepting this phenomenon because of the feeling of futility in effecting change in our complex social structure. Instead, the focus has been on trying to help clients adapt to the system.

In Chapter 1 Pearson states that the primary objective of this book is "the consideration and extension of social support-focused theory and research to counseling practice." In my opinion, he has certainly fulfilled his objective. This book should raise the consciousness of practicing counselors and counselor educators to the need to utilize natural and social support groups when dealing with gaps resulting from non-client based barriers. It also offers many illustrations for the application of natural and social support groups in the counseling process.

Although Pearson is careful to stop short of advocating that counselors take more responsibility for attempting to change unhealthy natural and social systems, I would have liked to have seen him tackle this issue and promoted this role as well, that is in Conyne's terms, focused more on remediation of *macro-system* causes of individual dysfunctions. Pearson's preference, however, is clearly described in Chapter 9 as follows:

> My concern with the impact of personal support systems leads me to focus on those social contexts that are closer to the individuals (closer in the sense that the people are known to each other as individuals, and typically have frequent, direct contact) as the contexts within which to apply the concepts and approaches of primary prevention.

Perhaps Pearson's next effort will be expanded to include remediation of macro-systems. In the meantime, *Counseling and Social Support: Perspectives and Practice* should produce a minor revolution in refocusing counselors to the importance of utilizing natural and social support groups in the counseling process. I am pleased to lend my support to this scholarly and, I believe, precedent-setting text.

— *George M. Gazda*

Chapter One

Introductory Perspectives

Edna, a 61-year-old widow, sought counseling for assistance with several life stage-related concerns: (a) She had an opportunity for early retirement, but was ambivalent about doing so; (b) her two children, married and living in distant cities, were not maintaining as much contact with her as she wanted; and (c) a long-standing relationship with a male friend was undergoing change because of his declining health.

The following excerpts reflect different facets of a central theme that wove through her counseling experience — a growing feeling of isolation from the persons whom she believed should care about her.

Wouldn't you think he [her brother] would realize that I'd appreciate some attention and help. He drove by the other morning while I was shoveling snow — just blew his horn, waved, and kept on going.

Besides the financial issue, the thing about retiring early that has me most up in the air is worry about losing a sense of belonging. It's not that I'm particularly close to anyone at work. My closest girlfriend retired two years ago and moved to Arizona. Yet it's sort of comforting to go to work every day, see the familiar faces, and know that if I'm out sick for a day, there are at least some people who wonder how I am, what I'm doing.

I'm not sure I could start again. I lost my husband, and now Gene's failing. It hurts too much to be left alone.

I remember how much I resented my mother-in-law's interference when we were first married — always there with the judgments, saying I shouldn't do this, or ought to do that. I vowed that when my children grew up, I'd leave them alone and not meddle in their lives. But now I hardly ever hear from them unless I call or write. I feel guilty about hinting that I have no plans for the holidays — fishing for an invitation — but if I didn't, I'm not sure I'd ever be asked to visit.

After Earl died, I felt I had to do it on my own — raise my kids, go back to work, keep things going. I didn't ask for help because I knew that they (her parents and brothers) had their own lives to lead. I didn't want them to pity me. So I handled things myself. I guess they still see me as a person who doesn't need their help.

Though Edna did not describe herself as having been abandoned, she said (in many different ways), "My relationships with people don't give me the emotional and material assistance I need." She had contact with many people, but they were not providing the amount, depth, and/or type of exchange she believed she needed.

There are many ways of conceptualizing Edna's concerns. Such perspectives as "developmental tasks" (Havighurst, 1972), "life transitions" (Schlossberg, 1981), "loss" (Simos, 1979), or "social skill deficit" (Phillips, 1985) could be used to illuminate one or another aspect of her experience. However, this book takes a different point of departure for considering the experience of Edna and other persons who seem to lack the sort of assistance from others that they, or we, might expect them to be receiving. "Social support" is a construct that, in my experience, provides a powerful base that counselors and other helping professionals can use to understand clients and to develop counseling responses to meet their needs. Social support is, then, the central, unifying perspective on which the following discussion of counseling practice is built.

Social Support Perspectives in
Contemporary Theory, Research, and Practice

The concepts of social support and natural support systems have perennially occupied an important place in artistic and scholarly considerations of the human condition, though perhaps under different names and labels. However, the past two decades have witnessed an astounding growth in attention focused on the nature, delivery, and consequences of social support for individuals facing ordinary and extraordinary life concerns.

Recently, it is nearly impossible to pick up a journal from any of the health, social, or behavioral sciences without finding at least one article (and often more) dealing with some aspect of social support and the natural and devised systems through which individuals obtain it. The programs of the professional meetings of these fields are sprinkled with presentations discussing theoretical and practical issues related to defining, measuring, and creating social support.

In applied settings, a concern with social support and support systems is reflected in an impressive array of formal and informal programs: for example, the creation and enhancement of neighborhood support systems by community mental health workers, the training of indigenous persons to serve as supporters, and the initiation of support groups. These and a host of other spontaneous and devised social support-focused field activities bear witness at least to the ubiquity, and probably the power, of social support as a construct with heuristic and applied relevance.

Where did all of this interest in social support and natural support systems come from? Where is this research and applied thrust going? What are its implications for me? Such questions come quickly to the casual observer as well as to counselors and other mental health workers.

This introductory chapter will provide an overview of historical and contemporary trends concerning social support and natural support systems. It serves as a point of departure for addressing the primary objective of this book; that is, the consideration and extension of social support-focused theory and research to counseling practice.

Social Support: Background Perspectives

In a very real sense, there is little new about the recognition that assistance received from, and extended to, others plays an important role in the development and maintenance of personal and group effectiveness. In the Judeo-Christian heritage, we find this theme surfacing often. The Old Testament Book of Leviticus is sprinkled with injunctions stressing the importance of offering assistance to neighbors, the poor, and strangers. Centuries later, John Donne asserted that no one is an island, and that each person's welfare is inextricably tied up with that of others. In a more recent expression of the ancient theme, the

Beatles explored the significance of connectedness among people in their "With a Little Help from My Friends." There is every reason to believe that an exploration of the oral and written beliefs of non-Western peoples would find a similar confirmation of the importance of social support.

Marie Killilea (1976) noted that the work of Prince Petr Kropotkin, a nineteenth-century opponent of conflict-centered Darwinian theory, provided an important articulation of the view that cooperation and mutual protection have played a central role in the development of successful species. The sociobiological view (e.g., Barkow, 1977) considers the phenomenon of social support to be deeply rooted in our biological inheritance, providing a central influence in our (to date at least) successes as a life form.

The Behavioral Sciences and Social Support

More narrowly, a concern for examining the effect of the social context on human development and behavior has been a central perspective of the social and behavioral sciences that have emerged and flourished in this century and the last. Anthropologists and sociologists have tended to see the social context as the predominant factor to be considered in understanding human functioning. In the field of psychology, a lively difference of perspective continues to assert itself regarding the relative importance of intra- and extrapsychic factors in the determination of behavior. Kurt Lewin's (1951) now-classic formulation, $B = f(P + E)$ (behavior is a function of the person and the environment), while recognizing the influence of both individual and contextual factors in determining behavior, allows a wide range of interpretation regarding the specific influence of each.

Given this background, the contemporary focus on the importance of social support and support systems (both natural and devised) can be viewed as simply the most recent swing of the pendulum on an issue of long-standing difference among social and behavioral scientists; namely, in understanding human development and behavior, are individual-based or situational factors most important? Psychodynamically oriented counseling and psychotherapy have tended to focus on individual, intrapsychic factors in understanding human behavior, while social psychology, sociology, sociobiology, and family therapy have emphasized the importance of the social context. Thus these latter fields have focused considerable attention on the role of family, friends, and other elements of individuals' social networks in the development and disruption of effective personal adjustment.

Practical Issues

The current interest in social support and natural support systems is, however, broader than the disagreements of academics. There also are contemporary social, political, and economic factors supporting the position that the impact of one's social context, especially as mediated by interactions with others, has a powerful (perhaps predominant) influence on the ability to meet the ordinary and extraordinary issues of life.

The presence of such factors is highlighted in Killilea's (1976) discussion of mutual help groups, one manifestation of social support and support systems phenomena; drawing from a broad literature, she outlined a variety of ways in which mutual help groups can be interpreted (pp. 40-66). Three of the views she identified seem particularly relevant to an understanding of the related, but broader, interest we now see in social support delivered by natural support systems. First, she suggested that mutual help efforts can be considered an expression of the democratic ideal; that is, a striving for participation, and a desire to provide and receive mutual help rather than depending on the assistance of professionals. Second, she pointed to mutual help groups as an alternative to the formal help giving system. This factor seems especially important in situations where the use of formal systems is avoided because they are viewed by potential users as noxious or irrelevant. Finally, she suggested that mutual help groups can be seen as a solution to manpower shortages in the human services. This perspective is based on the belief that there are many aspects of maintaining and restoring physical and mental health to which peers can respond more effectively and with more relevance than can professionals.

Taken in sum, Killilea's views highlight important factors contributing to the current interest in assistance from natural support systems. However, perhaps it is important to point out again that while they may be important in understanding the current upsurge of interest in social support from natural systems, none of these factors (i.e., the need to participate, suspicion of professionals, or unavailability of professionals) is really new. The belief that it is important to "look after one's own" and the feeling that there is a stigma attached to receiving assistance from persons not of one's own immediate circle of family and friends are ancient themes that continue to run deep in the lives of many contemporary people. These beliefs support the choice of kith and kin as supporters on the basis of both preference and obligation. Many service providers and researchers in counseling and other human service fields (e.g., Fischer, 1976; Hawley, 1973) have recognized that in our concern about the impact of urbanization and technology, we have probably been hasty in declaring the demise of natural helping systems made up of family, friends, neighbors, and co-workers. The use of these systems, supported as it is by powerful, deep-seated attitudes, continues to be an important preventive and remedial resource.

Primary Prevention

Beyond the sociological, political, and economic factors, there are issues of professional ideology that contribute to the growth of interest in social support and natural support systems. The long-standing concern of many scholars and practitioners in the mental health fields for encouraging primary prevention-oriented interventions represents an important force that is ideologically compatible with an interest in the contributions of social support and natural support systems. A number of writers (e.g., Golan, 1981; Gurin et al., 1960) have noted that the natural system tends to be the first source of assistance sought out when self resources prove inadequate. As the "first line of assistance," the adequacy of these systems can have an important bearing on whether the difficulties individuals experience are resolved quickly and well. If preventive assistance is received quickly, the development of dysfunctions requiring remedial interventions can be avoided. Although the mental health field has predominantly reflected a preoccupation with pathology and remediation (Albee, 1978; Cowen, 1983; Sarason, 1974), there has also been a parallel concern for emphasizing primary prevention. This tradition, rather than being suspicious of natural support systems or grudgingly reaching out to them as a way of coping with funding cutbacks, tends to affirm their role as an important element of primary prevention-oriented programming.

In light of the above discussion, the current attention devoted to social support and natural support systems can be considered a reflection of both long-standing and recent influences. Perhaps this convergence accounts for the vigor and richness of the conceptual, empirical, and practical efforts we now witness; that is, current interest in social support phenomenon draws its vitality not only from the urgency of contemporary realities, it is also nourished by the force of perennial concerns in human affairs, and the social and behavioral sciences.

The Literature of Social Support and Natural Support Systems

An examination of the relevant scholarly and practice-oriented literature reveals an impressive collection of texts and articles. It is an interdisciplinary literature, involving (to cite a few) the fields of anthropology, sociology, psychology, medicine, education, biology, and business administration. Three issues with important implications for support-oriented interventions in counseling and other human services occupy a central place in this literature:

· What is the nature of the interpersonal ties that make up the context of individuals' experience?
· What is the impact of, and function served by, the social support that persons receive through their interpersonal relationships?
· How can social support from natural or devised support systems be made more available to individuals?

Interpersonal Ties

Anthropologists and sociologists have focused considerable attention on the task of describing and analyzing the nature of relationships among people in a group. Who knows whom? Who interacts with whom, for what purposes, and with what results? Such questions have long been significant to social anthropologists and sociologists as entry points to understanding group structure and organization. The concept of "social network" was, as Mitchell (1974) noted, introduced by Barnes (1954) as a way of clarifying the system of social ties within which persons exist. Barnes's approach gave impetus to subsequent studies—for example, those of Bott (1955) and Mayer (1961)—in which the construct of social network was used as a perspective for analyzing field data gathered in a wide range of cultural contexts.

Not only have anthropologists and sociologists done the important work of casting commonplace observation of interaction among individuals into concepts that allow interpersonal contact and interaction to be described in a precise manner, they also developed measures that have aided the systematic analysis of these contacts. Mitchell noted that these measures are of two sorts: structural measures describing the quantitative characteristics of systems (e.g., size of the system, extent to which the members of the system know each other, subgroups of members who are frequently in contact with each other)and transactional measures describing the qualitative characteristics of social networks (e.g., purpose served by the relationships, degree of importance the persons attach to particular relationships, emotional tone of relationships). These measures have been adopted and elaborated by researchers and mental health practitioners as tools for describing the interpersonal context of particular individuals, and for examining quantitative and qualitative dimensions of the interaction taking place within groups of individuals. The application of structural and interactive measures to counseling practice will be examined in Chapter 3.

Consequences of Social Support

By far, the largest component of the literature relating to social support is made up of studies that examine the relationship between the availability of social support and the physical and/or mental health status of individuals. Such studies can be considered a direct extension of that position in the social and behavioral sciences that emphasizes environmental factors in understanding human behavior. These studies center on the hypothesis that the supportiveness of the social context within which individuals exist exerts an important influence on whether they will develop a wide range of physical and/or psychological illnesses.

This genre of study seems to have been set into motion by the work of John Cassel (1974), an epidemiologist whose professional concerns focused on the effects of urban living. Cassel noted, as had others before him, that noxious urban conditions seem to exert deleterious influence on residents' physical and emotional health. He hypothesized that an important consequence of such conditions is that the social ties of urban residents are disrupted. Such disruption serves to reduce the amount of information that individuals receive about their situation and interferes with feedback concerning the accuracy of their perceptions and the effectiveness of their behavior. Cut off from such feedback, individuals are apt to feel that they don't know "what's going on" or how well they are doing. This uncertainty can lead to heightened stress and subsequent physical and emotional disorders.

Gerald Caplan, a psychiatrist, found Cassel's formulations highly compatible with his own interests centered on preventive, community-focused interventions. Accepting Cassel's "buffering" hypothesis (i.e., that an important effect of social support is to ameliorate the negative impact of physical and psychological stressors that persons face), Caplan, in his book *Support Systems and Community Mental Health* (1974), turned to the business of clarifying the specific manner in which social support imparts such benefits. He suggested that support systems assist individuals by (a) helping them mobilize their own psychobiological resources as stressors are encountered; (b) providing assistance in meeting the demands of their situation; (c) making such material resources as money, needed materials, and skills available; and (d) giving cognitive guidance and advice (p. 6).

Though this description of the nature and function of support systems seems somewhat undifferentiated in light of later formulations (e.g., Gottlieb, 1978; Kahn & Antonucci, 1981), Caplan began the important process of moving understanding of social support and natural support systems beyond the very general delineation provided by everyday use of the words.

Building on the seminal views of Cassel and Caplan, the past decade has seen a steady accumulation of theory and research aimed at expanding understanding of the nature and effects of social support. House (1981), in an exploration of the role of social support in helping persons cope with work stress, has summarized current understanding of the specific ways in which social support aids individuals:

· As supportiveness increases, the presence of noxious influences in individuals' life situations is eliminated or reduced.
· A supportive environment serves to increase the general health of individuals, thus increasing their ability to withstand the negative effects of noxious physical and social factors.
· Social support serves to aid individuals by buffering them, fully or partially, from the negative impact of environmental stressors.

To illustrate these three processes, consider the experience of a young person who leaves her home to enroll at a distant university — a person not unlike many who come through the doors of college or university counseling centers. First, to the extent that her family members are psychologically sound, mature persons, the new student is not apt to be faced with parents who make her transition more difficult by (for example) acting in ways that might cause her to feel guilty about going so far away from home. The absence of such parental pressures serves to minimize at least one class of stress that might exacerbate the difficulties of college adjustment.

Second, as a consequence of her supportive upbringing, we might expect that the student would come to her college experience equipped with such beneficial personal attributes as high self-esteem and effective interpersonal skills. These will serve to ease the process of adjusting to her new situation. Having the interpersonal resiliency that comes from high self-esteem, and possessing skills that allow her to contact and develop relationships effectively, we would expect she could quickly establish a school-based support system. That new system would be a source of many of the resources needed in her transition to college.

However, even with her positive background and personal strengths, it is possible that she will experience some stress as she adjusts to college. In that case, the continuing ability and willingness of her family to provide her with reassurance, confirmation of her worth, and encouragement will serve to buffer her against the full negative impact of these stressors.

The last of these three effects of social support (that is, its ability to buffer people against the negative consequences of environmental stress) has received most of the attention in the theoretical and empirical literature (Eckenrode & Gore, 1981). The reason for this interest lies in the fact that in many (perhaps most) human enterprises it is actually (or practically) impossible to eliminate all possible negative factors. Also, before the fact, it is often impossible to provide persons with the skills and attributes that would allow them to cope with such stressors. Given these realities, a resource that helps persons bear up under, and come to terms with, unavoidable stress has enormous practical importance. Social support is, as House (1981) has suggested, a prime candidate for consideration as a resource that can act as a buffer against the deleterious physical and emotional effects of many types of environmental stress.

A very extensive literature has focused on tracing the impact of social support on persons' ability to cope with a wide range of life events and crises. While the adequacy of the findings and conclusions of many studies can be questioned (Heller, 1979), the consistency of the finding that persons dealing with ordinary and extraordinary life issues do so better if they have access to social support is impressive. The main issue seems to be why and how this occurs rather than if it occurs. For counselors and other human service workers, all three effects (i.e., reducing or eliminating negative factors, improving health, and providing resources that buffer against negative effects) have definite preventive and remedial applications.

Increasing the Availability of Social Support

Considering the mounting evidence that social support is a resource with powerful potential in the prevention and remediation of a wide range of psychological and sociological ills, it is understandable that the means through which social support can be made more available to individuals who lack it would be a focus of the literature of the social and behavioral sciences. Logically, there are two broad strategies for accomplishing this task: increase the amount and quality of social support available to an individual by intervening with actual and/or potential supporters to increase their willingness and ability to offer social support; and increase the willingness and/or ability of individuals to gain access to support from others.

Returning to Edna, whom we met at the beginning of this chapter, the first of these approaches (i.e., intervening with supporters to increase their willingness and/or ability to offer assistance) would center on some sort of effort directed at increasing the responsiveness of her brother, children, and (perhaps) her co-workers. The second approach (i.e., "doing something" to clients that enhances their ability to elicit assistance from others) might focus on helping Edna acquire the willingness and skills to be more assertive in expressing her need for assistance and recognition from her family.

Preference for one or the other of these general strategies seems to rest on whether one views the availability of social support to individuals to be determined primarily by environment-based (e.g., availability of supporters, characteristics of supporters, characteristics of the broader social context) or individual-based (e.g., physical attractiveness, sociability) factors (Rook & Dooley, 1985).

The strategy of promoting positive change in persons by focusing on changing their social network is, as Pattison (1973) noted, at the heart of the family therapy movement. Also, we can trace the strategy in the psychotherapeutic approaches of Attneave (1969), Rueveni (1979), and Speck & Attneave (1973), all of whom stress the importance of assembling and involving the social network of patients in the treatment process.

The effect of considering social support to be an environment-based variable is also seen in the field of community psychology (Heller, Price, Reinharz, Riger, & Wandersman, 1984; Rappaport, 1977) and in its parallel, community counseling (Lewis & Lewis, 1983). Community-focused conceptualizations of helping services stress the important impact that social and physical contexts can have on the mental and physical health of individuals. Therefore, these perspectives lead to the position that remediation of pathology and fostering positive health should center on the elimination of noxious environmental factors, and the enhancement of positive influences. In counseling and other human services, the community focus leads us to center attention on the persons who make up our clients' social environment. This is done in the belief that the status and characteristics of these individuals exert an important influence on the amount and quality of social support available to the people we serve.

The enthusiasm of some practitioners regarding the helping potential of natural support systems stands in sharp contrast to the views of many human service workers who regularly work with clients experiencing family conflict. As Heller (1979) rather cogently pointed out, clinicians have a tendency to take a rather negative view of families, peers, and friends. Perhaps that is because counselors and other human service workers are typically at the end of the help-seeking process. Before seeking formal help, clients often have engaged in considerable, but ineffective, coping activity. Often, natural support systems that are absent, nonresponsive, or deficient have a prominent place in clients' inability to function effectively.

Theory and practice can be used as a basis for viewing natural systems as either cause or cure of many of the difficulties bringing individuals to counseling. Perhaps a desirable stance to take is that both perspectives and approaches have relevance and utility in counseling practice. Counselor versatility will be enhanced by the acquisition of understandings and techniques that open up the possibility of using both approaches. Use of context-focused or client-focused interventions (or a blending of both) should reflect the realities at hand rather than being the consequence of the counselor's conceptual or technical restrictedness.

Purpose and Structure of This Book

This overview of the literature concerning social support and natural support systems indicates that there is already a wide body of theory, information, and opinion that can be drawn on by counselors who see the relevance of support-related issues to their preventive and remedial work. In this book, counselors will find material that specifically addresses issues encountered in pursuing support-oriented interventions. My intent is to provide a practical guide that describes procedures and materials useful in day-to-day work with clients. However, the book's development has also been guided by my concern for setting practical material against a backdrop of conceptual and research literature from which it has been derived.

The chapters that follow are organized around a general model for analyzing support-related issues in counseling and other human service activities. Figure 1.1 presents this model in its most general form.

Each element of this model will be further elaborated and discussed by one or more of the subsequent chapters.

- Chapter 2 focuses on a consideration of the sort of life situations in which the lack or misapplication of social support will often be found to play an important role in the development and continuance of concerns that bring clients to counseling.
- Chapter 3 considers methods and materials that can be used to assess the characteristics of clients' informal support systems that have a bearing on the amount and quality of social support available to them. Also, methods for identifying particular support deficiencies causing or worsening the concerns individuals bring to the counseling situation will be examined.
- Chapter 4 identifies and describes client-based barriers (e.g., shyness, aggressiveness, stigmatized status) that can reduce the willingness of past or potential supporters to offer assistance.
- Recognizing that support deficiencies often result from factors based within the client, Chapter 5 examines counseling strategies and interventions that can be used to remove or ameliorate the effect of such barriers.
- Chapter 6 identifies and discusses context-based barriers (e.g., limited resources of others, social disruption) that can reduce the availability of social support to our clients.
- Using the previous chapter as its springboard, Chapter 7 moves on to consider counseling strategies that can be used to eliminate or reduce the

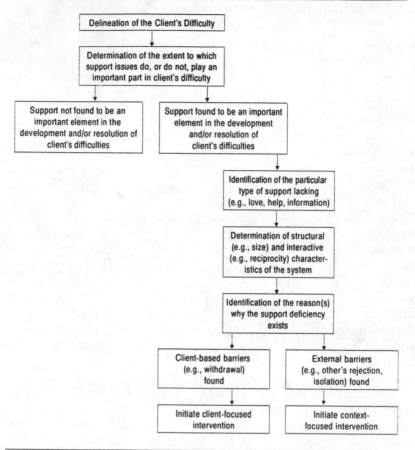

Figure 1.1. A Model for Using Social Support-Oriented Concepts and Procedures in Counseling Practice

impact of barriers housed in various sectors of clients' social and physical contexts.

- Chapter 8 centers on an extensive case study that illustrates the operation of client- and context-based barriers, and traces how counseling interventions designed to remove them can be planned and carried out.
- Finally, Chapter 9 considers a variety of issues raised, but not extensively explored, in the preceding chapters. Such matters as psychological health, primary prevention, research, and counselor education will be discussed

from the perspective of constructs and understandings developed in earlier portions of the book.

Some Cautions

Near the beginning of *Work Stress and Social Support*, House (1981) cautioned that the conceptual and empirical footings of his topic were still at a formative stage and thus his book ought to be viewed as "an exploration and assessment of new and varied ideas, scattered empirical facts, and selected (sometimes untested) practical applications of available knowledge" (pp. 9, 10).

The reader of this book would do well to entertain the same caution. Though there is an extensive, ever-growing empirical literature tending to support the positive effect of social support in the development, maintenance, and reestablishment of personal effectiveness, there is, as Heller (1979) noted, a wide variation in the strength of the design and implementation of the studies of which it is constituted. There is also variation in the degree to which the conclusions at which the studies arrive seem to be warranted. The adequacy of this literature as a base for understanding and practice rests, therefore, less on the unassailability of all the constituent parts and more on the consistency with which the positive effects of social support have been confirmed over many settings and with many populations.

Moreover, many of the intervention strategies discussed in Chapters 5 and 7 are individual and group procedures that, while familiar to practitioners in a variety of settings, have validity generally resting more on having met the test of clinical practice than on a foundation of empirical evidence supporting their effectiveness and/or their superiority to other intervention approaches.

If considered with due respect for these cautions, and if approached with a willingness to view the findings of existing research and clinical practice as a body of understandings and practices that can be tested against one's own experience, I believe the polar errors of uncritical acceptance and immobilizing tentativeness can be avoided.

Chapter Two

When Are Social Support Issues Important?

To say that many of the concerns that individuals bring to counselors and other helping professionals center on the quality of their social interaction with others is, at once, to say a great deal and to say little. As social creatures, dependent on our interaction with others for physical survival and psychological identity, how could it be otherwise than that our difficulties (as well as our successes) somehow involve past, present, and/or anticipated experiences with other people? This recognition, as Pattison (1973) noted, underlies those therapeutic approaches that stress consideration and involvement of the social contexts within which individuals function.

The purpose of this chapter is to call attention to one aspect of the enormously broad recognition of the impact of the interpersonal context; namely, what are the particular sorts of situations in which a knowledge of the constructs of social support and personal support systems will be particularly useful in helping counselors to develop understanding of their clients and to plan and implement helping interventions?

Awareness of Social Support Issues

In general, we become aware that social support issues may play an important role in the concerns of our clients in several ways:

- Clients themselves explicitly call our attention to their lack of supportive relationships through such statements as, "My husband doesn't give a damn whether I get my degree or not"; "My parents couldn't care less if I'm having a tough time"; "I'm just so tired of not having anyone who cares about me."

- Social support issues, though not initially apparent, are discovered to play an important role in a client's presenting concern. For example, we may find that an adolescent's low academic performance is tied strongly to a disrupted family situation. In such a family, parents and siblings may be preoccupied with their own reactions to an impending divorce; as a result, they have few emotional resources to give to the adolescent as she struggles with the tasks of college adjustment.

- Other persons alert the counselor that the client seems to be experiencing difficulties coping with life demands; for example, a teacher might call the counselor's attention to a student whose academic performance has dramatically decreased in the wake of his father's job loss.

Concerning self-referral, not seeking help does not necessarily mean individuals are free of difficulties (Gross & McMullin, 1983). Nor does it always mean that they have adequate social support resources available to them. Brown (1978) found that non-help seekers fall into two groups: the self-reliant (those who believe they can handle their difficulty themselves) and the reluctant (those who believe that getting help would be too difficult or impossible to acquire, or who associate undesirable consequences, such as criticism and shame, with seeking assistance). Brown's research indicates that the self-reliant tend to have more social and psychological resources than the reluctant non-help seekers. A third group, those who seek help, falls between the two non-help seeking groups in the level of their social and psychological resources.

Generalizing Brown's findings, it seems clear that many of the persons who are most deficient in terms of their social support resources (as well as their personal, psychological resources) are least apt to present those concerns to the counselor.

Support-Relevant Events and Situations

Since clients themselves may not alert us that they are experiencing support deficiency (either because they are reluctant to seek help or because they are not clearly aware of the role that a lack of social support plays in their difficulties), counselors will often have to look behind clients' presenting concerns to probe the possibility of social support deficiency. Adapting the work of Gerald Erickson (1975), the following general circumstances may be cited as those in which the concepts of social support and natural support systems are apt to have particular heuristic and practical use for the counselor:

- life transitions (e.g., moving, divorce, job shift) that result in disruption of, or isolation from, former or potential supporters;
- changes in the situation, responsiveness, or status of significant supporters (e.g., death of a spouse, relocation of a confidant, arguments with or among family members); and
- attitudes, behavior, or other characteristics of the client that tend to exert a negative effect on the willingness of others to be supportive (e.g., anger, counterdependence, lack of social skills, deviance).

Each of these situations will be examined in detail. Case examples drawn from my counseling experience or that of my colleagues and students are provided to suggest how counselors and other human service workers may encounter these circumstances in their work with clients.

Life Transitions

Transitions come in a wide array. They vary in the intensity and depth at which they affect individuals. They also differ in the nature of the changes with which they confront individuals. Some transitions focus on changes in the physical situation, as when a person moves from one community to another. Other transitions, dominated by changes in one's social situation (as when an important role change occurs), may involve little or no change in the physical situation but profoundly change one's daily experience. Changes in physical setting and social context are usually inseparably connected, with changes in one domain affecting the other.

Nancy Schlossberg (1981) developed a model that specifies the major factors influencing the impact that transitions have on persons: the transition itself, the person experiencing the transition, and the physical and social context within which the transition occurs. Of particular relevance to a consideration of transitions as a cause of support deficiencies is that aspect of the social context that she calls the "internal support system" (p. 5). Schlossberg asserts that this system (composed of close relationships, the family, and friends) has an important influence on the ease or difficulty with which transitions are made. Thus the experience of a mid-life executive who gives up a secure, lucrative position with the encouragement of spouse, family, and friends is apt to differ in process, if not in outcome, from that of a similar person doing so in opposition to the desires of family and friends.

Beyond the broad recognition that transitions affect individuals' physical and social situations, what are the specific ways they affect the availability of social support? Perhaps the most obvious manner in which transitions may affect the amount and type of social support to which individuals have access is that they often thrust people into new situations where their prior learning is inadequate or inapplicable. For example, lack of information about the new setting can reduce persons' awareness of formal and informal sources of support. We observe this when a transferring college student struggles with the many tasks of adjustment, unaware of the existence of student services that could ease the transition to the new campus.

Moreover, the changed situation into which the person in transition moves may have informal rules governing the formation of relationships of which the individual is unaware. A person coming from a work setting where it was expected that questions concerning work rules and expectations would be answered by fellow workers, may, in a new job setting, be confused when requests to colleagues for such information are ignored or rebuffed. The co-workers' behavior becomes comprehensible only when the newcomer recognizes a prevailing local norm requiring those questions be addressed to a supervisor. Lack of information about the resources and norms of the new situation can, therefore, isolate individuals from available social support, even given a disposition on their part to seek out and gain access to assistance.

Finally, transitions are often accompanied by a reduction in individuals' social support resources because persons making the transition find their own coping resources so tested that they lack the energy to institute activities that might open up new sources of support. Grieving persons often deny the reality of the loss of a loved one. They may refuse to acknowledge the necessity of reestablishing former social contacts or forming new relationships. Individuals often cope with the massive stress of a transition by "shutting down," withdrawing, and distancing themselves from former or potential supporters.

The net result of such patterns is that individuals' access to social support is reduced at a time when it could be of great use. The recognition that transitions restrict the availability of support by affecting both individuals in transition and their supporters has important implications for counseling interventions. Though these implications will be developed and examined in Chapters 5 and 7, it may be useful to point out that in addition to the client-focused interventions with which counselors are familiar, procedures involving significant others may help to increase the availability of needed social support to clients.

Geographic Relocation

Joan, age 28: I had moved a long distance before, from Minnesota to Arkansas, but in some ways this move has been more difficult. I think it's because I had developed such a close circle of friends at Riverton. I was part of a women's collective that really became very important to me, personally and professionally. I was establishing myself as a professional for the first time, and the women in the collective offered me a great deal of advice and encouragement — several really good role models. Also, I was going through a lot of thinking about just who I was and the kind of person I wanted to be. My friends offered a feminist perspective that helped me clarify a lot of my experiences and my options. The first two or three months here I had horrendous phone bills, but I needed to keep in contact with my friends. I hadn't yet built the new circle of friends I have here now, and I often felt that I had made a big mistake coming here. I had my cat, she provided a kind of continuity and gave me something here to love and be loved by, but I really felt lonely and cut off from the important people in my life. Things are much better now. I've made some really good friends, I've learned my way around the community, I know I can do my job, and I'm beginning to understand people in the Northeast.

When transitions involve moving, individuals' ability to come into contact with the persons in their support networks (as they existed prior to the transition) can be seriously disrupted. "Out of sight, out of mind" goes the saying, and even a continuing willingness to be supportive is made difficult by the problems associated with physical separation. Individuals with sufficient financial resources can take frequent trips "back home," make phone calls, or arrange for their supporters to visit. Lacking such resources, individuals are isolated from the support of their distant supporters and have to endure the loneliness and disorientation that transitions often cause.

Although the disruptive effects of transitions not involving a move may not be outwardly disruptive, they may still have a marked impact on persons' support resources. A worker who assumes a management position may find that former co-workers who provided extensive amounts of companionship and guidance now tend to be distant and formal in their interaction with her. Similarly, it is common for persons going through divorce to find that former friends feel they have to choose sides and, siding with the former spouse, either withdraw from or rebuff attempts to maintain relationships with both parties (Putney, 1981).

Changes in Others

While our attention often is focused on the impact of transitions on persons who are our clients, it is important not to lose sight of the reality that often the same transition is either directly experienced by, or has heavy impact on, our clients' supporters, affecting their ability to provide social support. For example, Gore (1978) noted that uncmployment affects the families of laid-off workers just as it does the workers themselves. Spouses and children, also struggling with the financial, social, and emotional adjustments required by a primary wage earner's unemployment, will often be found to have fewer material and emotional resources to make available in support of the worker. Thus, while the support system apparently remains available, there is actually a reduction in the amount of support to which the individual can gain access. The ability of former supporters to be of assistance is attenuated by their preoccupation with their own difficulties (Riley & Waring, 1976).

Death and Illness

Ben, age 87: I still miss her as if it were just yesterday that she passed on. Sometimes, sitting in the parlor, reading my morning paper, I swear I hear her rustling around the kitchen, making my breakfast. Then I realize that it's just the wind or some other noise from outside. Wouldn't you think I'd be used to her being gone by now? It's been sixteen years, but I can honestly say that hardly an hour goes by that something doesn't remind me of her. Maybe because we never had children; maybe that's why I miss her so much. I was the center of her life, she tended me, spoiled me, and she was happy doing so. I did the same for her, liked to make her happy, do things with her and for her. There were so many things we were going to do that we never had a chance to — travel to Europe, remodel the kitchen. Somehow the heart to do those things has gone out of me. My brother and his family are nice to me, try to include me in their doings, but it's not the same, of course. How could I not miss her? There's no replacing her in my life. I'm not anxious to die, but I'm ready — not much that really interests me without her.

While it is true that change affects relationships bilaterally, it may also be observed that the primary focus of change is often with one person. Subsequently, this change precipitates changes in other persons with whom he or she interacts. Death, serious illness, and accidents are striking instances of unilateral change that can reduce the amount of support received from a relationship. The impact of such events is influenced by the amount of support generally available to the individual, as well as the uniqueness (as judged from objective and/or subjective perspectives) of the support lost or diminished (Gottlieb, 1988). The death of an isolated elder's sole confidant might be expected to be experienced more deeply than would the loss of a similar person by another elder possessing an extensive, effective personal support system.

Even when there are many supporters, the loss of one who uniquely provides a particular type of support will typically have deeper practical and emotional disruption than that of a person whose support can be easily duplicated by others. For example, one might regret the death or disability of any business associate; however, the loss will be much more limited if this person is an occasional contact rather than a long-time partner who possesses a detailed knowledge of one's thought patterns, nonverbal behavior, and value preferences.

It is important to recognize that an individual's perception of the uniqueness of the lost supporter is often a more important factor in determining its impact than the objective uniqueness. It may have little effect to point out to a bereaved person that there are many other people who are willing and able to fill the emotional and material gaps left by the death of an old friend. The response to this will likely be, "It's just not the same." Indeed, from that person's view, a friend is not a friend, is not a friend. Subjectively, we invest many of our supporters with uniqueness. Facts notwithstanding, their loss by death, relocation, or serious disability creates a void that cannot be entirely filled by persons who could, and would, provide the same type of support.

In addition to a consideration of the extent to which the support loss is relatively unique or represents a large proportion of the client's support resources, there are other factors that might alert the counselor to the possibility that support is important to understanding and working with a client. For example, Bernice Neugarten's (1977) concept of "on time" and "off time" developmental occurrences highlights the fact that the emotional and practical impact of a life event is often strongly affected by the degree to which a person is able to anticipate its occurrence. The death of a parent when one is a child is, typically, more traumatic than at mid-life, when one is more apt to anticipate such an event. Schlossberg (1981) also called attention to this issue when she pointed out that one of the factors that affects the impact of a transition is the extent to which it can be, or is, anticipated by the individual. One may never be entirely prepared for the death of an important supporter; however, when a supporter's death is preceded by a long illness or intellectual decline, it allows time for the development of alternative means of filling the support needs that person provided.

Recognition of the differing effects on anticipated and unanticipated support loss has both preventive and remedial implications for counseling practice. Remedially, we might expect that the sudden death of an important supporter, especially if such occurs "off time," will leave a client with important deficiencies in support resources. In such instances, it is appropriate to help individuals work their way through the usual stages of grieving (Kubler-Ross, 1969). Also, helping them to focus on the specific nature of the support they have lost and to identify alternative sources from whom (in a broad sense) the same type of support can be obtained may be an important focus for counseling.

Lest it appear that the only manner in which death and disability affect support issues is in terms of the support one receives, it is important also to point out that most long-standing support relationships are reciprocal in nature. Therefore, one of the issues a person may confront on the death or disability of a loved one is what to "do" with the love, affection, companionship, material assistance that had previously been expended on the lost one. The curative, self-enhancing value of altruism has been widely noted (e.g., Frank, 1961). With the loss of a person who has been an important recipient of one's support, an individual may find that life has become empty and meaningless. Working with individuals to complete their grieving is often a helpful contribution of counseling. Additionally, the ability to reinvest support resources in other individuals is an important goal for many people. Doing so reinvolves them with others, allowing the recapture of a view of themselves as someone whose life has real purpose and significance.

Disaffection

Arlene, age 22: I knew he had really strong feelings about this interracial dating thing. You know, "Don't you ever let me hear of you so much as talking to a black guy" (only you know he didn't say black). So what did I do? I not only got involved, I married a black man. My dad told everyone in the family to stay away from the wedding and still barely talks to my brother who told him to go to hell and came anyway. I thought in time he would come around, would at least be civil. But it's as if I've fallen off the end of the earth. My mother says he never asks about me or the baby, that he leaves the room or gets angry if anyone at home says they've seen me or talked to me. I can't believe he'd shut me out like this; we were so close. He always encouraged me to set goals for myself and believe in myself. I'm angry and hurt. I just miss not having my dad there to enjoy my accomplishments, to pat me on the back.

In the extreme, emotional estrangement can be as final and absolute as the separation caused by death. After a quarrel, close relatives have been known to avoid any contact with each other for the remainders of their lives, even though living in close proximity. A casualty of such situations is the support that the individuals had previously provided to each other. Short-lived family quarrels, arguments between friends, and misunderstandings among co-workers disrupt the exchange of help and assistance among the individuals involved. Even when the relationships have been resumed, it is often true that some of the more delicate, fragile types of interpersonal support (affection, for example) may continue to be affected.

As is true with the impact of death and serious illness, the specific impact of interpersonal disaffection is apt to vary as a function of the robustness of the individual's general support resources and the uniqueness of the support lost. If our only, or most special, friend is angry with us, we are affected much more deeply than if a nodding acquaintance takes offense at something we do. For an adolescent, the loss of a girlfriend or boyfriend is a shattering experience. From the perspective of youth, obviously there will never be anyone else as special or loved as deeply. Our greater experience may lead us to counsel (or at least think) that the pain of lost love is short-lived; however, the limited experience of the adolescent does not allow such a loss to be viewed as just one experience among many.

Disagreement and estrangement are a common part of human experience. They are often repaired or adapted to without great difficulty; nonetheless, they constitute an important focus of attention for counselors and other human service workers. For many clients, the counselor's willingness to provide encouragement, understanding, and an acceptant place to air feelings of loss and disappointment will be sufficient to help them make it through until the relationship is reestablished or until newly formed or enhanced existing relationships can fill the void. However, for individuals with very limited support relationships and/or those with low-level skills and resources for developing new supporters, the loss of a close friend, confidant, or lover can represent a serious (perhaps disastrous) disruption of their interpersonal world. In such cases, counseling intervention will have to offer more than temporary palliation. Typically, the counselor's assistance will need to focus more deeply on the intra- and interpersonal factors causing, or exacerbating, the client's isolation.

General Disruption of the Personal Support System

It is not uncommon to find impaired relationships between specific individuals in such small, face-to-face groups as families, peer groups, and work groups. We've seen that these impaired relationships may significantly reduce an individual's social support resources. This is especially true if the particular other is a key person in the personal support system. However, since the loss or impairment is localized in specific relationships, individuals will often be able to offset the support loss by turning to other relationships that continue to be rich in support potential.

A much different situation exists for the person whose access to social support is reduced because one or more of these groups displays a general pattern of indifference and/or conflict among its members. "Sick" families, vicious peer groups, and cutthroat work environments are examples of situations where solidarity and mutual assistance are largely absent, and interpersonal experience is dominated by such stress-producing factors as self-preoccupation, insensitivity, exploitation, and competition. It is beyond the scope of the present discussion to trace the manner in which such noxious group climates are established in the first place. However, it is interesting to note that though internal and external crises and stressors have the effect of increasing the cohesiveness and mutuality of some groups, they exacerbate the negative interpersonal climate of others.

Elaine, age 55: It's as if my mother was the glue that held us together, kept us in contact with each other, soothed the feelings, saw that everyone got what they needed emotionally and materially. As I see it now, we really didn't care for each other so much as we wanted to please her, get her approval. When she died, the family turned upside down. First there were the squabbles about who would get what. Each of us had carved out what we wanted — the car, a particular piece of furniture, Dad's guns. Of course there was no will — you'd think with all the land, barns, equipment, and animals that there would have been one, but I guess she just never thought she'd die. All the hurts and resentments that had grown up over the years, all the jealousies that she had kept a lid on, out they came. We were at each other's throats. Mean, spiteful things were done, and we were glad to do them, glad that at last we could have our way. The scars have never healed. Out of the seven kids, there are only a couple of us who have anything to do with each other. My brother Bill and I are still here; everyone else took their share of the final settlement and moved away.

One can speculate that, generally, crisis and stress would tend to heighten preexisting support patterns of the group. Thus, while the death of a key member, a financial reversal, or a natural disaster would tend to place any face-to-face group under stress, those already characterized by competition and lack of reciprocity will be further fragmented by the event. In contrast, those with strong traditions of mutual assistance will generally heighten their supportiveness as a response to crisis. Gottlieb (1983) called attention to the network's potential for negative influence in his discussion of "the balance of support to stress" in the primary social network (pp. 112-113). Using the support-to-stress ratio as an index, we can say that the noxious groups we have been discussing are those in which the support a member receives is outweighed by the stress experienced.

When individuals have physical and emotional resources, we would expect that they would move out of contact with these unsupportive networks. However, just as it is often difficult for persons to move out of noxious individual relationships, so it may be difficult to break off ties with an unsupportive group. Lack of perceived alternatives, fear of the unknown, and feelings of obligation may all serve to keep individuals enmeshed in networks that deliver stress rather than support. Encouraging individuals to break off contact with the noxious relationships may be the most logical solution to such situations; however, doing so is often problematic. Clients cling to their impaired relationships, and the other persons making up those relationships cling just as tightly to them. Network-focused interventions (Pattison, 1973; Speck & Rueveni, 1969), though another apparent means of reducing network dysfunction, are in reality very complex, demanding of counselor time, and often resisted by network members.

Noxious family networks have been a major focus of the foregoing discussion. It should be pointed out that networks in which the balance of support to stress is weighted toward stress may be encountered in other contexts. An academic program where the possibility of failure is high is apt to create competition, individual striving to the disadvantage of others, and aggression. Similarly, work situations in which the possibility of a layoff is high or in which a harsh, insensitive organizational climate exists may stifle the tendency toward mutual help that might otherwise exist.

Such situations exact a high toll from the physical and emotional resources of individuals. Given this, we would expect students to transfer to other schools or workers to take other employment. Indeed, high worker turnover and student attrition often are observed in such situations. However, as with pathogenic families, individuals will often consider themselves to be (or actually may be) without other alternatives. Since (as will be discussed in Chapter 7) system-focused interventions may be beyond the preferences, resources, and expertise of some counselors, it may be useful to help individuals examine whether their lack of alternatives is actual or self-imposed. Even when they choose to continue membership in a stressful group, clients may be helped to develop strategies for maximizing the supportive contributions of unconflicted areas of the network.

Client-Based Factors

While it is true that persons sometimes lack social support from others because of factors that are based in the physical setting or in the attitudes and actions of others, support deficiency can also often be tied, in whole or in part, to their own attitudes, behavior, and/or status within the network. In practice, the distinction implied between behavior and attitude is not an absolute one. The belief that others are dangerous and exploitive very quickly translates into a variety of distancing behaviors that serve to separate the individual from supporters. That belief can also alienate others and make them unwilling to extend social support. Also, inappropriate behavior can lead to rejection and punishment, causing individuals to develop a generalized distrust of others. While recognizing the interdependence of attitude and behavior, each will be considered separately as a source of support deficiency. Different intervention strategies may result, depending on whether one takes an internally focused (attitudes and beliefs) or externally focused (behavior and action) perspective for understanding the persons with whom one works.

What are some of the attitudes and beliefs that are apt to affect others' awareness of a person's needs negatively, and to reduce their willingness to extend social support? Perhaps those most commonly encountered by counselors and other helping professionals are low self-esteem, fear and suspicion of others, self-centeredness, and fear of dependency. In actual practice these attitudes may be found to cluster together, as when fear and suspicion of others is closely linked to low self-esteem (e.g., "Why would anyone like me? This person seems nice, but what is he really after?"). However, because they often stand as a focus of attention in practice, these attitude or belief clusters will be considered separately.

Low Self-Esteem

Carl, age 14: No, I don't have any friends — why would anyone like me? I'm ugly, I'm bad in sports, and even my good grades in school get me nothing but grief from the other kids. Even when I try to stay to myself, like on the bus or in the cafeteria, someone makes fun of me, calls me a loser. If I could just play basketball, or were bigger or stronger, maybe it would be different, but I'm just a nerd and the only kids who will hang around with me are nerds too — who needs that? Sometimes when I'm listening to music in my room I try to imagine what it must be like to be all right, to be the kind of a person other people like, to have friends. Why did I have to be born such a loser?

The close association between positive, confirming interpersonal relationships and high self-esteem has been noted by a number of personality theorists (e.g., Combs, 1962; Jourard, 1970; Maslow, 1954). The pervasive belief that one is of little worth is both cause and effect of social isolation. Not valuing oneself, the assumption is made that others will feel the same way. Individuals withdraw from situations where there is the potential for significant social interaction because they expect rejection, criticism, or humiliation. If it is impossible to avoid such situations, they "fade into the woodwork," functioning in a manner that will draw as little attention to themselves as possible.

Many shy, interpersonally inhibited persons avoid close relationships because they don't like themselves and believe others will feel the same way. The process of distancing from others may allow one to escape anticipated negative actions; however, it also serves to isolate the individual from positive contributions others might make (Nelson, 1980). We see this effect in the aftermath of many suicides. People who have had some superficial contact with an individual express dismay that the deceased person was so distraught, and say that they would have been glad to help if only they had known.

Another consequence of low self-esteem that may influence the availability of social support to individuals negatively is the tendency toward self-deprecation in social interaction. Apologizing and calling attention to one's own deficiencies, even when there is no actual need to do so, are as apt to cause disdain and rejection as they are to engender acceptance and tolerance. In their attempts to make others more responsive to their needs, self-deprecating persons may actually diminish the willingness of others to be supportive.

Fear and Suspicion of Others

Rita, age 34: I just don't want them to know my business! All they do is criticize, anyway. The only time my brother and his wife have anything to do with me is when they want something from me. Sure, if they want someone to take care of their kids when they go off to the city for a weekend, they're right on the phone. But where are they when I need them? Criticize me — that's all they've ever done. Why should I be the one that never got an education? Why was I the one who had to stay home and take care of my mother? And what sort of thanks did it get me? None! But why expect anything different? That's the way the world is — everyone looking out for themselves, trying to boost themselves up by putting someone else down. Well, I've had it! I'll keep my business to myself and let my relatives do the same. I'm tired of giving, giving, giving, and getting nothing in return. How would you feel?

The belief that others are dangerous is another of the attitudes that can lead individuals to isolate themselves or to interact in ways that discourage potential supporters from establishing or maintaining contact. A reality-based, situation-specific cautiousness about potentially harmful interpersonal interaction is functional. It allows individuals to avoid exploitation and physical and emotional abuse. However, a pervasive, fear-filled assumption that others are dangerous is detrimental to the development of relationships in which one can receive social support. Just as rejection and criticism by significant others during childhood often lead to the development of low self-esteem and the tendency to distance from others, so the experience of being physically and emotionally hurt (especially during the formative years) can lead to a generalized fear and distrust of others.

At the extreme, we can observe individuals preoccupied with deep-seated paranoia, in which elaborate, threatening designs are assumed to be at work in interpersonal situations. At a less extreme degree, we observe a pattern of fearfulness, suspicion, and/or cynicism toward others that often leads individuals to reject or avoid meaningful contact with others and can alienate and antagonize potential supporters. Verbal and nonverbal communication of suspicion often causes persons who have offered (or who might offer) support to feel that their well-intentioned efforts are questioned. Reacting with anger and hurt, the likelihood of their offering assistance again is reduced: "Why you ungrateful ass, I was only trying to help! See if you get anything else from me!"

However real and painful the circumstances under which generalized attitudes of fearfulness and suspicion may have been developed, the continued, inappropriate application of these attitudes to subsequent situations disrupts the seeking and reception of assistance from the support system. Without any reduction of client fearfulness, counseling interventions that focus simply on encouraging network members to be more supportive or to "try again" will often be counterproductive. Clients will continue to respond to supporters in a manner that discourages assistance, rather than reinforcing it. Similarly, simply encouraging a client to ask for help or to be less suspicious of others is not apt to be productive unless the deep-seated (often long-standing) fears that have disrupted the client's interpersonal relationships to begin with are addressed.

Fear of Dependency

Walter, age 32: I got where I am by handling things myself. In my line of work, you're expected to know what you're doing, to take charge. That's what leadership means in the business world—rising to the occasion, making your own decisions, and taking responsibility for them. Sure, you can delegate tasks, but there can never be any doubt about who's in charge and whose decision is being implemented. Teamwork is fine up to a point, but in order to function effectively there has to be a strong leader calling the shots, setting the goals, and making sure people are doing their parts. The thing I've found is most important—the thing I pride myself on—is to be in touch with other people, to know what they're doing and feeling, but to not need them. If you're uncertain about what the next step is, thrash it out with yourself, but never let other people see your uncertainty. People want, and respect, certainty. They don't have much confidence in a leader who has to take a vote to make a decision. I believe that's true not only in business but also in family relationships. I didn't become a husband and father to be a nice, but wishy-washy, guy who needs the approval of his wife and kids.

The ability to "do for oneself," to make one's own way, is generally a valued attribute in our culture. Needing assistance is often viewed as weakness and inadequacy (Fisher, Goff, Nadler, & Chinsky, 1988). The encouragement and reward of individual striving underlies many of the remarkable accomplishments of persons in our society. Nevertheless, stressing individual accomplishment can block awareness of (what seems to me, anyway) a basic truth — however extensive our own efforts, many of our gains rest on noticed and unnoticed contributions of others. Internal and external pressure to stand strong, and on one's own, is pervasive in this society. The need to depend on others for comfort, guidance, or material assistance viewed as weakness (Lewis, 1978), especially for men.

Fear of dependency, and the rejection of help that it often leads to, takes many forms. It can range from a quiet, "toughing it out" alone to an angry, vociferous rejection of assistance offered by others (Nelson, 1980). To the extent that individuals do, indeed, possess extensive psychic and material resources to deal with the daily demands of their lives, their rugged individualism may not be dysfunctional. As a matter of fact, self-sufficiency is likely to be admired and rewarded by others. However, sooner or later most people are faced either with a decrease in their own resources, or with a life situation (for example, a serious financial reversal or a natural disaster) that overwhelms their resources. In such circumstances the ability to acknowledge and act on the need for support contributes to successful coping, while the inability to do so is apt to be dysfunctional. Rathbone-McCuan and Hashimi (1982), for example, described the suffering of rural elderly persons who resist (to the extent of using physical force) offers of critically needed social services. The physical and emotional well-being of these elders was reduced because they were unyieldingly locked into a self-view that emphasized taking care of oneself.

Without devaluing the worth of individual responsibility and self-direction, it is important to call attention to the fact that there are many situations in which help from others is a practical, perhaps critical, necessity. When individuals withdraw from, or drive away, needed assistance, they often do a disservice not only to themselves, but to others whose well-being may depend on them. A functional stance toward receiving support from others would seem to reflect the ability to deal with situations flexibly, standing on one's own when that is possible, and being willing to accept assistance when that is realistically necessary. William Schutz (1958) addressed this sort of flexibility in interpersonal relationships when he discussed "interdependence" as the ability to be both dependent and independent, as the situation realistically demands.

Insensitivity to Others

Wilson, age 18: I think they're the ones who are selfish. I've got really expensive things, and it's a lot different if you get a spot on one of my shirts than on one that costs less. My roommates just can't seem to get the point — I'd be glad to let them borrow my clothes, but they're really special. My folks bought most of them in Europe, and there's no way I could replace them easily. I mean, its not as if we're talking about a fifteen- or twenty-dollar shirt from Sears or some other place! Why is it being selfish to have nice things and to want to keep them that way? And then when I ask my roommate if I can use his notes for the English class I cut, he tells me, "The door swings both ways," that if I'm not going to share things I shouldn't expect others to. As if the two situations had anything to do with each other!

A number of writers have recognized that the lack of social support experienced by many persons may stem from their own alienation of persons in their social network (e.g., Froland, Brodsky, Olson, & Stewart, 1979; Nelson, 1980; Turkat, 1980). Erma Bombeck's humorous but poignant resolution, "I will try to remember that those who need love the most often deserve it least," points, more colloquially, to the fact that people often drive away the people who can and would, at least initially, offer support.

I have already suggested that low self-esteem, suspicion of others, and fear of dependency can drive away actual and potential supporters. Behaviors that others find noxious can also alienate and antagonize others. Selfishness, insensitivity, poor personal hygiene, annoying speech patterns, manipulativeness, and making unreciprocated demands are examples of the sort of interpersonal attitudes and behaviors that tend to reduce the willingness of others to extend or continue offering support.

My experience as a counselor suggests that most adequately functioning adults describe the majority of their support relationships to be reciprocal in nature (i.e., relationships in which social support is both received and given). In contrast, Froland and his colleagues (1979) point out that many chronically disturbed persons take, demand, and/or elicit social support, but do not return it to their supporters. People tend to move out of relationships that are not symmetrical in terms of their getting roughly the same amount of social support back as they give (Fisher et al., 1988). Exceptions to that general pattern are relationships built around strong ties of obligation (e.g., family relationships) or those in which the support giver is filling a formal role centered on the provision of assistance (e.g., human service work).

We can observe, then, that individuals themselves are often the primary cause of their lack of interpersonal support. They lack caring friends and relatives because people who might otherwise provide various types of assistance believe their interests, needs, and preferences are not met in the relationship. "Spoiled brats" who always demand to have their needs satisfied are a frequently encountered example of an interpersonal style that serves to diminish the offering of social support.

Stigmatized Status

Tammy, age 17: I'm a trailer park kid. That means the kids from the Village look down on me and the other kids from the Park. They call us dirt balls, they say we smell, they make fun of us. Maybe we don't dress as good as they do, but that doesn't mean we're trash. Kids from the Park don't ever get elected to class office; we don't get invited to their homes. Sometimes if a guy is good in sports, or if a girl is really pretty, they may be liked or paid some attention to, but not usually. They say that we're bad, that people from the Park drink and do drugs, sleep around; well, at least we're not hypocrites the way a lot of the kids from the Village are. We don't sneak around playing goody two shoes the way they do. I could tell you some stories that would change your opinion of some of the kids in this school! Sometimes it gets to me, being treated as if I was covered with scabs or something. Even some of the teachers act the same way — "What can you expect? She's one of the kids from the Park." So we stick to ourselves, and make fun of the Village kids. Personally, I can't get out of this place fast enough. I'll graduate, but only because I need to if I'm going to get into the type of training I want to in the army, not because I really like this dump!

Prejudice of all sorts serves to set up barriers to the giving and receiving of interpersonal support. The willingness to extend caring and assistance often stops at the boundaries of our own group. This is especially true if the other persons in question are viewed as not simply different, but deviant. The different can be ignored; however, persons considered deviant often become fair targets for indirect or direct aggression. Those labeled deviant are often not simply confronted with quiet ostracism and withholding of assistance; they may also have to deal with overt hostility. Others who might be inclined to be supportive withdraw as well. Hostility from others often forces persons labeled deviant to look to other persons like themselves for acceptance and assistance, strengthening the identity and solidarity of the group.

The danger and vulnerability associated with being different is seen in the reluctance of many persons to make their membership in rejected groups known. The soul-searching associated with making the decision about whether or not to "come out of the closet" or to come to the defense of persons identified as deviant is a common theme of literature. We also see evidence of the vulnerability associated with deviant or devalued status in the growth of mutual help groups for rejected persons (Killilea, 1976). Groups for persons with particularly devalued physical handicaps, ethnic and nationality affiliation, or political orientation offer a context within which access to social support denied by the wider society is possible.

Counseling strategies used with persons who lack support because they are considered to be deviant are as apt to reflect the values and preferences of the helper as the actual alternatives available to the client. The counsel to stop being deviant and "return to the fold" may indeed point to an effective, appropriate way for an individual to reestablish social connectedness with important people in his or her life. However, though easiest and most pragmatic, this alternative often ignores the reality that individual growth sometimes depends on individuals' ability to define what is really important to them, to think through the consequences of their beliefs, and to stand publicly for those beliefs.

In the long run, accommodation to general values may be in the best interests of neither the individuals identified as deviant nor the broader society. History gives ample support to the view that important contributions to social growth and development have often come from individuals and groups that were initially considered to be deviant. However, a counseling strategy that focuses on self-definition and self-direction will have to recognize that the decision to maintain an identity generally judged to be deviant will often be accompanied by the onset or continuation of support loss. In such cases, methods of enhancing self-support and of linking up with mutual help groups or other forms of peer support may be useful directions for counseling to take.

Conclusion

Whether focused on conditions residing in individuals themselves, in their significant supporters, or in their physical and/or social contexts, the situations that have been discussed exemplify those in which our clients are apt to experience support deficiencies. Sensitized to these situations, counselors can monitor the status of clients experiencing them to identify persons whose support resources have been negatively reduced or interrupted. Remedial programs designed to counteract the negative effects of support deficit can be begun before the physical and psychological disability commonly associated with lack of social support (Caplan, 1974; Cassel, 1974) becomes chronic or widespread.

As we will see in Chapters 5 and 7, support-focused counseling interventions can vary greatly in their targets (i.e., the person or persons at whom the intervention is directed) and their strategies. Movement from a broad recognition that social support seems to be an important element in a client's presenting concerns to the design and implementation of a specific intervention depends on assembling information concerning the particular nature of the client's existing support resources, deficiencies, and preferences. Chapter 3 will examine concepts and procedures that are useful in gathering such information.

Chapter Three

Assessment of Social Support Resources

Realizing that social support issues are exerting, or are apt to exert, an important influence on a client or a client group, a logical next step is for the counselor to gather specific data on the availability of social support to the client, and to assess the characteristics and functioning style of the natural support system made up of family, friends, neighbors, and co-workers (Froland et al., 1979). Clearly, it may also be important to determine the extent to which the natural system is or is not interfacing with formal systems (that is, human service workers, agencies, or organizations). However, the focus of this chapter will be the assessment and description of the natural system that stands as the first resource to which most people turn. The system represents a continuing pool of resources drawn on for facing the tasks of normal development (Golan, 1981; Gurin et al., 1960).

The examination of clients' relationships with such persons as family, friends, and co-workers is often a consideration in counseling practice. In many settings, intake procedures focus on developing a picture of the objective and emotional features of the interpersonal context within which clients function. For example, Cormier and Cormier (1985) cite the importance of developing an understanding of clients' "relationships and significant others" (pp. 186-187) as an element in understanding the problem behaviors that often bring individuals to counseling. In this vein also, Heller (1979) noted a tendency among many practitioners to see the natural network as a negative influence that is pathogenic in its impact on the emotional health of individuals; thus information concerning the natural network is considered to be important in developing an understanding of the causes and characteristics of the difficulties leading people to seek, or to be referred for, assistance.

Pattison (1973) noted that interventions based on this negative view of the natural system's effect are apt to stress the importance of separating the client from the social network as a way of reducing negative factors. In contrast, viewing the natural system as (actually or potentially) a positive resource in clients' lives casts a different light on the assessment of that system. Now assessment can be viewed as a matter of exploring how the system can be used as a resource in furthering clients' growth and development.

Support Assessment and Counseling Intervention

This chapter examines the concepts and procedures that counselors and other helping professionals can use to develop a picture of the social support resources available to clients, the role these resources have played in the development of clients' difficulties, and the way the natural system might be mobilized or enhanced to further clients' growth. Such a picture can contribute to the helping process in a number of ways. A knowledge of the social support resources available to clients, and an understanding of the characteristics of the informal social system through which these resources are delivered, can serve as an important basis for developing interventions aimed at helping clients find new support resources. This knowledge can also be used to help them make more effective use of currently available support. Specific support-focused strategies and procedures will be considered in subsequent chapters. For now, our focus is on the gathering and analysis of data on which such procedures can be built.

General Issues in Assessment of Social Support

There are a number of issues with which counselors must come to terms as they approach the development of an understanding of clients' social support preferences, needs, and resources. Most of these issues are not unique to the assessment of social support phenomena. For example, the matter of the relative worth of subjective and objective measures discussed below is ultimately an aspect of a metaphysical issue cutting across all facets of human endeavor: What is real, that which we can determine to be so by objective, quantitative means, or that which the sensing, experiencing human being believes to be real?

Four issues that seem particularly important and form a backdrop to an examination of the role of social support in the functioning of our clients are as follows:

  · How specific is it necessary to be in defining the properties of social support that guide the inquiry into clients' social support preferences, needs, and resources?
  · What are the comparative advantages and disadvantages of global and situation-specific assessments of social support and support systems?
  · Should subjective or objective strategies be used to assess clients' social support needs and resources?
  · What are the relative strengths and limitations of structured and unstructured approaches to assessing social support and support systems?

Each of these issues will be discussed, with particular consideration given to how each is apt to affect counseling practice.

General and Differentiated Views of Social Support

As pointed out elsewhere (Pearson, 1982), common use of the word *support* reflects a somewhat undifferentiated view of what support is. Typically, it connotes that it is a resource to boost up faltering individuals by alleviating the intensity of their feelings of sadness or despair, or to help them by taking action to improve their material situation (e.g., loaning them money, providing child care assistance). While most theoretical and empirical considerations of the nature of social support do, indeed, include dimensions similar to comforting and material help, theory and research in this area also have identified a number of additional facets that go far beyond relatively undifferentiated, everyday views.

For example, both Caplan (1974) and Cassel (1974) asserted that information from others that allows individuals to get a clearer understanding of their situation and feedback about the consequences of their actions supports individuals in their attempts to cope effectively with a variety of life situations. In examples presented previously, we've seen how the lack of "appraisal" support (i.e., feedback about the appropriateness or effectiveness of their actions) may be involved in the difficulties of some clients; however, the supportive potential of information-giving and feedback may not be recognized by clients whose views are dominated by a focus on comforting or material assistance.

Given the usual focus on social support as comfort and material help, the counselor should not assume that clients' views of social support will be differentiated enough to allow them to discuss their preferences, needs, and resources in detail and depth. There may be forms of social support that they receive from others but do not recognize, and there may be forms of support they lack that, because of a variety of factors, they do not realize.

Perhaps cultural influences warrant particular mention here as factors that may lead clients to hold limited views of the nature of social support. There is enormous variation among cultural groups with regard to which attitudes and actions are considered to be supportive and from whom such actions may appropriately come. Giordano (1976), describing the variations among urban ethnic groups, noted that some groups respond warmly to outside offers of material assistance, while others view such efforts as threatening or demeaning. We should be careful to enter our work free of too many assumptions about what clients do, or do not, view as supportive. Individual, family, or cultural factors may lead clients to overlook or discount extensive amounts of support they are already receiving or could potentially receive.

When it is determined that clients' narrow or undifferentiated views of social support are limiting their ability to recognize their needs or resources, it will often be necessary to move discussion with them beyond matters that are apparently relevant to the client. A query such as "How did you find out about that job opening?" may reveal that a client has access to a number of working friends who are alert to openings in their workplaces, informing her when people are being hired. Through such exploration, the counselor learns a bit more about the client's informal support network, and can also help the client "see" a type of support (i.e., information-giving) not previously considered in exactly that fashion.

Global and Situation-Specific Assessment Approaches

In terms of social support issues, should we concern ourselves with determining clients' general needs and resources, or is it more important to get a picture of these matters as they apply to specific issues or situations? Many of the instruments and techniques developed to assess social support phenomena yield global pictures. For example, many of the initial studies in this area used measures of "social embeddedness" as evidenced, for example, by whether or not a person was married (Eaton, 1978), the number of friends or relatives reported (Berkman & Syme, 1979), or membership in voluntary associations or fraternal organizations (Lin, Simeone, Ensel, & Kuo, 1979). Such general measures assume that the more socially embedded individuals are, the greater their access to social support will be.

Clearly, such measures provide only a very general indication of support resources (apparently) available to the individual. There is no way of knowing, for example, whether the specific voluntary organization to which an individual belongs considers its mission to include the amelioration of the particular sorts of difficulties the individual in question is facing. Moreover, while a marriage may or may not be generally supportive, one cannot tell, solely on the basis of knowing that an individual is married, whether or not the spouse is offering a form of support that is particularly important in a specific crisis situation.

The work of counselors and other human service workers typically begins with a concern for particular situations. As we saw in Chapter 2, people lose loved ones, are rejected by peer groups, alienate others, or make life transitions. The disruption that such events cause to the availability of social support from the natural system may lead such individuals to seek assistance from counselors and other helping professionals. When social support issues are determined to play an important role in those situations, we are naturally drawn to a consideration of what type of support is or is not available to the client, and from whom. It is, perhaps, only later that we have the time to pull back and pay attention to the manner in which the support issues at hand relate to broader aspects of the client's functioning.

Therefore, counselors are initially most apt to be concerned with a situation-specific examination of clients' support needs and resources. Rather than asking, "How important is it to you that people accept, not judge, you?" we are apt to ask, "Are you concerned that your parents will get down on you because you've flunked out of college?" Or, rather than asking, "Do you have friends with whom you can talk?" we focus more on the situation at hand by asking, "To whom do you go to talk out your worries that you may be laid off?" If rating scales or questionnaires are used to get a picture of a client's support needs and resources, those requiring respondents to indicate their status in terms of particular types of support from specific persons, for the particular issues they are facing, will typically be most relevant and useful in counseling practice.

Having noted that clients often come to counseling with concerns focused on particular situations, it is also important to point out that at some point we will begin to wonder whether or not the patterns and issues that are observed in the situation at hand also affect the client in other contexts. For example, do the patterns of social isolation individuals experience in the work situation also extend to their family or peer group relationships? Determining whether or not clients' strengths and limitations are confined to a particular situation, or are more generally manifested, is important in understanding the true dimensions of clients' needs. This understanding may also have implications for the development and implementation of helping interventions.

Subjective and Objective Support Assessment Approaches

Concerning ourselves with clients' views of social support, and its importance and availability to them, rests on the belief that how individuals view themselves and their surroundings is an important determinant of their behavior. The importance attached to subjective, phenomenological experience is reflected in assessment approaches that rest on individuals' self-reported experience, beliefs, and opinions. In contrast, practitioners and researchers who stress objective aspects of individuals' functioning are apt to rely on external assessments of behavior, believing that by doing so they gain access to data about individuals that are not distorted by the vagaries of biases, misjudgments, and lack of candor.

Cohen and Syme (1985) pointed to these two approaches to assessing clients' social support resources by distinguishing between functional and structural measures. Functional measures provide data about individuals' perceptions of support that is actually, or potentially, available to them. In contrast, structural measures describe the objective characteristics of individuals' social contexts. For example, the size of an individual's network and the number of persons contacted during a particular period are structural measures. It should be noted that this use of the term *structural measure* is somewhat different from that proposed by Mitchell (1974). As will be discussed more fully later in this chapter, Mitchell's structural measures relate to the form that the system takes (e.g., size, composition) in contrast to interactive measures that describe how the system operates (e.g., frequency of contact, density). The structural measures described by Cohen and Syme are distinguished by the fact that the data on which they are based are objective, rather than subjective, in nature. Such structural measures include indices that would be identified as both structural and interactive by Mitchell.

Without entering into the long-standing discussion in assessment circles about the relative advantages of objectively or subjectively oriented approaches to understanding human behavior (e.g., McClintock, Brannon, & Maynard-Moody, 1979), it will simply be noted that the majority of the procedures developed for assessing social support rest ultimately on self-report. That self-report may be gained through the use of questionnaires (e.g., the author's Personal Support System Survey, presented in Appendix A), checklists, interviews (e.g., the Social Stress and Support Interview, developed by Jenkins, Mann, & Belsey, 1981), and other procedures. However formal or informal the format, all such approaches essentially come down to asking individuals to express their views of their support status through such questions as, "How much support (in terms, for example, of financial help) do you get?" or "Who is offering support to you in this situation?"

In contrast, objective assessment approaches might, for example, have an observer view the individual and record the number of times social support (objectively defined) is sought or received from others. Or, we might gather data to determine the individual's social embeddedness, a construct previously discussed in this chapter. As has been discussed, the use of measures of embeddedness rests on the assumption that the greater the number of ties the client has to other individuals and groups, the greater the amount of social support he or she will receive. Not only is this assumption often open to question, the difficulty with objective approaches in general is that they are based on the position that generalized conceptualizations of what is or is not supportive have validity for any particular individual.

The possible pitfalls of applying general notions of support to particular individuals (however objective the process used) is apparent when we realize that attitudes and actions, ordinarily considered unsupportive in impact, sometimes may actually be experienced as quite supportive. For example, usually a refusal to offer comfort or material assistance would be considered unsupportive; yet, in retrospect, many persons will say that such actions were "exactly what I needed to stop feeling sorry for myself; they had more faith in me than I had in myself."

Similarly, attitudes or actions that to someone else may seem obviously supportive may be experienced by individuals as unsupportive. For example, while the willingness to intervene and promote clients' interests with significant others might serve to resolve a situation with which clients are struggling, such intervention may sometimes be experienced by them as demeaning of their competence or intrusive on their privacy.

While there are many theory-based reasons for concerning ourselves with individuals' subjective views of their support resources, there are practical reasons for doing so as well. Often, clients are the only source of data to which the counselor will have easy access. Moreover, the fact that clients' views of their support needs and resources may subsequently prove erroneous does not reduce the significance of those views. Indeed, helping such clients to gain a more accurate view of their support needs and resources may come to be a major focus of the counseling process.

Structured and Unstructured Assessment of Support Resources

There are many approaches, techniques, and instruments for determining clients' views of their social support needs and resources. Another broad distinction that can be made among these approaches is that some are primarily structured in nature while others are more unstructured in their character.

What the various structured approaches have in common is that their focus and procedures are determined before the gathering of information actually begins. Typically, the information gatherer already has the essential features of the area being studied clearly in mind, has decided the particular types of information that must be acquired to give a reading of the client's status, and (to varying degrees) will have specified the particular information-gathering procedures (for example, questions, checklists, rating scales) to be used.

In contrast, less structured assessment approaches are based on the view that the assessor should approach gathering information with as few preconceptions and predetermined activities as possible so that the data obtained will reflect the (perhaps) unique characteristics of the individual or group at hand. Clearly, data gathering must have some point of departure, but preset questions or procedures are kept to a minimum lest the investigators end up with data about what they, rather than the respondents, consider to be important.

To give an example of the difference between structured and unstructured strategies, consider two interviews, each of which is intended to help the counselor develop an understanding of (a) clients' notions of what social support is, (b) the types of social support they consider most pertinent to their current concerns, (c) the extent to which they actually consider themselves to be receiving such support, and (d) the persons from whom they are, and are not, receiving that support. In the first interview, the counselor guides the discussion by using a series of questions (perhaps a detailed extension of the four points just presented), making sure that information is obtained from the client concerning each of the predetermined areas.

The second interview proceeds from a decision by the counselor to focus on the client's views of social support and support availability, but to do so in a relatively open-ended manner. Thus, instead of following a set of predetermined questions or topics, the counselor allows the client to choose which aspects of her personal functioning have an effect on the nature, role, and availability of social support. Such an interview would be based on an invitation to the client to talk about her relationships with other people and the assistance they provide, rather than following an interview protocol. Open-ended questions would predominate rather than questions focused on obtaining specific information predetermined to be of significance.

Berit Ingersall (1983), contrasting the strengths and benefits of quantitative (structured) and qualitative (unstructured) data-gathering strategies, has suggested that each has its own unique contributions to make. The quantitative approach is efficient, can be used to gather data from many individuals, and thus can result in findings that are highly generalizable. In contrast, qualitative approaches, while tending to be more time-consuming in their implementation, result in findings that are rich in detail and capable of providing information unrecognized by persons not actually experiencing the sort of events under consideration.

Ingersall makes a case for using both quantitative and qualitative research strategies in a way that capitalizes on the strengths of each.

The same position can be translated into the work of counselors trying to develop an understanding of the role that social support variables may be playing in the presenting concerns of their clients. We might, for example, use checklists or questionnaires to develop a broad overview of clients' situations. Next, we might follow up with a discussion of the findings with clients, determining specifically how they interpret the variables introduced by the questionnaire, and examining the particular influence these variables exert on their lives. By skillfully blending both quantitative and qualitative approaches, it is possible for counselors to have both the advantages of the efficiency and generalizability of objective approaches and the detailed, individual-specific findings of the subjective.

Assessing Clients' Support Resources: General Aspects

Whatever assessment strategy is used (e.g., structured/unstructured or objective/subjective), assessing clients' support resources begins by identifying a set of questions, the answers to which will provide the counselor a clear view of how support variables might be affecting clients' ability to cope with life issues. The following questions, based on an examination of the research and practice-oriented literature, and on my counseling experience, can provide both an understanding of clients' status and a base for developing counseling strategies:

· What are the client's views of social support, its importance and availability?
· Who are the client's supporters?
· What particular types of social support are being provided by various supporters?
· How does the social support system, made up of these supporters, operate?

The first question focuses on getting information concerning support preferences and availability specific to the individual with whom we are working. The second and third questions provide a basis for extracting what Mitchell (1974) has called "structural measures" (for example, size, family proportion). In contrast, the final question yields data from which "interactive measures" (for example, how often supporters are contacted and who in the system knows whom) can be developed.

The P3S: An Instrument for Assessing Social Support Variables

The Personal Support System Survey (P3S) is a multifaceted assessment instrument I've developed for clinical and research purposes. It is designed to yield information on which answers to the four questions just posed can be based (the P3S can be found in Appendix A in its entirety). Though clearly not the only means of assessing clients' views of the nature of social support, its availability to them, and the characteristics of their natural support systems, the P3S is representative of other instruments. It will be used as a basis for examples in the following discussion of assessment procedures. Other approaches will be mentioned from time to time in this and subsequent chapters, and the reader can seek out Heitzman and Kaplan's (1983) excellent review of a number of social support assessment approaches for a broader introduction to assessment options.

The P3S is built on a differentiated view of social support. The rating scales respondents are asked to complete in the first part of the instrument focus on 12 different types of social support, ranging from "comfort," common to everyday conceptualizations of support, to "guidance," the supportive function of which is often overlooked. These 12 different types of support were initially identified by giving a group of 33 individuals a general description of what a natural support system is, asking them to identify the persons in that system, and, finally, asking them to indicate (using single words or short phrases) what it was that those persons provided to them that had supportive value.

From the resulting pool of responses, a comprehensive set of "support types" were identified that were specific enough to avoid extensive overlap among categories, yet not so narrow that respondents would be overwhelmed by the necessity to make fine distinctions. Extensive clinical and research use of these categories supports their usability. Additionally, rating scales based on the categories have demonstrated acceptable levels of reliability (Pearson, 1982; Esperon, 1985/1986). Their predictive validity is supported by the finding of expected differences on support variables between various demographic groups (Claudio, 1983/1984; Cruz-Lopez & Pearson, 1985).

In the most recent form of the P3S, the support areas were slightly modified to include three scales representative of each of the four types of support identified by House (1981); that is, emotional support (love, comfort, companionship), informational support (information, guidance, example), appraisal support (honesty, acceptance, encouragement), and material support (resources, advocacy, tasks).

Social Support Assessment in Counseling Practice

To illustrate the manner in which data concerning clients' support preferences and resources can be developed and summarized, the P3S results of Rose (a person whose protocol actually blends data from several clients) will be used. As presented here, Rose was a 28-year-old single woman who sought counseling assistance with concerns focused primarily on dissatisfaction with her current social life. Although she came from, and had ready access to, a large extended family, she reported she had few friends of her own age. Most importantly, she had no current, intimate male relationship.

Rose indicated that many of the women who were her long-time friends were now married, which she believed interfered with her access to the companionship she previously received from them. Their marriages also served to accentuate to her that time was passing in her own life, and she was still unmarried.

In general, Rose believed that she was not making adequate progress toward important life goals related both to marriage and her career. Initially, counseling focused on the possibility of going back to school to open up new alternatives to her current unchallenging job in a large insurance office. Somewhat later, Rose focused more on her interpersonal situation. She examined the loss of an intimate relationship two years before and probed the reasons for its end. Finally, she moved on to consider the more general difficulty she had developing close nonfamily relationships.

Rose's P3S protocol can be found in Appendix B. Data from the protocol will be drawn on to illustrate how various types of support-relevant indices can be derived to describe clients' social support preferences and resources.

Clients' Views of Their Support Preferences and Needs

Lakey and Heller (1988) noted that many researchers have tended to assume that measures of perceived social support are equivalent to the amount of support actually received by an individual. They also noted, however, that a number of investigators (e.g., Kiecolt-Glaser & Greenberg, 1984; Sarason & Sarason, 1986) have avoided such an assumption. Rather, they have attempted to explore the effect of social support by objectively controlling the amount of assistance available to individuals coping with a variety of tasks and demands.

By varying the level of objective support (variously operationalized as interviewer warmth or the amount of assistance offered by a friend or experimenter) available to an individual, such studies are able to examine the relationship between received social support and performance. Additionally, some experimenters following this "social support-as-objectively-measured-variable strategy" have also gathered data relating to the individuals' perceptions of the amount of social support available to them in the experimental situation. Using such an experimental design, Lakey and Heller (1988) found no significant relationship between perceived and received support. They also found these two types of social support (i.e., perceived and received) showed a different pattern of association with different types of dependent measures. For example, perceived support showed a significant positive relationship with individuals' perceptions of the stressfulness of the experimental task (a problem-solving task), but bore no significant relationship with the measure of objective support. Conversely, the measure of objective support was found to have a positive relationship to the individuals' advice-seeking behavior, but not to their perception of the amount of help received.

Within the limits of their study, Lakey and Heller concluded that perceived and received support should not be assumed to be equivalent either in composition or in effect. They speculated "whether received support might operate primarily by influencing coping behavior and whether perceived support might operate primarily through appraisal processes" (1988, p. 820). To the extent these findings are found to be generalizable, they suggest that (as counselors) we might contribute to clients' access to social support by helping them become more active in seeking support across a variety of situations. Conversely, we might help them experience less stress in many situations by helping them acquire a generally positive outlook on the amount of social support available to them. Thus a differentiated approach to working with individuals' support needs and resources will (as we will see in Chapter 5) have both attitudinal and behavioral dimensions.

Without discounting the importance of gathering both objective and subjective data concerning support resources and needs, my own approach begins with getting clients' own views of their situation vis-à-vis social support. Later I investigate the extent to which those views correspond to objective reality; however, initially I concern myself with seeing the world as they see it. I believe there are good reasons for examining clients' perceptions of situations. Phenomenological theorists (e.g., Snygg, 1941) assert that we respond to life on the basis of what we perceive our situation to be, not necessarily in accordance with the way that situations may, objectively, be. If behavior is guided by perceptions, then in order to understand our clients' difficulties, and their responses to those difficulties, we need to enter their frames of reference, seeing the world as they do. Doing so may help us to understand why a particular client consistently avoids seeking or accepting supportive assistance from individuals in her environment, or why another client persists in trying to get emotional comfort from an individual who, objectively, is not concerned about his welfare.

The first section of the P3S (see Appendix A) focuses on obtaining data concerning the importance that respondents attach to various types of social support . Also, the degree to which they are satisfied with the availability of each is determined. An example of the rating scales used to obtain those data is presented in Figure 3.1.

I have chosen to get information from clients concerning both their views of the availability of different categories of social support and the degree of importance they attach to those categories. Logically, a knowledge of clients' satisfaction with the availability of a type of social support does not tell the counselor as much as that same information in combination with the knowledge of how important that type of support is to them. For example, two clients might indicate that they are somewhat dissatisfied with the amount of "guidance" available to them. However, one client indicates that guidance is very important to him, while the other indicates that it is of little importance. These ratings are illustrated in Figure 3.2, with the X representing the first client (i.e., high importance, low availability) and the * representing the second client (low importance, low availability).

In the first case, something of importance is lacking, while in the second the client has indicated its lack is of no great importance. A counselor considering ways of helping these clients deal with their support deficiencies would focus on expanding the first client's access to guidance, while that type of support, even though lacking to the second client, would not be of major concern since the client attaches little importance to it.

There are a number of additional ways in which these support importance and availability ratings can be used. Numerical values (1-5) can be assigned to segments of the rating scales, ascending from "very important" and "completely available" to "of no importance" and "completely unavailable." Since the individual scales represent one of four

We receive many kinds of social support from others. The type of support listed below is one of those most commonly mentioned by individuals.

You are provided with two rating scales. The first scale is for you to tell how <u>important</u> that type of support is to you. The second rating scale is for you to indicate how <u>available</u> this type of support is to you.

<u>Companionship</u> - the sharing of activities, the sense of belonging or togetherness you get from contact with others.

very important :____:____:____:____:____: of no importance

completely :____:____:____:____:____: completely
available   unavailable

Figure 3.1. **Example of P3S Directions, and Importance and Availability Scales**

broader support areas identified by House (i.e., emotional support, material support, informational support, appraisal support), the sum of ratings for an area may reflect (for individuals or groups of individuals) broader areas of importance and deficiency.

Whether one uses the ratings for the 12 individual support types or those for the four broader areas, it is possible to identify categories of support in which clients indicate they have important support deficiencies. This knowledge opens the door to discussions in which the counselor can develop a deeper understanding of the nature and causes of the deficiencies. Such understanding can provide a basis for developing ways of alleviating those deficiencies.

Rose's Importance and Availability Ratings

To use Rose's responses as an illustration, we can get a picture of her status vis-à-vis emotional support by finding the average of her importance and availability ratings on the "love," "companionship," and "comfort" scales. In doing so, we observe that emotional support is very important to Rose ($X = 1.0$), but not seen as readily available ($X = 3.3$). In contrast, on the informational support scales (that is, guidance,

Companionship - the sharing of activities, the sense of belonging or togetherness you get from contact with others.

very important : ___X___ : ___ : ___ : ___ : ___✷___ : of no importance

completely : ___ : ___ : ___ : _✷_ : _X_ : completely
available   unavailable

Figure 3.2. Example of Contrasting P3S Importance and Availability Scales

information, and example) we find a mean importance rating of 3.0 and a mean availability rating of 1.7. This suggests that informational support has little salience for Rose and that she considers it to be relatively available to her.

Indices of Support System Structure

Having obtained an overall picture of a client's social support preferences and needs, perhaps the next logical matter with which to concern ourselves is the determination of the people from whom support is received. Information about the structural characteristics (e.g., size) and composition (e.g., percentage who are family members) of the system can be helpful both in understanding its current functioning and in highlighting aspects that should be changed in order to improve the client's support resources.

In a conversation-based approach to obtaining information about the characteristics of the natural support system, we could ask the following questions:

· Who are the people in your life helping you deal with [the situation]? (Either a specific situation or a more general focus can be supplied.)
· Tell me a little about who these people are. For example, are they family members, friends, co-workers? Also, are they your own age, younger, or older?
· How long have you known each of these people? Are they recent acquaintances or long-time supporters?

On the P3S, a more structured approach to gathering data about the structure and operation of the support system, respondents are instructed to list the people who make up their support systems, indicate the nature of the relationship they have with each of these people (e.g., wife, friend, neighbor, admired well-known person), and indicate the others in the system whom each person knows and with whom there is interaction. Respondents are later asked to indicate how long each person has been a source of support.

There are a variety of descriptive indices that may be used to summarize the information obtained from clients concerning the characteristics of their natural support systems. Each of these will be considered, and their derivation and use discussed.

Size

The size score is determined by simply counting up the number of persons or objects (note that respondents often will identify animals or objects as sources of support) listed by the individual. Thus, in Rose's response to the P3S, we find that Rose has listed nine people in describing her general support system.

My experience suggests that there is considerable variation among individuals in support system size, and that one should not assume a direct relationship between size and support satisfaction. For example, Esperon (1986) found a .27 correlation between system size and the overall level of satisfaction that recently graduated college students expressed with the amount of social support received from their systems. There seem to be various styles of building a support system: Some people have just a few supporters, from each of whom they receive many different types of social support; others have relatively large systems, with each person supplying a distinct type of support. In terms of producing a satisfying support system, either strategy seems to be successful, perhaps reflecting the individual's general interpersonal style.

However, the counselor should follow up general questions to determine if there is any significance to unusually small (I use three or fewer supporters) or large (in my experience, more than ten) systems. Sometimes clients will express dissatisfaction with small systems, indicating that they want more people as supporters, but don't know how to go about forming relationships with new people very well. In other cases, clients will indicate that their large number of supporters is reflective of the fact that they have many acquaintances but no real friends, and that they'd like to have fewer, but closer, relationships. Either of these statements could serve as a point of departure for developing a counseling direction (e.g., skills training, helping the client examine the advantages and disadvantages of moving).

Size of Rose's system. Referring to Appendix B, we note that on the P3S, Rose has listed nine people in her support system. At first glance this would seem to present a favorable picture, since this is a relatively large system. However, as has been mentioned, the face-to-face exchange of counseling allows us to push beyond generalizations about whether "more is better." We observe that all but one of the persons listed are family. Also, Rose has indicated dissatisfaction with her support system because all the people are too similar. These observations provide us with directions to pursue in seeking to understand how Rose is experiencing her interpersonal relationships.

Composition Percentages

Often it will be useful to examine the proportion of supporters who belong to one or another particular group. Depending on the situation, the following proportions may be of significance:

- proportion of supporters who are also members of the respondent's *immediate* family;
- proportion of supporters who are members of the respondent's immediate and *extended* family;
- proportion of supporters who are of the respondent's sex group;
- proportion of supporters who are of the same age group; and
- proportion of supporters who are of the same racial, ethnic, or religious group.

Though we would ordinarily think that a support system composed primarily of family would be an indicator of a person's having access to rich, personalized support resources ("Just one big happy family!"), whether or not such is actually true depends on the characteristics of the family in question. For example, families dominated by the alcoholism of one of its members may discourage closeness with outsiders for fear others will discover the concealed pathology. Fisher et al. (1988) noted that the social network will often discourage behavior considered to conflict with its assumptions and norms. Thus a family that believes help from outsiders represents unwarranted interference or indicates family inadequacy will tend to discourage individuals from seeking (or accepting) assistance from outside. Not only is the family not a source of assistance, it also acts as a deterrent to members' gaining support otherwise available.

In such cases, what Gottlieb (1981) called the "stress-to-benefit ratio" may be very high, reflecting the fact that members are locked into a conflicted system in which the support achieved is outweighed by interpersonal turmoil. Wilcox (1981), in a study cited in Chapter 1, found that women with family-dominated personal support systems tended to have more difficulty dealing with the consequences of divorce than did those whose systems had a smaller proportion of family. His explanation of these findings was that the women more dependent on their families often found that there were strings attached to the assistance that family provided. Having to rely on family threw them back into a position of dependency, often a circumstance with negative consequences.

As with the size score, we should not make too many prior assumptions about what a high or low proportion of any of these groupings in the support system means. Again, we can explore the significance of any pattern noted with clients. This allows us to determine its influence on clients' current concerns and assess the degree to which the pattern needs to be taken into account in subsequent problem-solving interventions.

Composition of Rose's system. We have already noted that almost all (89%) of the persons whom Rose identified as making up her support system are family. This leads us to recall the comments of the women in Wilcox's (1981) study, which indicated that there were both advantages and disadvantages to depending primarily on family for support. Family closeness can be expressed in such forms as meddling and unsought control, as well as in caring and concern. One meaning of Rose's statement that her supporters are "too similar" could be that they are nearly all family members.

However, there are other composition proportions we can examine that also may shed some light on Rose's dissatisfaction. For example, four (45%) of the persons whom Rose listed in her support system are male. This is not a remarkable figure until we realize that all of these males are family members. This lends another dimension of meaning to Rose's identification of the lack of a romantic relationship as one of her chief life dissatisfactions.

A similar situation holds with reference to the age group composition of her natural support system. Though the P3S does not ask for the ages of the persons listed, we can assume that probably four (three siblings, one friend), and perhaps one more (co-worker), supporters are of her age cohort. If face-to-face conversation confirmed such an assumption, the "same age cohort" percentage would be 45%, again not a remarkable figure. However, when we realize again that only one or two of those persons are nonfamily, the extent to which Rose is dependent on her family comes clearly into focus. Whatever the benefit she derives from her relatives, it is apparent she is dissatisfied with the lack of access to relationships with nonfamily persons, perhaps particularly persons of her own age. Even more specifically, her dissatisfaction is related to the absence of a male with whom she could have a romantic relationship.

Stability

Another characteristic of the system that may have importance for the concerns on which counseling focuses is whether the people in the system are newly acquired or long-standing supporters. The most common pattern I have encountered is that of a stable core of supporters (usually family), with the remainder of the system made up of more recent additions. Those more recent additions represent the dynamic, growing edge of the support system. Some individuals are sloughed off, and others are added as time goes on and life situations change. Often, it is possible to trace past transitions (e.g., going to college, taking a job at a particular company) by noting clusters of persons who entered the system at the same time. Such life shifts tend to put the individual into contact with new people, some of whom enter the system. Often these additions are, in turn, replaced at a later time as the individual's life changes.

What is a "good" pattern in terms of the stability of a personal support system? As has been true with other aspects, it is impossible to provide a single, definitive answer to this question. The research provides no relevant findings, and my own work with clients suggests that people express satisfaction with systems that vary considerably in terms of stability. However, extreme patterns (for example, systems completely composed of long-time supporters or, conversely, those made up entirely of very recently acquired supporters) should catch our attention.

The lack of anyone of recent acquisition in the system may be indicative of such factors as low-level social skills, which make forming relationships difficult. It might also reflect the effect of a tight, controlling system that discourages any significant contact with outsiders. The absence of long-time supporters may also reflect an inability to form deep, lasting relationships, or be the result of sharp schisms in individuals' relationships with their families and other long-standing relationships.

Discoveries of such significance to predominantly long-standing or recently acquired systems may be an important element in understanding the development of clients' current difficulties. This background can provide the basis for planning changes in their outlook or behavior and/or their physical or social context. For example, Cruz-Lopez (1985) found that 87% of the supporters listed by a sample of Puerto Rican elders from the Mayaguez area were of their own age cohort. He explained this high proportion by noting that the area in which they lived was characterized by intact neighborhoods in which social ties among individuals and families were stable and long-standing. Also, a mild climate and the custom of gathering outside for conversation and playing dominoes tended to support the importance of age-related ties for these elders.

Noting that a large proportion of a client's supporters are of recent acquisition should lead us to wonder about the relative absence of long-time support persons. Is the client a person who has been rejected by kith and kin and thus has had to repopulate the support system with new people? Has the client recently undergone a change of physical (e.g., geographic move) or emotional (e.g., mid-life crisis) life context, causing a withdrawal from former supporters?

Though the reasons for a scarcity or overabundance of long-time supporters may vary, observation of these patterns can serve as a departure point for gathering information that can help us understand clients' social context and the manner in which they establish and maintain relationships with support persons. Such information may also provide the counselor with information that will be helpful in developing a direction for intervention.

Stability of Rose's system. We note that Rose has a very stable system. Only one of her nine supporters is of recent acquisition. In her case, this is an obvious consequence of having a system dominated by family. With little other information about Rose, we can only speculate about the significance of this pattern. Is she a shy, socially inept person who has few relationships other than those she "inherits" by consequence of family membership? Does she come from a religious or ethnic group in which family unity and cohesion are central? Has the family moved frequently (as is often the case with military or corporate families), serving to limit or discourage significant relationships outside the family? The flexibility of the counseling relationship allows us to follow up any pattern, determining its meaning and possible significance for the course of counseling.

What Type of Support from Whom?

A knowledge of which types of social support are typically provided by each of the persons in the support system provides counselor and client with an overview that may be useful in identifying specific types of support the client believes are not currently available. Also, this information can reveal a pattern of redundancy among supporters and raise the possibility of adding persons to the system who could provide more diverse types of assistance.

Gottlieb (1988) noted research indicating that supporters cannot be assumed to be interchangeable with regard to providing the specific sort of social support clients need in order to deal with particular life stresses. Gottlieb suggests that in attempting to expand clients' support systems, we need to be sure that the additions are "people who are either naturally best equipped to help the focal individual respond to the demands imposed by the stressor, or who can be trained to offer relevant resources for resisting stress" (1988, p. 16).

On page 7 of the P3S respondents indicate which of the 13 types of support each person in the system provides. We can go down the column of each support type to determine if one or more persons are providing it. If there are few checks in any column, we might refer to the importance and availability ratings in the first part of the instrument to determine if this is considered to be an important type of support and if, in spite of the fact that few people are providing it, the client is satisfied with the amount available. Working the other way, we can note the support areas the individual considers to be most important, then use this section of the P3S to identify who, if anyone, is providing that type of support.

Rose's specific sources of support. Noting that Rose has three persons (no males) providing love, and only one person (Carol) providing companionship, we can check back to find that both love and companionship are of highest importance to her. We begin to get the picture that Rose is feeling the lack of close relationships outside the family circle. Again, we must recognize that simply noting these patterns does not provide us with definitive information about why they exist. However, a number of possibilities are beginning to come into focus that we might begin to pursue.

Interactive Measures

By examining dimensions of the system such as size, composition, and stability, we can develop a picture of the structural characteristics of the system. Another dimension of systems that can be examined is the manner in which interaction among members of the system takes place. Indices describing this dimension are called "interactive measures." Those most useful to the work of counselors and other human service workers are density, the actual/vicarious ratio, and reciprocity.

Density

Anthropologists have developed a number of measures for describing and quantifying the interpersonal relationships they observe among the groups they study (Mitchell, 1974). One of these measures is "density," defined as the number of the group in question who know (or perhaps have any significant contact with) each other, as contrasted to the maximum number of such pairs that could exist. Density is computed by use of the following formula:

$$density = n/([N(N - 1)]/2)$$

where n = the number of unique pairs of people who know and have contact with each other and N = the total number of individuals in the system.

Density is an index of how tight or focused a system is. Highly dense systems (i.e., those in which most of the members know and interact with the others) are typically characterized by readily available lines of communication, shared information, and similarity of perspective. As with family-dominated systems (and we should note that family-dominated systems tend also to be dense systems, though dense systems are not necessarily composed primarily of family), there may be disadvantages to dense systems. In these systems there is typically an increased likelihood that members will overlap each other in ways that reduce desirable diversity. For example, if a client has been laid off, having a personal support system primarily made up of former co-workers who have also been laid off may serve to limit the amount of emotional support available ("Don't cry about your problems to me, I've got my own."). A dense system may also be restricted in the availability of certain types of important information ("What can I tell you? I haven't been able to get any job leads myself!").

Though there is some evidence to suggest that dense systems are disadvantageous in situations that involve a significant transition (e.g., Hirsch, 1979, 1980; Wilcox, 1981), the particular significance of a density score should be explored with the client.

Density of Rose's system. When we examine the data shown about Rose in Appendix B, we observe that there are 24 unique pairs of persons who have frequent contact with one another. In a group of 9 people, there are a possible 36 unique pairs; that is,

$$[N(N - 1)]/2 = [9(8)]/2 = 36$$

Therefore, the density of Rose's system equals 24/36, or .67. This is a relatively dense system, and (as we have seen) the fact that there are few nonfamily with whom she has supportive relationships was a source of dissatisfaction for her. We can speculate that this predominance of family support and the resultant gap the availability of certain salient types of support were the likely reasons for her coming to counseling.

Support from Actual and Vicarious Supporters

The concept of social support seems to assume actual interaction with the persons from whom support is derived. Indeed, we might wonder how support could be received from someone or something never actually encountered. While it is rare that an individual will report vicarious supporters (those with whom there is no current contact or there has never been any contact), there are situations in which such support is not only observed, but is an important part of the individual's support resources. Perhaps the most extreme example would be that of prisoners in solitary confinement who are physically separated from their support systems and lack any opportunity to meet new individuals to supplement that system. Less drastically, we can consider individuals who, because of ostracism, isolation, physical disabilities, or membership in a devalued subculture, are restricted in the degree to which they can come into actual contact with their preferred supporters, or are limited in their ability to develop new support persons. In such cases, individuals are apt to have systems composed of persons with whom there is no current contact.

In point of fact, elderly persons are often found to draw heavily on religious and inspirational figures as sources of comfort and acceptance. Could this be related to the fact that the older one gets, the fewer and fewer of the age cohort with whom one has shared so many formative and rich experiences are still alive? Decreased physical mobility stemming from infirmity and/or lack of access to transportation may make it necessary for the elderly to depend more and more on vicarious support (Majerovitz, 1988). Such vicarious support is often accessed through recollection and prayer. Age-focused prejudice and a pattern of age segregation in many families, neighborhoods, and communities may have the same effect (Rathbone-McCuan & Hashimi, 1982).

Given the relative infrequency with which substantial dependence on vicarious support is encountered when examining individuals' support resources, its appearance warrants the counselor's attention. In some instances it will simply reflect a high level of religiosity or a sensitivity to the inspirational impact of historical or contemporary figures. However, in other cases dependence on vicarious support indicates social, physical, and/or psychological isolation that may be an important issue in the development and remediation of the difficulties that have brought the individual to counseling.

Rose's direct and vicarious support. The "direct support ratio" is determined by using the data recorded in the second column (headed by the question, "Do you actually see or talk to this person?") on page 8 of the P3S. In Rose's case, we observe that she reports actual contact with all of her supporters. Her direct support ratio is thus 1.0. While this figure may seem somewhat high, my experience is that most adults who are physically and socially active have a clear majority of supporters with whom they have actual contact. Data I have gathered for several adult American samples yield direct contact ratios ranging from .333 to 1.000, with 40% to 50% of respondents indicating actual contact with all of their supporters. Thus there is probably little significance to the fact that all of Rose's relationships are characterized by direct contact, and likely reflects the fact that she lives in a family-focused context.

Contact with Supporters

Natural support systems can vary considerably in the frequency with which individuals are in actual contact with their supporters. Conceivably, a person could have a support system primarily composed of supporters who were contacted only infrequently, though this would be rare in my experience. On the P3S this can be operationally defined as having a majority of supporters described on page 8 as falling into the "few times a year" or "every few years" categories. Some interesting patterns may be noted when we combine the frequency of contact score with the actual/vicarious ratio previously described. In the case of isolated elderly persons, we may find that the actual/vicarious ratio is quite low, indicating the individual has few supporters with whom there is actual contact, but that most of the contact with those vicarious supporters takes place on a daily basis. This suggests that the individual in question is probably using recollection as a means of coming into a kind of contact with absent (perhaps deceased) supporters or is contacting religious figures through prayer.

Difficulty in making a transition may be reflected in a relatively large proportion of a respondent's support contacts falling into the less frequent categories. A person who never really puts down roots in a new community may depend on letters, phone calls, or occasional trips back to the home community for contact with supporters. If distances are great and money for phone calls or travel is limited, support (though actual when it occurs) may be essentially vicarious in nature.

Rose's contact with supporters. Examining Rose's responses to the "frequency of contact" portion of the P3S, we note that one-third of her supporters are contacted on a daily basis, while another 55% are seen weekly. There is no one whom she describes as being contacted on the less frequent "few times a year" and "every few years" categories. Her support thus comes from supporters with whom she interacts on a fairly frequent basis. This probably reflects the fact that Rose lives in the city of her birth. Many of the family (from whom she draws virtually all of her support) still reside in that city. However, in spite of reasonably easy access to the persons in her support system, we find she expresses dissatisfaction with that system (see page 9 of her P3S results presented in Appendix B).

Rose's results point out that (as with support system size) more does not necessarily mean better. While separation from support persons and the consequent infrequency of contact that separation causes are usually experienced as unsatisfactory by individuals, frequent contact with supporters who cause as much stress as they do benefit, or who lack the ability to provide types of support that are particularly salient, may also be quite unsatisfactory.

Reciprocity

Fisher et al. (1988) noted that the norms of most social networks do not demand immediate reciprocation of benefit received from others; however, my observation suggests that, except in special circumstances, people tend not to stay in relationships in which the giving of benefit (e.g., support) is not eventually reciprocated. Special instances in which asymmetrical relationships (vis-à-vis exchange of support) are continued include those dominated by powerful obligations, such as family ties, or those in which one person holds a social role, the function of which centers on the offering of assistance. However, even in the latter case it should be noted that in addition to whatever altruism helpers may be acting on, they are also usually paid for their efforts. One-way relationships, vis-à-vis the giving of social support, are difficult to maintain because givers who receive little in return are apt to feel exploited and to conclude that there are few benefits to their efforts. Even human service workers, whose work it is to be the source of support, often cite the condition of being drained dry emotionally as an occupational hazard. Professional burnout in these fields often results from the seemingly endless needs of clients for support.

Hirsch (1979) noted that persons who end up needing the assistance of mental health workers are often demanding, needy individuals who have alienated and driven away many past and potential supporters. It is not so much that there are not persons available to them who could offer them support; rather, they have worn out their welcome and depleted the goodwill of persons in the natural system. Thus they must move beyond informal sources of social support to connect with professionals whose role assumes the giving, but not receiving, of assistance.

In light of these observations, the proportion of individuals' relationships that are reciprocal in nature may hold deep significance for the future stability of their social support resources, as well as giving an indication of their general interpersonal adequacy. We note that while Rose is not certain of the reciprocity of the relationships she has with some of the persons in her support system, she lists no one-way relationships.

When clients describe relationships in which they provide support but receive none in return, we should be alert to the possibility that their personal resources are being overtaxed. If the outflow of support is not counterbalanced by its reception from reciprocal relationships, clients may find themselves suffering from the same type of emotional and/or material depletion that human service workers often experience. Assistance in limiting such relationships, or in expanding the system to include persons with whom more mutuality can exist, may be beneficial to overburdened clients who feel obligated to stay in nonreciprocal support relationships.

I've pointed out that using clients' self-report as the basis for building understanding of their situations is subject to deliberate and unknowing distortion by the clients themselves. We can attempt to minimize this distortion through such strategies as stressing confidentiality or emphasizing the manner in which clients' interests will be served by candor. However, in spite of our assurances, if the issue at hand is strongly colored by the issue of "social desirability" (Edwards, 1957), clients may find it difficult to avoid presenting a more favorable picture of themselves than is actually the case. Given the strong negative value usually attached to taking without giving back in relationships, the counselor may want to check clients' self-reports against other, more objective, sources of data (Cohen & Syme, 1985). This is especially true when there is some reason to believe that clients may be sensitive to how others view and evaluate them.

Conclusion

Whether the search for fuller understanding of our clients uses subjective or objective, structured or unstructured strategies, the ability to describe and analyze their support preferences and resources is often an important prerequisite to developing counseling interventions. In the face-to-face exchange of the counseling session, it is possible to follow clients, letting them reveal the aspects of their support-related experience that are of significance to them. Even if we choose such structured approaches as questionnaires, or interviews that follow a predetermined sequence, the opportunity should not be lost to follow up the data obtained to determine their specific meaning for particular clients.

The measures that have been described will also be useful to counselors in developing broad pictures of different demographic groups with whom they work. Many of these measures have been found to vary across subgroups. Noting these differences may lead to adaptations that make individual counseling style or programmatic efforts more responsive to the needs of a particular group. For example, Stokes and Wilson's (1983) finding that women in their sample had larger percentages of relatives in their support networks than did the males might suggest the importance of family-focused interventions in programs designed for women whose concerns relate to social support issues.

Chapter Four

Client-Based Barriers

When individuals seek counseling, or are encouraged to do so by others, it is clear that someone believes a problem exists. Also, we can usually assume that the client and/or others believe the problem exceeds the client's own ability or willingness to resolve the difficulty. Moreover, seeking the assistance of an outsider, a person not of the client's informal support network, generally indicates that assistance sufficient to resolve the problem is, for one reason or another, unavailable within the natural network.

To the degree that these conditions hold in any given situation, seeking or referral to counseling can be viewed as an attempt to gain access to a supplementary source of social support. Two questions arise naturally from such a support-centered view of clients' entry to counseling:

- Why aren't the individuals able to deal with these life concerns themselves?
- Why aren't they receiving the needed support from their informal support systems?

The first of these questions is an important one in counseling and other human services. Given the value that our society places on personal independence and self-sufficiency, it is quite understandable that assisting clients to develop the willingness, understanding, and skills required to stand on their own should be a frequent concern in counseling.

However, the issue of the supportiveness of clients' social network raised by the second question also is a common focus of attention in counseling practice. As much as we prize self-sufficiency and try to enhance our clients' ability to stand on their own, assistance from others also has an appropriate place in coping with life concerns. When the lack of social support appears to be an important contributor to the emergence or lack of resolution of clients' difficulties, it is reasonable to turn to identifying the causes of that deficiency. Understanding the reasons why our clients are not receiving the amount or type of social support that would be beneficial can serve as a point of departure for developing strategies to increase its availability (Sarason, Sarason, Hacker, & Basham, 1985).

Barriers to Receiving Social Support

Why do some people not receive the support of others as they attempt to deal with the life problems they encounter? Rook and Dooley (1985) identified two broad perspectives on the nature of social support that may be helpful in answering this question:

> Two alternative views on the origins of social support are dominant in the analytic literature. One view holds that support is an environmental variable in that its causes are largely external to the individual. The second view holds that support, although manifested in the response of the social network, is largely a function of characteristics of the individual. (p. 15)

This individual/environment split is also found in House's (1981) more multifaceted view that the availability of social support varies as a function of the characteristics of individuals, the relationships among individuals, and the social or cultural context within which individuals function.

In the complexity of individual lives, neat distinctions among individual-based, other-based, and context-based factors that reduce the availability of social support received by individuals often break down. When we find individuals who are rejected by their families it is often difficult to tease out whether any dysfunction we observe in the client is cause or effect of that rejection. At the point in time when the counselor enters the scene, mutually reinforcing barriers to the exchange of social support are often found in the functioning of both client and family.

Also, if we find clients mired in social or physical contexts that are detrimental to their need for support (e.g., socially disrupted neighborhoods, physically isolated places), it is often difficult to determine the source of their dysfunctionality. Does it flow from the nonresponsive situations, or does personal inadequacy keep them trapped there, as when persons with deep fears of others retreat to an isolated area that lacks opportunities for informal or formal assistance.

Nevertheless, the individual/other/context distinction can be a useful one in getting an overview of the factors that need to be taken into account in understanding clients' functioning and in moving toward the development of interventions aimed at increasing the social support resources of clients. Variation in such "client-based characteristics" as personal attractiveness, level of social skill, or willingness to ask for assistance can strongly affect the likelihood that past or potential supporters will respond in a supportive fashion. Also, differing levels of such "other-based characteristics" as supporters' interpersonal sensitivity, general level of altruism, or personal adequacy can influence their ability or willingness to offer support.

In this chapter, the characteristics and impact of three types of client-based barriers (withdrawal from others, social ineptitude, and moving against others) will be discussed. Chapter 6 will turn to an examination of the nature and operation of other-, social context-, and physical environment-based barriers to the exchange of social support.

Client-Based Barriers to Social Support

Sarason, Sarason, and Shearin (1986) commented on how individuals' characteristics can reduce the amount of social support they receive:

> Social support correlates positively with extraversion and negatively with neuroticism. Individuals high in neuroticism tend to be neither initially attractive to others nor the source of particularly rewarding experiences in ongoing social relationships. Both depression and hostility are inversely related to social support. There is also evidence that neither of these affective states is appealing to others. . . . The negative feelings toward others that are characteristic of hostility are logically inconsistent with the attraction of others and the development of supportive relation-

ships. Pervasive depression and hostile feelings are logically inconsistent with a lack of satisfaction in most kinds of interpersonal relationships. The negative relation of anxiety to both availability of and satisfaction with social support also helps flesh out a picture of the personality characteristics associated with perceived support. (p. 845)

In Chapter 2, several clients were mentioned who illustrate different forms these individual-based barriers can take. Carl presented a client-based barrier that can be described as "withdrawal from others." Expecting rejection and disapproval from others, he withdrew rather than give them the chance to make fun of him. In Rita's case we observed another person who withdrew from others, but for different reasons. Her fear and suspicion resulted in a tendency to distance herself from others in order to avoid what she believed was their prying and exploitation.

Walter displayed yet another pattern in his withdrawal from his supporters. His strong need to be viewed as self-sufficient led him to believe that accepting, or even showing a need for, assistance would reflect weakness. A strong, socially facile person, his withdrawal (unlike that of Carl and Rita) took the form of censoring any communication of uncertainty or feelings of inadequacy.

The attitudes and behaviors of all these persons are examples of factors that can reduce the ability, and/or the willingness, of others to offer support. Through their physical or emotional distancing, such persons decrease opportunities for others to offer assistance. Also, their characteristics increase the likelihood that the need for support will be actively or passively hidden from supporters (Fisher et al., 1988).

With other unsupported individuals, a lack of social skill, or "social ineptness," can generate feelings of discomfort in persons who have provided, or might provide, support. Such discomfort can interact with clients' feelings of ambivalence about relationships to produce a pattern of sparse social exchange, even when physical proximity exists. In a study of the relationship between children's behavior and their social integration in play groups, Dodge (1983) suggested a typology that is relevant to the present discussion. Describing children who showed varying degrees of isolation from their peers, Dodge made a distinction between "neglected" and "rejected" children. Neglected children were those who displayed distancing (i.e., leaving the setting or hanging on the fringes of activity) or mildly annoying, inept behavior. In contrast, rejected children were those who related to others in noxious ways (e.g., markedly inappropriate behavior, aggression, manipulation). Such noxious behavior led to punishment or ostracism by their peers.

Ansel (the focus of a case study to be presented in Chapter 8), though showing a clear pattern of withdrawing from others, also presented an example of social ineptitude. He described himself as feeling tongue-tied, not knowing what to say when he was with other people. He believed his discomfort was apparent to others and would lead to his rejection if they got to know him. We can imagine that many of Ansel's casual contacts saw him as a quiet, somewhat strange young man with whom it was difficult to talk. Eventually, his apparent discomfort led them to just nod, or smile, as they went on about their business. In Dodge's typology, Ansel's withdrawal and ineptitude resulted in his being a neglected person.

Social isolation, and its concomitant negative impact on the exchange of social support, can also result from "moving against" others. If an individual's behavior is sufficiently noxious to cause others to feel antagonized, they may move from the more tolerant response of neglect to an active rejection of the individual. For example, in Chapter 2 we met Wilson, whose insensitivity and self-centeredness tended to antagonize others. Similarly, Arlene lost the support of her father because she took an action to which he was deeply opposed. For that he rejected her and withdrew his previous support.

In these instances, we observe the loss of social support as a consequence of clients' actions that alienated past or potential supporters, reducing their willingness to respond in helpful ways. Returning to Dodge's (1983) typology, Wilson and Arlene were rejected rather than neglected.

Table 4.1 describes these three client-based barriers to social support (i.e., withdrawal, social ineptitude, moving against others) in terms of their attitudinal and behavioral correlates. Each of these barriers will be examined, and their attitudinal bases and behavioral expression will be explored.

Withdrawal from Others

My interaction with clients suggests that some types of assistance can be derived from vicarious processes; for example, a person may feel comforted by reading an inspirational book, or may receive useful career information by viewing a television program. However, by definition, social support rests on actual contact with others. Distancing from others reduces the amount of social support a person receives because it limits opportunities for social interaction, the medium through which support is exchanged. Withdrawal from others can be defined as distancing (physically and/or psychologically) from past or potential supporters. Withdrawal diminishes the amount (and, perhaps, quality) of the social support the individual can receive. There are a variety of internal processes (i.e., perceptions, beliefs) underlying withdrawal. Also, withdrawal can be expressed through a range of behaviors. What are some of the internal and external aspects of this client-based barrier?

Attitudinal Dimensions

Withdrawal from others is clearly apparent in shy, reticent persons who go out of their way to distance themselves physically from others or are quiet and retiring as a way of minimizing physical, verbal, and emotional contact. What is behind such behavior? Why do people (apparently voluntarily) cut themselves off from the very resource (other people) that could provide assistance with the feelings of loneliness, lack of being cared for, and being overwhelmed by the life demands they report?

Generally, withdrawal from others stems from the expectation that, in one way or another, harm will result from physical and emotional closeness. Tolsdorf (1976) found that such a negative expectation (which he labeled "negative network orientation") served to inhibit emotionally disturbed individuals from seeking assistance from their informal support network. As Gottlieb (1983) noted, Tolsdorf's methodology does not allow us to determine whether the patients did not ask for help because their past experience with the network had taught them they would be refused, or if they simply never asked for help because of an unfounded expectation that they would be refused. Whether cause or effect of persons being unsupported (and clinical experience suggests that both patterns operate), negative network orientation represents an attitudinal set that acts to bar the flow of social support. The orientation takes several forms:

- Because I am unworthy others will reject me (low self-esteem).
- If I ask for, or accept, help from others, I will be viewed as inadequate and less worthwhile by others (fear of dependency).
- Other people are hurtful or exploitive (fear or suspicion of others).

Table 4.1.   Individual-Based Barriers to Social Support: Attitudinal and
              Behavioral Correlates

Barrier	Attitude	Behavior
Withdrawal	Low self-esteem Fear of criticism Expectation that others won't help	Avoiding others Self deprecation Quietness Aloofness Low self-assertion Not asking for help
Ineptness	Ambivilance toward others	Mildly inappropriate behaviors
Alienation	Self-centeredness Suspicion Insensitivity	Annoying others Demanding Manipulating Nonreciprocation Exploitiveness Aggressiveness

In general, these beliefs act as barriers to receiving social support because of a double-barreled effect. First, the physical and/or emotional distance resulting from withdrawal increases the likelihood that individuals' need for assistance will be invisible to potential supporters (Fisher et al., 1988; Goffman, 1963). Also, even if the need for assistance is perceived and support is offered, individuals' apparent discomfort (e.g., embarrassment) at the offer of support may discourage or "put off" the would-be helper (Mitchell & Trickett, 1980; Nelson, 1980; Shapiro, 1983).

While each of these attitudes will be discussed separately, overlapping elements of each are often found in the functioning of clients. For example, low self-esteem often leaves individuals feeling vulnerable to exploitation by others. Low self-esteem can also cause individuals to believe that they have to adhere strictly to social expectations (e.g., be independent, stand on their own) to avoid rejection. Indeed, perhaps it is a generalized sense of vulnerability that leads people to be cautious in their relationships with others. This cautiousness, whatever form it takes, can lead to a distancing from persons who could provide them with assistance in dealing more effectively with life concerns they face.

Self-Esteem

Fisher and his colleagues (1988) pointed out that the theoretical literature focused on the relationship between self-esteem and help seeking presents competing hypotheses. The first (the "vulnerability hypothesis") holds that low self-esteem individuals will tend to avoid seeking assistance because to do so would require them to expose their inadequacies. The second view (the "consistency hypothesis") leads to the prediction that high self-esteem individuals would be least likely to seek assistance because to do so would be inconsistent with their preferred view of themselves.

Fisher et al. (1988) suggested that the consistency hypothesis is most clearly supported by the empirical literature:

> Given the same need state, low-self-esteem individuals are less threatened by seeking help and approach others for aid faster, more frequently, and with larger requests than high-self-esteem individuals. The reluctance of high-self-esteem individuals to seek assistance has been corroborated by field observations. (p. 273)

While not wishing to dispute the assertions of Fisher and his colleagues regarding research trends and the results of naturalistic observations, my work with clients suggests that both vulnerability and consistency hypothesis are useful in understanding clients' reactions to the need for assistance. It is true that viewing oneself as helpless can lead to a sense of entitlement that causes individuals to abuse the willingness of others to help. This often results in the burnout and alienation of supporters that Tolsdorf (1976) and others have noted. However, it is also common to encounter clients who, like Ansel, withdraw from others because they feel unworthy of the attention and assistance of possible supporters. Therefore, in the following discussion of client-based attitudinal barriers to receiving support, both low self-esteem and high self-esteem (i.e., fear of dependency) will be examined.

Low self-esteem. Low self-esteem reflects a negative evaluation of one's own characteristics, qualities, and capacities. As a determinant of behavior, it leads to responses that center heavily on protecting oneself from the consequences of that perceived inadequacy. Individuals may disparage themselves to decrease the likelihood that others will do so. What is commonly called shyness can represent an effort to avoid any real contact with other people as a means of preventing criticism and rejection. Because they devalue their worth and competence, persons with low self-esteem often avoid precisely those situations in which they could experience success or positive responses from others. Thus they continue to be cut off from positive events that could modify their negative view of themselves.

With regard to social support availability, the primary impact of low self-esteem, as Nelson (1980) noted, is to lead individuals to distance themselves from others. This often results in a decreased likelihood that they will seek, or be able to seek, assistance from their supporters. Because of this withdrawal, potential support persons may be largely unaware of shy persons' need for assistance. Even if the need for assistance is recognized, supporters may be hesitant to offer assistance for fear of causing them discomfort. Persons characterized by low self-esteem often face life situations without access to emotional and material support from others because of self-defeating assumptions. Low self-esteem can lead individuals to believe that they don't deserve assistance and, therefore, that others shouldn't be imposed on. These individuals, reflecting Tolsdorf's (1976) negative network orientation, may also believe that others wouldn't be disposed to help even if they were asked.

Finally, the self-protectiveness of persons with low self-esteem often negatively affects the receiving of informational and appraisal support. Persons often avoid relationships with others that could provide needed information about the situations with which they are coping (or will cope) and corrective feedback about their characteristics and/or performance.

Fear of dependency. I have noted that Fisher et al. (1988) found strong support in empirical studies (e.g., Burke & Weir, 1976; Gross, Fisher, Stiglitz, & Craig, 1979) and naturalistic observation for the assertion that high-self-esteem persons tend to avoid seeking assistance. They do not seek help, apparently, because doing so would be inconsistent with their preferred view of themselves as competent, effective persons. My observations in counseling practice have led me to think of this resistance as taking the form of "fear of dependency."

Sometimes a concern about control and power issues is behind a client's hesitancy to take a the help-receiver role — confident, assertive clients view the counseling situation as one in which they are required to give up power and autonomy. However, just as often, fear of dependency seems to be tied up with issues of public image. Resistance to depending on others for assistance is an effort to avoid being viewed as weak or ineffective.

Observers, both foreign (e.g., Alexis de Tocqueville) and native (e.g., Ralph Waldo Emerson) have noted that a strong emphasis on independence and self-sufficiency is a central element of the American ethos. In general, to be able to stand on one's own is evidence of competence, while needing assistance is viewed as indicating inadequacy and weakness (Spense, 1985). To the degree that individuals internalize this societal value, it is difficult for them to ask for or accept supportive actions from others because they believe that doing so puts them in the position of being judged as less than competent. Thus individuals will often be found doing those things (e.g., keeping their distance, not revealing pain, or deprivation) that keep others from becoming aware of their justifiable needs (Gross & McMullin, 1983). The words of a social worker, cited in Eloise Rathbone-McCuan and Joan Hashimi's book *Isolated Elders* (1982), point to this pattern among elderly people and trace its affect on the help they receive from supporters:

> People, particularly the elderly, don't like asking for help. I think that attitude extends to both the informal and formal sources of support. I know that many of my clients simply won't ask their willing friends, family, or neighbors for assistance until there is absolutely no alternative. Not asking for help serves to keep people's behavior consistent with their values but it stands in the way of their receiving help. (pp. 90-91)

However dysfunctional this rigid insistence on self-sufficiency may come to be for many persons, it is important to realize that the beliefs underlying it are not only widely held, they are also often reinforced in formal and informal interaction. A study that focused on elders in Quebec identified what Corin (1982) called the "poor dear" phenomenon. Within this group of elderly persons, when it became apparent that someone was experiencing unusually high levels of the problems associated with advanced age, he or she would come to be referred to as "poor dear" by the peer group. Concomitantly, the individual was assigned a low position in the group's informal status hierarchy. The message of this pattern was not lost on many of the elders, and (as was true of the Arkansas elders described by Rathbone-McClean and Hashimi) they adopted a position of keeping their problems and needs to themselves.

Such withdrawal from supporters can lead to a variety of negative consequences. The individual is apt to slip into physical and psychological isolation. This not only leaves problems and concerns unresolved, it also allows them to become more serious. Moreover, potential supporters, observing the individual's withdrawal or (perhaps) being rebuffed, often withdraw in turn, leaving the individuals even more isolated.

Fear and suspicion of others. Fear of disapproval and consequent rejection is often a factor in individuals' resistance to asking for, or accepting, assistance. Generally, we would expect that persons who consider themselves to be rejectable — vulnerable, in Fisher et al.'s (1988) terms — would demonstrate a pattern of withdrawing from supporters, fearing the contact of helping interactions would carry with it the potential for rejection. Such self-focused attitudes as low self-esteem and poor body image lead individuals to anticipate negative reactions from others.

It is important to recognize that while anticipation of rejection often has its base in the subjective beliefs of individuals (e.g., reasonably attractive adolescents who, like Ansel, fear rejection because they believe they are ugly), it can also have an objective basis. We can cite clients who, as members of stigmatized groups, may come to us with a long history of rejection. Also, clients from critical, demanding families often transfer anticipations of criticism from the family context to their broader relationships.

Although defensiveness and suspicion can lead a person to be hostile and hurtful toward others (a reaction that will be considered in a subsequent section of this chapter), these attitudes often lead individuals to withdraw from others. Suspicious of hurt or exploitation, clients leave or fade into the background to reduce their exposure to the harmful intentions they attribute to others.

Rita (whom we met in Chapter 2) believed she was exploited and taken advantage of by her family. Though she could, and sometimes did, become hostile toward her perceived tormentors, more often she simply avoided them, keeping her "business" to herself. She spent a great deal of time ruminating about the selfishness of others. Her self-pity spilled over into a whining bitterness that (apparently) her brother and his family found annoying and difficult to handle. They would not hear from her for months on end, then suddenly she would appear at their door, or call on the phone, denouncing their lack of concern and insensitivity. Rita's withdrawal served to keep her family uninformed of her needs, even those to which they might have been inclined to respond.

Behavioral Dimensions

Social isolation is a common denominator among many persons who lack supportive relationships. Though such isolation may be forced on individuals in some instances (as when a person must reside in a remote, rural area), individuals often contribute to their isolation because they lack, or are unskilled in, behavior that fosters the development of relationships.

One broad class of behaviors that decreases the likelihood of developing supportive relationships can be described as "failure to contact others." Some ways in which persons remove themselves from others are as follows:

- avoiding contact with others;
- leaving the presence of others;
- declining offers of inclusion; and
- accepting offers of inclusion, but failing to follow through.

Such behaviors are dysfunctional for a number of reasons: (a) They separate individuals from supportive resources, (b) they discourage or prevent the development of ongoing support relationships, (c) they prevent potential supporters from becoming aware of individuals' need for assistance, and (d) they "teach" possible supporters to leave the individual alone (Harker, 1972).

A variant of avoiding or minimizing actual contact with others is seen in the behavior of individuals who psychologically distance themselves by "fading into the woodwork" through their silence or minimal participation, even though they actually stay in the presence of others. Such individuals (often described as shy) hang on the fringes of social interaction, seemingly wanting the benefits of contact with others, but unable or unwilling to actively participate. As with any contact, their behavior (e.g., failure to talk, looking uncomfortable when others attempt to include them in discussion or activities) often influences the subsequent behavior of others. Potential supporters may leave shy persons alone, not wanting to make them uncomfortable. Ironically, quiet persons may be viewed as aloof, and feelings of superiority may be attributed to them. This may cause others to dislike and reject them.

Moving Against Others

At the other extreme from withdrawal from others is a barrier to the reception of social support that, earlier in this chapter, was described as "moving against others." Rather than removing themselves from the presence of past or potential supporters, persons manifesting this barrier tend to misuse and/or overuse contact with others. Their contact is generally experienced by others as noxious, causing them to react with rejection, punishment, or ostracism.

It is clear that a relationship begun is not necessarily a relationship continued. In a broad sense, unless a relationship is rewarding, the people involved usually find ways of ending or circumscribing it (Thibault & Kelley, 1959). Even draining, seemingly unrewarding relationships will, if they continue, ultimately be found to be supported by helpers' access to such rewards as a sense of being of service, a paycheck, or the meeting of the need to be a nice person. The paths of many unsupported persons are littered with relationships from which the other persons have withdrawn because they found that the cost/ benefit ratio was not running in their favor.

The matter of moving against others emerged as a central issue in a study carried out by Froland et al. (1979). Their research examined the support resources of mental patients. They found that persons who displayed chronic emotional disorders typically had alienated the members of their natural support network so thoroughly that the flow of assistance from those past or potential supporters was severely restricted. Comparing the composition and operation of the natural networks of disturbed patients to those of a group of less impaired outpatients, the researchers found that while the systems of the more disturbed group displayed a larger proportion of family members, their relationships with their supporters were described as less intimate and less reciprocal (that is, the patients received more support than they gave). The researchers suggested that, over time, the depletion of the emotional and material resources of kith and kin resulted in their eventual refusal to provide help. This refusal often was the crucial influence in chronically impaired patients' assistance from formal helping sources (i.e., mental health professionals and agencies) — since they were no longer able to get assistance from their informal networks, they had to turn elsewhere.

Attitudinal Bases

Many of the same attitudes put forth as factors causing withdrawal from others (e.g., low self-esteem, fear or suspicion of others) can also lead to moving against others. Whether fear of others leads clients to flee or to attack may vary as a function of the situation at hand, or it may reflect broader, more persistent patterns in individuals' functioning.

The corrosive impact that many clients have on the goodwill of others often stems from their preoccupation with their own needs and experience or from their belief that since they cannot meet their own needs, others must do so. This observation translates into the assertion that two broad attitudinal sets form the basis for moving against others: narcissism and the view of oneself as helpless.

Narcissism

The importance of reciprocity to the continuance of social relationships has been cited by a number of writers (Garrity, 1973; Hyman, 1971; Lewis, 1966). If we examine the operation of continuing relationships it will typically be found that the roles of supporter and support receiver shift back and forth between the participants (i.e., when one is "down" the other can be counted on to be "up" and vice versa). Clark (1983) noted that in informal networks an expectation of reciprocity operates. However, assistance or other forms of benefit are not expected to be reciprocated immediately, as is the case when assistance is received from someone outside the network.

In the persistent absence of reciprocity, one member of the relationship will usually come to feel drained, dry, or exploited and move to terminate or limit the interaction. While reciprocity often involves exchange "in kind" (for example, two persons lend each other money when either is short), we also observe patterns in which the exchange, while equally valued, involves different types of resources. For example, individual A provides individual B with information needed to make a pending decision, and individual B provides A with child-care assistance at a later time. Whatever the specifics, the sense of relative balance between cost and benefit in a relationship seems to be essential to its continuance, unless a reward system outside the relationship itself is operating.

The self-preoccupation suggested by the term *narcissism* can be the basis of a lack of reciprocity in a relationship. One facet of this self-preoccupation is that so much of individuals' attention is focused on their own concerns and experience that they are unable to recognize that others also have needs. This insensitivity to others makes empathy difficult. In turn, lack of empathy increases the likelihood that narcissistic individuals will function in ways that are exploitive of others. Because they are unable to put themselves in the place of others, they have difficulty realizing the impact that their demands or manipulations are having on their supporters. Sympathy is also limited, except as a ploy to increase others' willingness to be responsive.

To the extent that one's attention is focused within, the likelihood increases that awareness of the physical and social context will be impaired. Ideas are less apt to be reality-tested, and the importance of other persons' ideas and perspectives are often ignored. In the extreme, this preoccupation with one's own inner world of sensation and thought characterizes the schizophrenic's loss of reality contact. Hallucinations and "odd" patterns of thinking, however real and appropriate to the individual, operate away from the influence of reality.

Helplessness

It is clear that the issue of needing help from others can be a part of the discussion of both moving away from and moving against others. Persons who have internalized a high positive valuing of self-sufficiency tend to resist taking the roles of help-seeker or of help-receiver (Fisher et al., 1988). As we have seen, this leads them to withdraw (physically and psychologically) from others in situations in which their self-sufficiency is, or may be, at issue. In contrast, persons who view themselves as helpless may throw themselves on the care and protection of others.

In moderation, depending on others can be a very functional coping strategy. In fact, it is the central thesis of this book that social support (both its giving and receiving) is a basic element of effective personal functioning. However, when the seeking of assistance becomes never-ending, or is put forth in the form of a demand, the reciprocity and goodwill on which relationships depend are reduced.

Helplessness can be viewed as a learned response. In a context in which there are responsive, willing helpers, the cues of "helplessness" (e.g., looking worried, crying) can mobilize others into helpfulness. The reward value of such help can quickly establish a pattern of expecting others to handle difficult situations for one. Supporters who are initially overprotective and overresponsive may find that they have had a hand in creating a relationship that becomes burdensome. Low self-esteem on the support-seekers' part, or continually facing situations that are greatly beyond, or independent of, their coping resources (Seligman, 1975), can be seen as predisposing individuals to learning helplessness as a way of maintaining themselves.

Behavioral Dimensions

If reciprocated benefit is a central feature of continuing support relationships, we can expect that many unsupported clients will be individuals whose behavior toward others can be described as "unrewarding." Unlike the merely socially inept whom we will consider shortly, the behavior of some clients is strongly noxious and pushes past and potential supporters beyond the level of tolerance. Their "moving against" others is sufficiently strong to elicit active ostracism and punishment. When requests for help become too frequent or demanding, or the emotional or material costs of continuing the relationship are too high, supporters will often move from simply turning a deaf ear to entreaties for help (neglect) to becoming avoidant and/or punitive (rejecting). What are some of the behaviors that current or potential supporters experience as noxious, leading them to reject clients?

Failure to Reciprocate

Everyday language has a rich store of words and phrases for describing individuals who take from relationships but give little in return. To be a "sponge," a "leech," or a "mooch" is to be a person from whom others distance themselves. Whatever the causes of a lack of reciprocity, its result is that others feel exploited or used.

Operationally, lack of reciprocity exists in a relationship when one of the participants judges that his or her contributions to the other person heavily outweigh those received. Failure to reciprocate is expressed through such behavior as the following:

- repeatedly asking for favors, but seldom returning them;
- failing to express gratitude for assistance or material goods given; and
- expecting return for assistance that is far out of proportion to the value of that assistance.

It is important to note the significant effect that verbalized gratitude or small offerings expressing thankfulness can have in softening the impact of imbalance in a relationship. Even when supported persons are limited in their ability to reciprocate, gratitude (whether expressed in words or conveyed through the offering of support, which has more symbolic than substantive value) is experienced by most supporters as a kind of benefit that can offset otherwise imbalanced relationships.

Failure to say "Thank you," or "I know this doesn't repay all that you've done for me, but I want you to have this little gift," can make imbalanced relationships even more noxious, while the expression of such amenities can maintain a type of balance.

Punishing Others

Returning to Dodge's (1983) research on the relationships between patterns of children's behavior and their status in play groups, we note that children who were aggressive and disruptive toward their peers eventually were rejected. The negative effect of aggressive and disruptive behavior on relationships in general, and support relationships in particular, is not limited to children. We often find counterparts to Dodge's rejected children among our adolescent and adult clients. Rejection is often directed against persons who

- are physically aggressive;
- are verbally abusive;
- flagrantly abuse others' property rights;
- invade others' personal space with unwelcomed contact and touching;
- intrude on others' privacy by spying and prying; or
- behave in ways that are disruptive to the flow of ongoing activity (e.g., interrupting, demanding attention, making inappropriate comments).

Again, we can look to everyday language for words and phrases indicative of behaviors that are apt to create barriers to the offering of support by others. To be a "pain in the neck," a "snoop," or a "kook" is to invite rejection and punishment from others.

Social Ineptitude

Social ineptitude can be viewed as a mid-ground between the other two client-based barriers discussed in this chapter: withdrawal from others and moving against others. Such behaviors as incessantly talking about oneself, interrupting others, dressing inappropriately, or avoiding eye contact can exert a negative influence on social exchange. These attitudes and behaviors are characteristic of individuals who, while not clearly withdrawing from or moving against others, think and behave in ways others find strange or somewhat noxious. The impact of these individuals is not extreme enough to lead others to drive them away or punish them — in Dodge's (1983) terms, to reject them; however, their interaction and presence is uncomfortable to others. Thus past or potential supporters will often be found taking a wary or disinterested stance vis-à-vis these socially inept persons.

The socially inept can be viewed as persons who are only somewhat dysfunctional. They underutilize or misuse their relationships, but they have relationships. While they are unskilled, their attitudes and behaviors are not extreme enough to force them out of something approaching normal interaction. We can conceptualize working with this group as focusing on what Cowen (1973) called "secondary prevention"; that is, intervention aimed at limiting and reducing the impact of already-manifested, but not deeply entrenched, dysfunction. Though barriers to the reception of social support are created by social ineptitude, the barriers have some permeability — the inept are neglected, not rejected.

In general, these persons have a more favorable outlook for improvement than clients displaying the more dysfunctional patterns of withdrawal and moving against others. In spite of their dysfunctional attitudes and behaviors, they can be expected to have at least the minimal resources required to maintain some semblance of interaction with others.

Attitudinal Dimensions

From a phenomenological perspective, the same attributions associated with withdrawal (e.g., others are hurtful) can lead either to social ineptitude or to moving against others. Wanglass and Prinz (1982), for example, suggested that social withdrawal can result from a variety of attitudinal factors, including fearfulness and anxiety.

With socially inept persons, the belief that others are harmful is, apparently, not strong enough to cause them to remove themselves from others or to feel that they must counterattack to protect themselves. Rather, the fear of others, while present, is moderate enough to allow them to participate (however cautiously) in social interaction.

Oddness, another aspect of social ineptitude, has also been encountered in the discussion of moving against others. Like the jarring, bizarre behavior that frightens or angers others, these less aberrant actions of the socially inept often flow from self-preoccupation. Almost any attitude relating to individual conduct or social interaction that is different enough to set individuals off from supporters can generate social distance. When adolescents make fun of someone they consider a "goody-goody," or adults criticize a co-worker they consider too conscientious, they are expressing annoyance and discomfort at those persons' different ways of looking at what is, and is not, appropriate. Of course, the concept of "odd" is a relative one. Oddness in one group may be normality in another. However, having odd ideas is typically a factor that leads others to distance themselves from the one viewed as different. As long as the different ideas are not too extreme, individuals will usually be tolerated, though perhaps at arm's length. However, when the oddness becomes excessive, and its expression experienced as noxious by others, tolerance (i.e., neglect) can turn to rejection.

Behavioral Expressions

Behaviorally, some socially inept persons withdraw, but not completely, from others. They alienate others through their inappropriate or annoying behavior, but not to the extent that others are moved to strike back at or ostracize them actively. Behavioral deficits with regard to socializing skills may make interaction with some of them difficult, but there is enough potential for exchange that at least shallow relationships can form. Their lack of skill and grace in social interaction leads them to be (again in Dodge's terms) neglected.

In general, social ineptness can result from either behavioral deficit or dysfunctionality. Clients may make others uncomfortable, or fail to engage others adequately in social exchange, because they seem to lack behavior skills (deficit) or because the behavior they manifest has a negative impact on others (dysfunctionality). Persons whose experience is limited (either generally or with regard to particular situations of importance to the exchange of social support) may have gaps in their interaction skills that strongly limit their ability to develop and maintain relationships. Consistent with this position, research conducted by Asher and Renshaw (1981) found that students identified as "less popular" were judged to be less friendly and less effective in solving situations relating to the entry and maintenance of ongoing interactions.

In contrast to ineptness that stems from deficits, we also see inept persons whose difficulties result from the fact that their responses are either clearly inappropriate or, while appropriate in a general sense, implemented in an inappropriate fashion (e.g., being overly friendly with a stranger who is clearly made uncomfortable by such familiarity). This is the oddness discussed above, expressed behaviorally.

There is a of body literature relating to social competence (e.g., Danish, Galambos, & Laquatra, 1983) that specifies the behavioral deficits and dysfunctionality displayed by socially inept persons. To summarize and organize that literature as it applies to the clients with whom we work in counseling, the following skill areas will be examined: (a) verbal skill, (b) nonverbal expression, and (c) appearance and personal hygiene. Deficits or dysfunctionality in these three areas can result in the sort of ineptness that leads our clients to be neglected by current or potential supporters.

Lack of Verbal Skill

Deficiencies in verbal skill can focus on either mechanical difficulties or the content of conversation. Stuttering, heavy accents, and convoluted language structure are often experienced by others as annoying. Faced with such mechanical issues, others may withdraw from our clients, making relationships difficult to establish or maintain. In turn, clients with expressive difficulties may come to anticipate that others will be nonaccepting, leading them to minimize verbal interaction with persons they do not know very well.

In contrast to social ineptitude associated with verbal difficulties of a mechanical nature, some clients are apt to be impaired with regard to the content of their verbal interaction. For example, Putallaz and Gottman (1983) found that popular children tended to behave in ways that were more relevant to ongoing action than did their less popular peers — they were more apt to adopt the frame of reference of the people around them, and more likely to say and do things fitting in with what was going on, rather than distracting from it.

Deficiencies and deficits with regard to the content of verbal interaction can have a variety of sources. The negative impact of narcissism on persons' ability to attend to the subtleties of events around them has already been examined. Such inability to "get with it" can result in non sequiturs or comments that are in bad taste in terms of the values of the persons with whom they are conversing.

Limited experience can be another source of inappropriate content. Such limitation can operate in two ways. First, lack of experience with a wide range of persons can lead individuals to approach verbal interaction with faulty generalizations about what is and is not appropriate conversational content. For example, persons whose main experience has been in social contexts in which sexual matters are openly and explicitly discussed may be puzzled when new acquaintances become uncomfortable or distressed by their sexually focused comments. Also, lack of experience may cause individuals to possess a narrow range of topics for discussion. Persons who spend most of their time in certain activities (e.g., hobbies or work) may have little else they believe they can discuss. Conversational persistence on these topics may lead to their being perceived by others as preoccupied or obsessed with those areas.

Nonverbal Expression

We can return to the construct of "odd" in examining nonverbal behavior that results in persons' being neglected by others. Such behaviors as facial tics, clumsiness, and unusual carriage or gait can trigger stereotypes that cause others to distance themselves. Also, tense, nervous actions (e.g., excessive hand movements, hair twisting) can strike others as odd and lead them to conclude there is something wrong with the person. In addition to these odd, nervous behaviors, others are also put off by physical contact that violates group or individual expectations about what is appropriate. Individuals who stand too close to others or touch them inappropriately (as judged by the other persons) will usually find others reacting with discomfort and, in the extreme, punishing or rejecting them. Whether done moderately or to an extreme, unwelcomed intrusion on other persons' physical "space" serves to create a negative impact.

Appearance and Personal Hygiene

While the old adages instruct us that "beauty is only skin deep" and that it is the "inner person" who really counts, physical attractiveness confers on the possessor at least an initial favorable impact on others (Gross & Crofton, 1977). Given the findings of a strong positive relationship between judgments of physical attractiveness and objective measures of social skill (Goldman & Lewis, 1977), and considering that physical attractiveness is a relatively static characteristic, one is led to speculate that we are dealing with a situation in which "the rich get richer, and the poor get poorer"; that is, physical attractiveness opens doors to social interaction in a manner allowing prosocial behavior to be established and polished.

Persons who vary markedly from the norm of their group in terms of personal attractiveness enter social situations with an immediate disadvantage. In some cases, unattractive persons may be able to compensate for their disadvantage through good grooming or the development or possession of some other attribute (e.g., athletic prowess, wealth, intellect). However, even in such instances, the person may be left with behaviors (e.g., withdrawal from intimacy) that make social interaction problematic.

The negative impact that the lack of physical attractiveness has on social interaction is particularly pernicious in the case of persons who are disfigured because of accidents, disease, or congenital defects. Pomerance's (1979) play *The Elephant Man* documents the barriers to acceptance and human contact that physical disfigurement typically causes. At the extreme, such persons may be rejected by even reasonably tolerant persons. At less extreme levels, the unattractive will often be found to be neglected — tolerated, but limited in the amount of positive attention and closeness they receive from their peers.

If beauty is not only skin deep (at least in terms of its ability to influence the reactions of others), neither are dress and personal grooming superficial issues. Clothing advertisements in newspapers and magazines suggest the continuing power of the old saying "Clothes make the man." While we can extol the virtue of persons whose clothing and grooming are simple but clean, the reality is that entry to, and acceptance in, many situations requires more than simplicity and cleanliness.

Tammy, the "trailer park kid" we met in Chapter 2, was acutely aware of the way in which the quality and cut of her clothes set her off from the "village kids" who were at the top of the social status hierarchy in her school. Especially in situations where considerable socioeconomic diversity exists, one often finds individuals setting up and maintaining interpersonal boundaries on the basis of such externals as clothing and grooming.

Perhaps the most sensitive expression of grooming is found in the area of personal hygiene. Smelling "nice" doesn't guarantee acceptance and popularity, but to be judged as smelling "gross" is to guarantee rejection and ridicule. Persons who are dirty or who have strong body odors tend to be viewed not only as disgusting, but also as morally deficient. After all, "Cleanliness is next to godliness." Pity the person who does not have access to hot water and washing equipment and yet must interact with those who do.

Beyond the issue of cleanliness, we can also cite the matter of slovenliness, a behavioral cluster that serves to cut down on the frequency and/or depth of social interaction. Having poor table manners, scratching one's genitals in public, using an overused handkerchief, and picking one's teeth while talking to others are but a few of the ways of getting labeled as a slob or a gross person.

Conclusion

As Tolsdorf (1976) noted, many of the people who need support most are least apt to receive it. In this chapter, the individual-based barriers of withdrawal, moving against others, and social ineptitude were examined in order to clarify the manner in which individuals themselves interfere with the flow of social support from others. To hold those attitudes and do those things that result in isolation, rejection, and neglect is to make it less likely that others who have been, or might be inclined to be, supportive will be so.

It seems obvious that working to modify the attitudes and behaviors involved with these three barriers would be a useful approach to helping clients who seem to be struggling with life concerns in the absence of social support (Sarason et al., 1986). Indeed, even if we do not conceptualize helping clients to become more socially effective as a way to increase their social support resources, such is often an important consequence of our efforts. As important as being less lonely, and more accepted from a personal happiness perspective, they are also important because of other consequences. With increased social contact and acceptance go greater opportunities for clients to receive assistance from others, to have dysfunctional attitudes modified, and to acquire the skill that will, in turn, open further possibilities for social support.

In Chapter 5, we will examine the manner in which counseling strategies and interventions can be used to reduce the negative impact of individual-based barriers to the exchange of social support.

Chapter Five

Client-Focused Interventions

Chapter 4 examined how individuals' attitudes, cognitions, and behaviors can act as barriers that reduce or eliminate available social support as they deal with ordinary and problematic issues of life. This chapter moves on to consider a question logically springing from that consideration of client-based barriers: What are the strategies and interventions that might be used by counselors to remove such barriers?

The broad conceptualization of barriers to social support outlined in Chapter 4 called attention to the fact that such barriers can be located either within clients or within their context (that is, the physical or social environments). In many instances a comprehensive counseling intervention will include both client- and context-focused elements. For the moment, however, our concern is with counseling approaches centered on removing or ameliorating client-based barriers.

The importance of fostering client change as a means of increasing and maintaining the flow of social support is highlighted in the following observation made by Sarason et al. (1985) in a discussion of the interrelationships between individuals' characteristics and the availability of social support:

> However helpful the provision of social support may be, making the social environment more supportive is not easily accomplished and may not be highly effective. An important factor is that the person to be helped must

possess certain characteristics needed both to gain and to continue interpersonal relationships. (p. 469)

If clients cannot, or will not, maintain relationships, putting them into contact with a new circle of supporters will simply result in their withdrawing from or alienating yet another set of people. The same internal and behavioral factors that caused clients to be unsupported in the first place are likely to reappear if we simply alter their context without helping them change. For example, fearful clients who continue to withdraw from actual or potential supporters are not apt to attend a support group with which we put them into contact.

Support-Focused Individual Counseling

To some extent (as suggested in Chapter 1), social support is a part of many past and contemporary conceptualizations of the counseling process. This is particularly apparent when support is viewed as a multifaceted phenomenon, rather than as simply the offering of reassurance or encouragement.

Those views of counseling that stress the importance of the emotional quality of the relationship between counselor and client emphasize the growth-enhancing potential of what House (1981) has identified as "emotional support" (e.g., caring, comfort reassurance). Relationship-oriented conceptualizations also focus on "appraisal support." The counselor's unconditional positive regard is an implicit confirmation of the client's worth and value.

Behavioral and cognitively oriented approaches view counseling as a learning situation that eliminates dysfunctional behaviors and beliefs and enhances adaptive, effective responses. Learning theory-based approaches emphasize what House has called "appraisal support" (i.e., feedback about the presence and effects of particular dysfunctional behavior and/or beliefs).

Also, "informational support" is provided in many counseling interventions, perhaps especially those that focus on life planning or decision-making situations. When clients face such issues, counselors often provide information about new alternatives of action and belief. Such information can help clients move toward more satisfying ways of dealing with life situations than those they currently are demonstrating.

Finally, the willingness of counselors operating from many theoretical orientations to move beyond verbal exchange and listening to advocate, troubleshoot, or offer needed material resources stands as an example of providing what House and others have called "material support."

The provision of social support can, then, be considered an important element in much of what counselors do, even if their counseling interventions are not conceptualized primarily from a social support perspective. However, in addition to viewing social support as an implicit element of counseling, it is also possible to use it deliberately as a perspective for understanding clients and for developing specific counseling interventions. This chapter examines the forms that such deliberate use of social support perspectives can take when we focus on working with individuals rather than on modifying their social or physical contexts.

In Chapter 4, a variety of client-based barriers to the reception of social support by clients (i.e., withdrawal, social ineptitude, moving against others) were examined. These barriers were considered in terms of their attitudinal and behavioral correlates. Those foci will be maintained in discussing strategies and interventions for removing or ameliorating the effect of client-based barriers. Table 5.1 identifies broad counseling strategies that can be used when such barriers are found to be operating. The table also presents specific counseling interventions that implement each of the broad strategies identified.

Strategies and Interventions

A word about my use of the terms *strategies* and *interventions* is in order here. Though some writers use these terms interchangeably (e.g., Cormier & Hackney, 1987, p. 24), I find it helpful to differentiate between the two. Counseling strategies (as I will use the term) are broad groupings of counseling actions that share some common perspective or theoretical base. For example, we can speak of "learning theory-based strategies" or "family-focused strategies" as a way of identifying a group of broadly related counseling actions that share a focus on learning theory perspectives or (in the second instance) a concern for family-related issues.

In contrast, an intervention is a specific counseling activity used to carry out a counseling strategy. For example, we might ask a client to keep a chart documenting the number of times he withdraws from potential supporters. This would be a counseling intervention used to implement a learning theory-based strategy. We might also carry out a

Table 5.1. Strategies and Interventions for Removing or Moderating Client-Based Barriers

Strategies	Interventions
Attitudinally-focused strategies	
Corrective experience	direct experience vicarious experience simulated experience
Self-exploration	establishment of a relationship of trust (reduction of threat through acceptance, understanding)
Confrontation	identification, and disputation of dysfunctional beliefs
Behaviorally-focused strategies	
Respondent conditioning	desensitization of anxiety
Operant conditioning	shaping of functional benavior (in vivo interventions, simulations)
Modeling	modeling presented in simulated situations fostering contact with positive models (in vivo modeling)
Skill training	teaching relationship-establishment skills teaching relationship-maintenance skills teaching support-focused skills (e.g., support system assessment)

desensitization procedure to reduce the anxiety a client feels in asking for assistance. In doing so, we would again be pursuing a learning theory-based strategy, but doing so by use of a different intervention; that is, using desensitization rather than charting. This strategy/intervention distinction will permit the consideration of counseling activities aimed at removing client-based barriers to proceed at different levels of specificity.

Strategies and Interventions Focused on Internal Barriers

Dysfunctional attitudes and cognitions (those that provide an ineffective basis for understanding and responding to the situation at hand) can be viewed as the result of

- limited or biased past experience (direct and vicarious) that makes accurate generalization to other situations unlikely; and
- cognitive and/or emotional barriers that prevent modification and broadening of dysfunctional attitudes and cognitions. (Such individual-based barriers often continue in spite of experience or information that would ordinarily lead to perceptual or cognitive change.)

This approach to individual-based barriers focuses attention both on the process through which attitudes and cognitions are formed (i.e., direct or vicarious experience) and the manner in which they are maintained (i.e., internal characteristics such as perceptual rigidity or denial). Specifying the source of attitudinal and cognitive barriers has practical importance for counselors. Doing so provides a point of departure for developing strategies and interventions aimed at increasing clients' access to supportive resources. Broadly, these strategies emphasize corrective experience, self-exploration, or confrontation as means of reducing or eliminating attitudinal barriers to the acquisition of needed social support.

Corrective Experience and Internal Change

As clients discuss their concerns and difficulties we often become aware that they systematically view or think about others, situations, and events in ways that reduce the likelihood others will respond supportively. Sometimes the internal barrier (i.e., attitude, cognition) is the result of a gap in the client's attitudinal or cognitive structures. For example, some individuals may never have heard of a support group; thus they will be unaware of, and have little existing attitudinal predisposition toward, the possibility of using such groups as a source of social support during various life transitions. Other times the internal barrier is based on attitudes or cognitions that (because they are either generally erroneous or invalid with reference to the situation at hand) prevent access to social support.

Three general strategies can be identified for reducing or eliminating the effects of dysfunctional attitudes and cognitions that serve to reduce clients' access to social support: providing direct, vicarious, or simulated experience.

Direct Experience

The counseling relationship itself can be viewed as a major source of direct experience. It can serve to fill gaps in clients' prior experience or correct inaccurate generalizations that guide their understanding of, and response to, situations. Counselors' attitudes and behaviors can provide clients with models of new, more functional ways of relating to others. Also, the safety and acceptance of the counseling relationship can encourage clients to try out and establish new response patterns, the lack of which had been causing difficulty. For example, by encouraging the awareness and expression of affect, the counselor can help clients begin building a body of experience with affective self-disclosure. Though initially limited to the counseling relationship, this experience may eventually be generalized to, and elaborated in, clients' daily functioning.

Also, the counseling relationship can be viewed as a place to set up experiences in clients' real-life settings that will add to and/or modify their existing attitudes and cognitions. The intervention of assigning homework is used by many counselors. We might, for example, assign a client the task of calling a mental health information hot line as a way of finding out whether or not there are any support groups in the community that would be useful in providing a needed type of social support. In another instance, by determining that clients have expectations and beliefs that lead them to avoid potential supporters (e.g., "They'd think less of me if they knew that I couldn't handle this myself"), we might encourage them to put their assumptions to the test by requesting assistance from the least threatening and most approachable of their potential supporters.

Group procedures have enormous potential as sources of direct experience. In discussions of the nature of group treatment, it is commonplace to refer to the group setting as a microcosm of life. Much of the gain from group treatment comes from interacting with others who (like oneself) are experiencing life difficulties and (unlike the single, trained helper) are apt to represent a variety of backgrounds and outlooks. Given the wider stimulus value the group is apt to represent, it can provide a rich source of direct experience for individuals as they explore and try out new ways of looking at themselves and interacting with others. For example, within the group situation, shy, retiring individuals are confronted with the same issue of communicating the need for help that they experience in their daily lives. They experience a gradual process of coming to trust their fellow group members enough to display their need and vulnerability. This can provide a counterbalance to the withdrawal that had cut these individuals off from social support available from their natural system. Also, some clients come to the group believing that requesting assistance for life concerns will lead to rejection and criticism from others. Feedback from other group members can lead to the realization that the clients are holding the values of independence and self-sufficiency in a rigid, undifferentiated fashion.

Clearly, in pursuing a direct experience strategy with clients, a concern for maximizing the chances of success is of major importance. A positive experience can provide a functional base for more effective awareness and use of support resources. However, an ill-advised or carelessly devised homework assignment or group experience can confirm individuals' worst fears about depending on others. This may harden their resistance to future attempts to increase their seeking assistance from others.

Vicarious Experience

Vicarious experience can be described as experience obtained primarily through such symbol-based channels as printed material, television, films, dramatic presentations, or simple verbal exchange. The client's role in vicarious experience is that of a passive receptor who takes in and then, it is hoped, integrates the information provided. Vicarious procedures provide information concerning events, objects, or situations that are not part of individuals' immediate life experience, or that focus on aspects of their experience to which they had not been attending.

Counselors' comments can constitute a major source of vicarious experience for clients. When we give advice, describe our own experience or that of others, or provide information, we are saying, essentially, "This is the way the world is, how things are set up, what you can expect." Such statements (or information) can be a valuable, efficient means for clients to gain data and perspectives that would be difficult or impossible to acquire on their own. However, there are cautions. We should be concerned that the material we are presenting is information and not misinformation; for example, is information based on our own undergraduate experience a reliable guide for current students?

Clients will often be found to lack past experience on which they can base valid expectations of the willingness or ability of others to be supportive in particular situations. Given an openness to new data, it is usually a fairly simple matter to provide vicarious experience that can change their attitudes.

With clients approaching life transitions (e.g., unemployment, job change, divorce, going to college), referral to a helpful big sister/ brother type of person can lend a speedy start to the process of adding new persons to the informal support system. Also, the information provided by such persons can open up access to supportive resources of which the clients had previously been unaware or had been mistakenly discounting.

Simulated Experience

Simulated experience can be defined as that resulting from the creation or recreation of life situations. The creation or staging of events and circumstances is carried out in the belief that while such experience is, in and of itself, artificial, it can foster understanding and skill acquisition that can be applied to real situations. The distinction between real and simulated experience can be illustrated by considering a group counseling session during which a role-playing activity is carried out to help a client acquire acquaintancing skills. The ongoing group counseling experience can be considered real or actual experience. As removed from members' daily comings and goings as group interaction may be, it is unstaged and proceeds on the basis of members' spontaneous implementation of themselves. In contrast, the role-playing activity is an attempt to create or recreate situations that are not actually part of the "here and now," and thus is a simulated experience.

Jacob Moreno is usually identified as the most important source of innovation in efforts to bring the power and versatility of the dramatic tradition to the work of psychotherapy. His theory and practice proceed from the assumption that situations and experiences can be created and recreated in the treatment situation to provide therapeutic, growth-enhancing experience for individuals (Moreno & Elefthery, 1975). Through the medium of psychodrama, time and place are transcended, allowing clients to have access to the people and situations they need to come to terms with life issues.

In its classical form, psychodrama is a complex treatment modality that uses a variety of "instruments" (e.g., director, group, stage) and procedures (e.g., direct soliloquy, role reversal, mirroring) to help individuals explore unresolved, problematic life concerns. Though psychodrama continues to be used as a treatment form in and of itself, its major impact in counseling and other helping professions is probably found in an adaptation usually called "role playing." Role-playing interventions are used by many counselors as an alternative or adjunctive way of helping clients deal with a wide range of concerns.

Psychodrama and role playing allow us to transcend the limits of time and place. Any context that clients need to expand their understanding of themselves and others, or to try out new responses, is available to the counselor and client. Shy, withdrawing individuals can, through role playing, be taken back to a recent situation in which they withdrew from contact with others. This allows them to reenact the situation, trying out a different, perhaps more assertive, set of responses. Such reenactment would also allow withdrawing individuals to step into the role of a potential supporter as a means of testing their assumption that a request for help would cause the other person to view them in a negative fashion.

Use of role playing can allow socially noxious individuals to step into the shoes of a person toward whom they have been exploitive or hurtful. In doing so, they can experience how their actions affect others. They see how their lack of concern can lead to rejection or counterattack from persons who might be sources of support if treated better. Such simulated experience can offer a point of departure for the development of a new, more reciprocal, manner of relating to others.

Self-Exploration and Internal Change

The persistence of dysfunctional attitudes and cognitions, even in the face of disconfirming experience, is a situation often encountered in counseling. The same ongoing processes that have resulted in clients' ignoring, distorting, or dismissing experience inconsistent with their beliefs are apt to be activated when the counselor presents new information or experience to prompt client change. For example, elderly persons who hold tightly to the belief that the only help worth having is help that comes from the primary family, are apt to discount the relevance of information about nonfamily sources of help. They are also apt to dismiss expressions of caring or encouragement from nonfamily (Chapman & Pancoast, 1985).

Day-to-day experience with persons in counseling and informal interaction offers ample support of the assertion that exposure to new information or direct experience gives no guarantee that existing attitudes will be modified (Lewin & Grabbe, 1948). Why this resistance to change? Why do people often continue to cling to attitudes and views that fly in the face of fact and reason?

Reduction of Threat

The construct "threat" holds a central place in phenomenological formulations about barriers to perceptual (and hence attitudinal and behavioral) change. The effect of threat is to make individuals' views of their situation more rigid and less differentiated. For example, persons who believe their economic well-being is threatened by an influx of new immigrants are often found to cling tightly to racial or ethnic prejudices. In their apprehension, they fail to make the differentiations among members of those groups that they might make in less threatening situations. From this perspective, a reduction of the subjective threat that individuals experience toward matters pertaining to the attitudes in question can support attitude change.

We've seen that clients sometimes reject offers of assistance because they believe that accepting help represents weakness and inadequacy (Fisher et al., 1988; Goffman, 1963) or is an undue imposition on the resources or goodwill of others (Harker, 1972). Efforts to change these attitudes by providing factual information supportive of a contrary view are often unsuccessful because clients believe that too much is at stake to risk change; for example, the possibility of alienating or causing difficulty for their kith and kin.

Fisher and his colleagues (1988) noted that the literature suggests a variety of strategies that make it easier for individuals to accept assistance. For example, emphasizing individuals' past, current, or future contributions to others may reduce the discomfort high-self-esteem individuals commonly feel about receiving unreciprocated support. Similarly, pointing out that the need for assistance is the result of external, noncontrollable factors (e.g., disease, economic conditions) may make it easier for self-reliant persons to accept help. However, such strategies may fail to "take" because making such distinctions calls for an ability to admit and consider new information, and anxious persons may find that impossible to do.

An understanding of how to get through to change the belief that accepting social support represents personal inadequacy, or is an unwarranted imposition on others, can be furthered by a consideration of the factors that contribute to individuals' feeling threatened. Threat can be the result of influences lodged in the social or physical environment, as when family members ridicule a person who voices the intent to seek assistance from a counselor or other mental health professional. Such sources of stress result from factors external to the individual, and will be considered in Chapter 7. For the moment, our focus is on how the counseling process can contribute to the reduction or elimination of intrapsychic barriers to attitude change as a means of enhancing social support availability for our clients.

The development of a relationship of trust to counterbalance the impact of external or internalized threat is emphasized, but not limited to, person-centered approaches to counseling (Blocher, 1987 p. 210). Varying views of the counseling process emphasize the importance of acceptance and understanding in the counseling relationship. This convergence seems to have its foundation in the recognition that positive change is fostered by an interpersonal context where clients experience safety. Stated somewhat differently, openness to change is enhanced when experienced and anticipated threat, which would otherwise rigidify perceptual and cognitive processes, are reduced.

Behaviorally oriented and person-centered theorists and practitioners view the positive impact of an acceptant, nonjudgmental relationship differently. Behaviorally oriented practitioners view a safe relationship as an effective extinguisher of anxiety. In contrast, phenomenologically oriented counselors tend to see the acceptant relationship as a means of promoting perceptual flexibility. However, both approaches share the view that providing a nonthreatening relationship is an important factor in counseling.

I have suggested that when there are no strong intrapsychic barriers to attitude change, a straightforward presentation of vicarious, simulated, or direct experience can produce desirable attitudinal and cognitive change. However, when clients cling tightly to dysfunctional beliefs (dysfunctional in the sense that they interfere with access to needed, available social support), attention must be focused on how we can use our relationship with them to foster a sense of safety. When established, this safety can help clients begin the process of genuinely considering information that is (and may have long been) available to them.

In a psychologically safe relationship, many clients increasingly find it possible to examine their assumptions about themselves, others, and the physical context. Through such examination, they often discover things of which they had not been aware and/or come to realize that some things they believed to be true are otherwise. For example, the counselor's recognition and acceptance of initial faint expressions of vulnerability and need for help can make it easier for clients to recognize, and then accept, their own feelings of inadequacy and their need for help.

In other instances, clients are able to use the safety of the counseling relationship to make distinctions they had not been able to make under the stress of self- or other-inflicted negative judgment. They may come to recognize that needing help with certain situations does not mean they are totally helpless or inadequate. Moreover, when clients can relax about needing assistance from others, they may be freed to devote attention to identifying the specific type of support they need. Rather than having a global, disquieting sense of needing someone to help them, clients can pursue the issue of whether it is emotional, material, informational, or appraisal support that their current concerns demand. Knowing what it is they need makes it easier for clients and counselors to identify strategies for pursuing those needs.

Confrontation

Relationship-oriented counselors emphasize the positive impact of acceptance and a nonjudgmental stance in moving clients beyond the perceptual, attitudinal, and cognitive barriers that lock them into such support-blocking behaviors as withdrawal, ineptness, or exploitation of others. Some practitioners take a very different tack, using confrontation of clients' beliefs and perceptions judged to be dysfunctional.

If, as the saying goes, the thought is parent to the deed, then changing how one thinks about a situation is one approach to changing the response to that situation. This is precisely the basic strategy of Rational Emotive Therapy (RET), an approach to promoting personal effectiveness developed by Albert Ellis. Ellis (1971) called attention to the manner in which irrational conceptualizations (beliefs) lead to dysfunctional emotional and behavioral responses to life situations. By replacing clients' irrational beliefs with beliefs that are more rational (and hence functional), many of the problems and difficulties clients experience can be ameliorated or eliminated.

Ellis identified a number of commonly held irrational beliefs that can lead to dysfunctional responses. Among them, the following would seem to have the greatest significance with regard to creating barriers to the flow of social support:

· It is a catastrophe of some sort if I am not perfectly loved and approved of by everyone.
· I must be completely adequate, competent, and effective if I am to have any worth.
· Most difficulties and responsibilities are better avoided than faced.

· Dependency, having someone who is more competent to rely on, is the best way to handle most difficult situations.

An examination of this list suggests that persons who catastrophize common life events and react to them with strong affect (e.g., anger, fear) have a dysfunctional life orientation. In seeking to neutralize the operation of such irrational cognitions, the counselor moves clients toward a style that eliminates unwarranted or self-defeating emotional reactions. This interpretation of Rational Emotive Therapy is strongly consistent with Hinkle's (1974) finding that "natural copers" (i.e., individuals who typically seem to have little difficulty in dealing with major life difficulties) tend to be persons who display a nonreactive stance toward life events.

Within the RET framework, the basic process through which irrational beliefs are changed is one that stresses the counselor's ability to convince clients that those beliefs are, indeed, irrational and dysfunctional. Such convincing takes place through verbal exchange that identifies, confronts, and challenges the irrational beliefs. Walen, DiGiuseppe, and Wessler (1980) have suggested that confrontation of irrational beliefs can be pursued by asking questions that challenge the assumptions on which the beliefs rest. In the case of cognitions that could serve as barriers to the reception of social support, a counselor might pose the following challenges:

· How do you know that people look down on any person who needs help or assistance?
· Even if there are some people who condemn others who ask for help, don't you think its an overgeneralization to say that everyone looks down on anyone who needs assistance?
· What are the consequences of your belief that the only reason someone would offer help is because they're setting you up to take advantage of you?
· What's so terrible about someone telling you that they're too busy to give you a hand?

Confrontation of clients' irrational beliefs does not have to be pursued in a relentless, badgering manner. Simple courtesy and a sensitivity to client readiness suggest the desirability of proceeding in a manner that communicates concern and respect for the importance of clients' experience. However, even when approached with concern for client sensibilities, there seem to be some clients for whom the confrontation of beliefs is not effective. Cormier and Hackney (1987) noted:

> Clients who are turned off to cognitive approaches may be in crisis or have more severe problems, want or expect a great deal of emotional support and warmth from the counseling relationship, process information kinesthetically, and react to issues and make decisions emotionally. (p. 166)

They also suggest that clients to whom cognitively focused interventions seem most comfortable tend to be "intelligent, witty, present neurotic symptoms, generate pictures or internal dialogue easily, and value the art of logical thinking" (p. 166). With such clients, confrontation and "cognitive disputation" of dysfunctional beliefs (Walen et al., 1980) can be highly effective in reducing or eliminating patterns of client withdrawal, ineptness, or lack of reciprocity that decrease the flow of social support.

Strategies and Interventions Focused on Behavioral Barriers

We have seen that some individuals behave in ways that reduce the likelihood they will receive support from others. Clients cannot be supported if they withdraw from persons who have provided support in the past or might do so in the future. Potential supporters are apt to be unaware of individuals' need for assistance if that need is unvoiced or hidden. Socially inept persons may lack the personal presence or conversational fluency to put other persons at ease in a way that encourages potential supporters to approach, initiate, and maintain contact. Clients who manifest such socially noxious behavior as insensitivity, exploitiveness, or cruelty cause others to withdraw. If they persist in engaging others, these clients elicit punishment and ostracism.

Such clinical observations about how behavioral gaps and dysfunctional behavior can interfere with the flow of social support are echoed in the literature on social support. Heller and Swindle (1983) observed:

> The level of support enjoyed by the individual depends not only on environmental structures and the actions of others, but also on the individual's abilities and predilections to link to others and elicit support from them. (p. 96)

The importance of focusing on the role of individuals' behavior in opening up or closing off the flow of social support is also reflected in Hirsch's (1981) observation that individuals may experience little support from others because they "lack the requisite personal or social competencies needed to capitalize on available opportunities" (p. 163). Rook and Dooley (1985) have discussed how social support research can be applied to individual-focused interventions aimed at improving the quantity and quality of social support received by individuals. They suggested that such interventions are best conceptualized as educational in nature and designed to focus on training individuals to cope with interpersonal situations, social competence training, and training persons to be more skillful in eliciting support from others.

If many of our clients struggle with concerns and difficulties without the benefit of social support because of the way they behave, how do we go about helping them acquire missing behaviors and/or eliminate those that are dysfunctional? An obvious answer is to "teach" them to stop doing what is dysfunctional and to begin behaving in ways that elicit and encourage the supportiveness of others. The obvious response is, however, not particularly useful in identifying specifically how our support-deficient clients can be helped; teaching can take many forms and vary in style and approach.

A variety of principles derived from learning theory can be used to help fill behavioral gaps or to modify dysfunctional behaviors that block the flow of social support. There are no behaviorally oriented strategies and interventions unique to the domain of social support-focused counseling. Rather, counseling practice in these cases takes standard, well-tried behavioral approaches and adapts them to the characteristics and demands of the specific support deficiency situation at hand.

Among the many behaviorally oriented strategies that might be used by counselors, three (respondent conditioning, operant conditioning, and modeling) will be examined as strategies for reducing or eliminating client-based barriers to support deficiencies. Additionally, "skill training," a broad, programmatic approach to behavioral acquisition and change that incorporates elements of operant and respondent conditioning, will be discussed.

Respondent Conditioning Applications

Typically, anxiety in interpersonal situations has a detrimental effect on individuals' ability to acquire and maintain prosocial behavior. As we have seen, anxiety leads many persons to avoid the very situations in which they could learn interpersonal skills. Even those who more or less remain in contact with others may have their ability to attend to moment-to-moment events reduced by anxiety. Thus the ability to recognize fine nuances of social interaction is impaired and a potential source of interpersonal learning eliminated.

Many persons who lack social support actually possess reasonable social skill, but have difficulty expressing it in situations that involve gaining access to social support because they are fearful or anxious. For example, clients may be able to function effectively in proven, safe relationships, but become anxious when dealing with persons with whom they are less familiar. In such situations, as Cormier and Hackney (1987, p. 189) noted, systematic desensitization is an effective intervention for eliminating debilitating anxiety.

Systematic desensitization is the underlying theoretical base for respondent conditioning. Respondent conditioning is a process through which new responses (such as relaxation) are linked to a stimulus (e.g., talking to a stranger) that previously had elicited some other response (e.g., withdrawal from contact). It is the classical conditioning procedure used by Pavlov in training animals to salivate at the sound of a bell or to lift a paw at the blinking of a light (Kanfer & Phillips, 1970).

As developed by Joseph Wolpe (1982), desensitization is a process for training individuals to respond to previously feared objects or situations with relaxation and lessened anxiety. Systematic desensitization can reduce or eliminate the anxiety of clients who withdraw from, or minimize contact with, potential supporters. Lessened anxiety allows such clients to build or expand supportive relationships more easily.

There are three basic elements of the systematic desensitization process: (a) relaxation training, (b) development of a stimulus hierarchy, and (c) vicarious presentation of increasingly anxiety-producing situations (i.e., items from the stimulus hierarchy) to the relaxed client. Specific materials and procedures for implementing systematic desensitization interventions are extensively discussed in the literature (e.g., Godfried & Davison, 1976; Rimm & Masters, 1979; Wolpe, 1982) and will not be detailed here.

Generally, systematic desensitization interventions can be very helpful when working with clients who are markedly deficient in behaviors related to the establishment and maintenance of social interaction because they have isolated themselves. Eliminating the fear they experience in the presence of others can allow these clients to feel sufficiently comfortable to begin the process of establishing and polishing their social skills.

Operant Conditioning Applications

Operant conditioning, an extremely robust approach to modifying behavior, is based on Thorndike's "law of effect." This principle states that if behavior results in consequences favorable to the actor, the probability increases that the behavior will subsequently recur in the same or similar situations. Behavioral theorists assert this simple paradigm constitutes the foundation of animal (human and otherwise) behavior, however complex that behavior might be — we do, and continue to do, what "pays off," and discontinue whatever results in neutral or negative consequences.

As simple as it seems, the law of effect has been used by Skinner and others as a point of departure for a wide variety of approaches to fostering behavioral change. The central strategy in the application of operant conditioning interventions is to create a situation in which the desired behavior occurs, and then to introduce circumstances (e.g., objects, sensory states) having positive value (reward) for the organism. The individual acts (or is caused to act) in the desired manner, and those actions are quickly followed by the introduction of something that has reward value. Operant conditioning interventions thus rest on (a) the ability to elicit the desired behavior, (b) access to objects or circumstances that have reward value for the client, and (c) the power to present those rewards in close proximity (but after) the occurrence of the behavior.

In practice, there are a number of issues that complicate the implementation of this apparently simple intervention paradigm. Often, one of the most thorny problems is getting clients to express the desired behavior so that it can be reinforced and thus strengthened. For many of our withdrawing clients, the pattern of removing themselves from social interaction is so deeply entrenched that the likelihood they will stay close to others and/or take a more active role in social interaction is very remote.

Also, in many instances, the final behavior we aim to establish with our support-deficient clients may be so complex that it is unlikely that clients could, right from the start, demonstrate the desired responses in a form that is complete or polished enough to have an actual, positive effect on potential supporters. For example, as one element in building

a repertoire of relationship maintenance skills, we might be interested
in helping a client become more effective in conversing with others.
Though some withdrawing clients may already have excellent conversational skills and simply have difficulty using them with persons
they don't already know and trust, many clients have serious deficiencies precisely because their contacts with others have been limited. In
the latter case, we should not expect the client to move from conversational inhibition to fluency in one jump. Rather, the task of establishing
the desired, but complex, behavior pattern could be accomplished
through the process of "shaping," in which successive approximations
of the final goal are established. Each approximation serves as the point
of departure for another expression of the behavior pattern that is closer
to the ultimate goal of conversational fluency. We might begin by
reinforcing a client's ability to stay briefly in the presence of a stranger.
When that is established, we would move on to lengthening the period
of comfort.

After reaching the point where the client is able to tolerate proximity
to strangers, we might begin the process of establishing the ability to
begin verbal exchange. The first step might be to encourage and reinforce relatively "safe" comments that focus on asking for the time or
commenting on the weather. As such relatively simple, limited verbal
exchange becomes established, we would move on to expand the complexity and open-endedness of the client's verbal exchange until something approaching our original goal of conversational fluency is established. In such a fashion, clients can be moved toward ultimate
acquisition of response patterns that initially would have overwhelmed
them.

The foregoing discussion of establishing complex behavior patterns
through the process of shaping also highlights another tactical problem
encountered in implementing operant conditioning procedures: moni-
toring a client's behavior closely enough so that a judgment can be made
as to the degree to which the behavior at hand actually approximates
what is being focused on at that stage of the training. If the training is
done in vivo, using situations that are genuinely a part of a client's life
experience, the counselor (or a representative) will have to shadow the
client, observe his or her actions, assess the appropriateness of these
actions, and dispense or withhold reward. Clearly, this can be very
time-consuming for the counselor, especially if one considers that the
situation to which the client is expected to respond may not occur on cue.

A way around problems encountered with in vivo training is to use simulated situations (e.g., staged or role-playing situations) that can be managed much more efficiently. However, the use of simulated experience introduces the problem of ensuring transfer from the training situation to real-life contexts. A combination of simulated and in vivo interventions is perhaps most necessary with clients who come to counseling with very low levels of social skill. Simulated situations provide a relatively efficient way of establishing basic proficiency with regard to relationship initiation and maintenance skills. Once clients have developed a level of competence that makes it reasonable to assume they will experience success in (initially) carefully chosen real-life situations, training can shift from simulated to in vivo interventions.

It will be noted that the shift from simulations to real-life enactments also can mark a shift from rewards managed by the counselor to controls mediated by clients' everyday contexts. The general strategy of setting up behavioral acquisition in a way that capitalizes on reward patterns operating naturally in the environment has tremendous value because it frees both client and counselor from the constraints of carefully adhering to an essentially unnatural treatment situation. Naturally occurring reinforcers of desired behaviors continue beyond the counseling situation, operating at times and in places to which access is virtually impossible or impractical for the counselor. If there are no natural reinforcers operating in clients' usual contexts, we may have to consider ways of altering those contexts. For example, we might change clients' circle of associates or intervene with those associates to enlist their assistance in noticing and positively reinforcing the newly established behavior.

In working with clients who withdraw from or alienate others, a central goal should be to establish sufficient social skill that they will be able to gain access to and/or maintain social interaction that has strong, positive reinforcement value. By definition, social support has a positive impact on the recipient — however well intentioned the actions of supporters may be, if they are not experienced by clients as beneficial, they are not supportive. Through operant conditioning interventions, we may be able to help our clients to stop running away from potential supporters and/or to eliminate noxious behaviors that lead others to respond with neglect or punishment. In doing so, we open those clients to social contact that will support and maintain those prosocial patterns we have established in our counseling intervention.

Modeling

One of the most pervasive learning strategies of everyday life is that of watching to see how other people handle a situation in order to determine how we should respond to the same or similar situation — find someone who seems to know what he or she is doing and do what they do. This is an instance of what Bandura (1977) called "social learning" — learning mediated by the viewing of, or contact with, others. Much social learning seems to be an implicit process — children learn to speak their native language by listening to the people around them and then imitating what they hear. Social learning can also be deliberately used (either by clients themselves or by other persons interested in expanding or modifying their behavior) as a strategy for helping individuals acquire behavior.

The power of social learning lies, I believe, not only in its being a basic, pervasive learning strategy, but also because it generally works. "When in Rome, . . . " the adage goes, and it conveys to us that there is advantage in taking on the behavior of those around us. That advantage may be gaining approval or avoiding criticism or punishment.

Within the framework developed in this chapter, modeling is a counseling strategy that depends on vicarious experience. Our clients learn new ways of responding to life situations by observing other persons handling those same or similar situations. Such observation may focus on an audio- or videotaped presentation of the behavior, simulated enactment of the behavior (e.g., role playing), or live, in vivo functioning of persons in their natural contacts. Whatever its form, modeling puts the client in an observer's role as a means of demonstrating new or more differentiated behavioral responses. Even the intervention called "self-as-model" developed by Hosford and de Visser (1974) rests on having clients observe their own taped behavior.

Characteristics of the Model

Though basically a simple strategy, the effectiveness of modeling seems to be influenced by a variety of content and process variables. For example, Perry and Furakawa (1980) have focused on the characteristics of the model (especially in relation to those of the client) as variable affecting learning outcome. A model viewed by the client as attractive and having high prestige has a positive impact on behavioral change or acquisition. Using a model with whom the client can identify strongly and positively typically increases the "take" of modeling. It also increases the likelihood that the behavior presented to the client will be relevant and appropriate.

Another variable that seems to influence the potency of the modeling process is the level of competence demonstrated by the model. The literature suggests that the model should demonstrate a level of competence that is good, but not too good. Hosford, Moss, and Morrell (1976) suggested, for example, that a "coping" rather than a "mastery" pattern should be demonstrated. A master is apt to be viewed as too superior to be a good identification figure for our novice clients. Also, the behavioral demonstration given by an expert is apt to be too fluid and rapid or to contain too many details to be internalized by the beginner.

Designing Modeling Interventions

Finally, we can focus on the design of the modeling intervention itself. As is also true with operant conditioning interventions, the final behavior, or behavior sequence, we are helping clients acquire is often complex. In such instances, it is not likely that clients would have sufficient understanding to pick up the many, sometimes subtle, aspects of a fully developed response demonstrated by a model. Two general strategies for overcoming the problem of complexity can be found in the literature.

First, the complex behavioral sequence can be broken down into simpler parts, and these parts modeled in a systematic program that builds toward the eventual integration of the constituent parts. For example, when helping a withdrawing client acquire relationship establishment skills, we might focus our modeling intervention initially on "opening lines" (e.g., "I'm not sure I got the math assignment right; was it questions 12 to 20, or 15 to 20?").

Our next focus might be on broadening the opening into a fuller discussion. Through a series of comments our model might demonstrate how a line of conversation can be continued by finding an issue that is common to both people (for example, "I really like math but I'm not sure about this stuff we're covering now. How about you?").

Finally, we might focus on establishing nonverbal behavior that serves to make conversation a positive experience for other people. Thus, during this sequence, our model could demonstrate the presence of such facilitative nonverbal behavior as maintaining eye contact or using minimal encouragers (e.g., "right," "I see," and "um hum").

A second strategy for dealing with the problem of modeling complex behavioral sequences is to build commentary and verbal instructions into the modeled presentation. Orienting statements can be inserted into the presentation by the models themselves ("I know this classmate is really interested in baseball, so I'm going to make a comment about last night's game as a way of establishing contact with her").

Or the counselor might provide a running commentary to a role-played or videotaped enactment, alerting the client to particular actions that are important in an upcoming or preceding segment (Perry & Furakawa, 1980). Such statements as "Now I want you to pay attention to the way Sally encourages the other person to stay in the conversation—she maintains eye contact, gives a hint of a smile, and says things like 'That's a really interesting idea'" can orient clients to the important elements of the action.

Modeling in Daily Life

Beyond the intentional, formal use of modeling interventions in the counseling situation itself, an appreciation for their fundamental power and versatility can lead us to consider how clients' ordinary life experience provides functional or dysfunctional models. For example, if clients have difficulty establishing and maintaining supportive relationships, we might explore the extent to which their families are characterized by aggressive or critical interchange. Such patterns, if incorporated by clients and directed at nonfamily, can act as barriers to the flow of social support.

Exploring the operation of clients' social network can yield insight into the sources and impact of client-based barriers and prompt us to consider the benefits of modifying or expanding the network in order to provide more positive models. As Gottlieb (1981, pp. 220-221) pointed out, the general strategy of fostering contact with peers (i.e., nonnetwork persons who are experiencing the same difficulty) can provide clients with positive models for coping. This strategy might take the form of a "big brother/sister" program or of putting clients into contact with a support group. Such interventions have the potential of providing clients with access to persons who, vicariously and directly, can demonstrate effective ways of dealing with problematic situations.

Skill Training Applications

Phillips (1985) noted that there are a variety of historical trends from which the skill training movement has drawn its impetus. Though some of its roots are clearly fixed in psychotherapeutic endeavors (e.g., the work of J. Wolpe), the position is often taken in its literature that skill training rejects many of the assumptions on which traditional psychotherapeutic approaches are based. Phillips (1985) has called attention to the fact that skill training approaches are being applied increasingly to individuals and populations traditionally viewed as candidates for group and individual psychotherapy and that this trend has "helped replace the traditional notions of abnormal psychology and psychiatry that people are lacking in social competence because they are 'sick' rather than the other way around" (p. 17).

Actually, it would seem that the distinction to be made is not between skill training approaches and traditional counseling and psychotherapy in general but, rather, between skill training and those approaches that focus on intrapsychic factors as the cause of individuals' dysfunctionality. It is clear that there is considerable compatibility between the skill training strategy and those of behavioral formulations of counseling and psychotherapy. Indeed, the work of Joseph Wolpe (1982), specifically his contributions to the broad intervention known as assertiveness training, is one of the major influences that has shaped the skill training movement. Also, many of the behavioral strategies discussed earlier in this chapter (e.g., operant conditioning, modeling) that are widely used in counseling and psychotherapy lend themselves well to use in skill training interventions.

As with behaviorally based approaches to counseling and psychotherapy, skill training strategy focuses on behavior as the source of individuals' dysfunctionality. The skill training approach considers that movement toward greater effectiveness is best accomplished by combinations of removing ineffective behavior, strengthening appropriate but weak or constricted behavior, and establishing new, effective behavior.

The notion that personal discomfort or difficulty often results from skill deficits is also found in the social support-focused literature. Heller (1979), House (1981), and Gottlieb (1981) suggested that the lack of those skills needed to gain access to and maintain relationships from which social support can be obtained is a frequent element of the difficulties suffered by socially isolated individuals. Once the relationship between the lack of social skill and low levels of social support received is noted, it is logical to share Heller's speculation that if "teaching social skills can increase social competency, might not a skills approach help individuals maintain themselves more appropriately in a supportive environment?" (1979, p. 371).

Developing Skill Training Interventions

A particular contribution that social skill training can make to the counseling strategy of expanding clients' social support resources is that of providing a systematic framework. Within this framework, the task of specifying the skills needed for effective functioning in a particular situation and for developing a program for clients' acquisition of those skills can be pursued.

As described by Eisler and Frederickson (1980), the process of skill training proceeds through the following steps:

- empirically identifying the skills on which effective functioning in the context in question rests;
- developing a set of learning experiences that will allow clients to acquire the needed skills;
- implementing the learning program; and
- evaluating the outcomes of training in naturalistic settings to determine the extent to which the client has indeed become "skillful."

Most counselors would not start from scratch in developing and implementing a skill training intervention with a client. The literature contains many detailed accounts of skill training programs that can serve, at least, as a point of departure for our work with clients. For example, Goldstein's (1980) Structured Learning Therapy (SLT) is a programmatic skill training approach designed to provide individuals with effective alternatives to dysfunctional behavior. Because of this focus, SLT would be a likely place to start in developing a counseling intervention to reduce or eliminate the client-based barrier to social support discussed in Chapter 4 as "moving against others."

There are many accounts of the specifics of training programs through which individuals can be helped to acquire such skills. However, a recognition of the extent to which prerequisite skills and training programs can be affected by situational and individual factors should cause us to be wary about assuming that a set of skills demonstrated to be effective with one individual or population (e.g., social skills characterizing effective conversationalists in an elderly population) can be extrapolated to another individual or population (e.g., an adolescent who is having difficulty communicating effectively with authority figures).

While it may be helpful to determine what the literature has to say about social skills generally required in the sort of situations faced by persons similar to our clients, a rigorous application of the skill training methodology requires that we go into the field to determine the extent to which the findings of past work actually apply to the specifics of our clients and their situations. We should use previously developed training interventions only after we have considered how compatible their process and content are with the particular client or client group with whom we are working.

For example, if one of our clients seems to lack social support because of a strong pattern of moving against others, we might start by getting a specific picture of what it is that she does to alienate others. This could involve observing the client in her natural settings or in simulations representative of the situations in which she experiences difficulty. In doing so, we might conclude that the primary problem stems from her inability to cope with differences in points of view — whenever someone disagrees with her, she becomes loud and abusive. We may learn that if the other person does not come around to her position, she typically resorts to pushing and shoving in an attempt to get the other person to leave the situation.

Armed with a fairly specific picture of what our client is doing to alienate potential supporters, our next task is to identify what it is she should be doing; that is, determining what would be skilled behavior for the client. It is too simple merely to say that the client should be nice to people. That she should stop getting angry when faced with disagreement and should find other ways of coping with disagreement than hitting and pushing seems obvious. However, we need more specific targets to guide our efforts. For example, within the client's social group, how much disagreement is allowed? Typically, how is disagreement expressed? How do people deal with disagreement — by negotiating, ignoring it, or appealing to an authority? Without some grounding in the client's social context, we run the risk of focusing our training on a conflict resolution approach that is fine in some situations, but is out of tune with those faced by our client.

Support-Focused Skills

Training programs focused on such social skill clusters as conflict resolution, assertiveness, or interpersonal communication, though broader in scope than the establishment and maintenance of support relationships, clearly will often have direct application to our social support-deficient clients. However, there are other important skills that are social skills only in the broadest sense, yet relate very specifically to the understanding and management of social support resources by clients.

Theoretically, all of the support system analysis techniques discussed in Chapter 3 could be taught to clients as a way of arming them with a set of perspectives for thinking about and acting on their social support resources. Indeed, a number of writers have stressed the usefulness of providing clients with support-relevant understandings and techniques. For example, Hirsch (1981) described workshops developed by Brennan (1977) and Gottlieb and Todd (1979) that "focus on imparting skills in network analysis and in linking multidimensional relationships, density, and so on, to participants objectives" (p. 168). Similarly, Brammer and Abrego (1981) noted that persons whose support resources have been disrupted by life transitions often display a specific need "for assessing the adequacy and scope of their network" (p. 28). They then describe several approaches to helping such individuals acquire these assessment skills. Such skills can serve as a point of departure for self-initiated remedial action.

In a somewhat different vein, Tolsdorf (1976) noted that individuals may lack support because their excessive demands have depleted family resources. He suggested that such persons can be helped to recognize their overuse of family support and then aided in identifying unused sectors of their support system. Identification and use of nonfamily segments of the system can result in clients' having access to new resources. It can also serve to take pressure off the family, opening the way to the reestablishment of more favorable relationships. Such a strategy (i.e., the identification of overused and underused segments of the support system and the shifting of requests for help from the former to the latter) is one that can be taught directly to clients. Combined with instruction in network analysis and relationship establishment, the strategy can provide clients with a way of dealing with one specific cause of support deficiency (overuse of one segment of the natural system).

Ashinger (1985) discussed how network analysis can be brought into the counseling process as a foundation for client action. She used an inventory that identified the persons in the support system, specified the type of support provided, and classified supporters into such categories as friends and neighbors, family, co-workers, and formal helpers. These data are converted to a visual device called the "network structure graph." Using the graph, the client can be encouraged to determine what changes in the social field would be helpful in his or her life. He or she can gain a new perspective on support, recognizing those who have been taken for granted in the past. Some members may have been underused and now may offer additional support. The client can also determine void areas on the inventory and be encouraged to analyze the degree of interaction related to positive and negative effects in social relationships. (Ashinger, 1985, p. 520)

This procedure can be implemented in a way that provides clients with an understanding of the situation at hand, as well as teaching them network analysis skills and interpersonal strategies. These skills can be carried away from the counseling situation for future use.

Conclusion

A range of strategies and interventions focused on the removal of client-based barriers to the reception of social support has been presented. I have made an effort to discuss those extensions or adaptations of well-established counseling strategies that have either demonstrated or apparent application to the expansion of clients' social support resources. That even this brief overview covers a wide range of views and procedures reflects, I believe, the central place that social support plays in the development and functioning of individuals. So much of what we are — the manner in which we function and the success or failure of our efforts — is affected by the contributions of others. Each conceptualization of human behavior, even if it does not directly use the construct "social support," seems to have something to say about how individuals encourage or discourage the supportiveness of others. To the extent this is true, we should expect that other counseling and psychotherapeutic approaches not extensively examined in this chapter will yield perspectives and interventions that are useful in removing client-based barriers.

Chapter Six

Other- and Context-Based Barriers

A number of people who were not receiving the amount or type of social support they wanted or that we might think appropriate were introduced in Chapter 2. Often, if we ask why our clients are not receiving the social support they need, the answer will be because there's "something" about them. For example, Rita's suspicion and bitterness tended to drive her brother away, and Wilson's selfishness was resented by his roommates. In these situations, the client-based barriers discussed in Chapter 4 can be observed.

However, in other cases presented, the barrier to the flow of social support stemmed primarily from the operation of factors not having to do with the persons themselves. For example, Elaine found herself cut off from contact and emotional exchange with her brothers and sisters because of family conflict precipitated by the death of her mother, a strong, dominant matriarch who had held the family together. Similarly, Tammy's rejection by what she called the "village kids" was primarily a result of the prejudice and bias of others rather than the consequence of her unacceptability.

For Elaine and Tammy (as for many clients), the answer to the question posed above about the causes of an observed lack of support is that they lack the social support they want because of "something" about other people or their physical setting.

We have already examined the manner in which clients cut themselves off from social support (client-based barriers). In this chapter, we turn to a consideration of how support deficiencies can be caused by factors external to clients themselves.

Other-Based Barriers to Receiving Social Support

House (1981), commenting on the effect of other persons' experience, attitudes, and resources on the social support available to individuals, noted:

> The major determinants of the socially supportive inputs provided to individuals by others are (1) their ability and motivation to provide support and (2) the degree to which the larger interpersonal and social context condones and supports such efforts. (p. 110)

The impact of other persons on our clients can range from the highly personal, face-to-face influence of a parent or close friend to the much more diffuse, depersonalized (yet nonetheless impactive) consequences of societal norms and values. Specifically focusing on social support issues, we sometimes find clients whose struggles with life concerns are made more difficult by the fact that a spouse or sibling is not able or willing to provide needed assistance in the form of emotional, material, appraisal, or informational support. Other times the disruption characterizes the natural system more broadly, as when the members of an alcoholic family are so wrapped up in their individual pain that they are unable to be supportive of one another.

Also, there are those clients whose coping is made more difficult by broadly based societal attitudes that result in the withdrawal or antagonism of others. Racial prejudice, societal prizing of a rigidly defined and applied individualism, or the presence of widely held fear and apprehension (as those that exist during times of war or economic disruption) can erect barriers. These factors interfere with the flow of social support generally or to particular individuals or groups of individuals.

Finally, though not strictly an other-based factor, the flow of social support to clients can be affected by barriers housed in the physical environment. Poor roads, lack of public transportation, bad weather, and poorly designed buildings are examples of environmental features that can make communication and physical contact difficult or impossible.

The levels, then, at which other-based barriers to clients' reception of social support can operate are as follows:

* barriers that characterize particular others (e.g., spouse, parent);
* barriers located more broadly in the client's informal network (e.g., the family, the peer group, co-workers);
* barriers located in the general social milieu (e.g., the community, "society"); and
* barriers resulting from features of, and conditions in, the physical environment (e.g., lack of roads, few public transportation alternatives).

Determinants of Other-Based Barriers

When we push beyond external descriptions of the level at which other-based barriers are operating (i.e., particular other, the informal network, the broader social context) to consider why the deficiency occurs, one of the following barriers or a combination thereof will be found operating:

* physical separation from others;
* others' limited resources; and
* others' dysfunctional attitudes and/or behaviors.

By considering these other-based determinants in conjunction with the previously noted levels at which they can operate, it is possible to generate the nine-celled matrix presented in Table 6.1. Depending on the counselor's theoretical orientation and/or preferred strategies for offering assistance, one or another cell or cells defined by the matrix will hold particular salience. For example, counselors oriented toward family intervention approaches will find the cells in the second row (informal network) to have the most relevance. In contrast, those who, like Caplan (1974) and Sarason (1974) focus on the importance of broader community and societal factors, the cells in the third row (society) will hold the greatest interest and significance. An understanding of the interaction of these factors and levels can contribute to our understanding of our clients' experience and serve as a point of departure for the choice of counseling strategies and interventions to be presented in Chapter 7.

Table 6.1.   **Interaction of Targets and Barriers in the Operation of Context-Based Barriers to Social Support**

	Separation	Lack of Resources and Skills	Attitudes and Behaviors
Particular Others	1	2	3
Informal Network	4	5	6
Physical and Social Environments	7	8	9

In discussing these permutations of other-based barriers to the reception of social support, the levels (i.e., particular others, network, social context, physical context) will at times be examined separately or collapsed, depending on the degree of overlap that exists among them.

Physical Separation
(Cells 1, 4, and 7 of Table 6.1)

Separation that results in a loss or decrease in the social support available to clients can occur for a variety of reasons. Death stands as the ultimate separation. As Golan (1981), commenting on the impact of the death of a spouse, noted, "It is stark finality, in that it is irreversible. One cannot turn back the clock or replace the loss; one can only adjust to it" (p. 171).

Though less final and irreversible, a relocation can have a marked negative effect on contact with persons who had previously been support providers. As a move is undertaken, friends often promise to stay in touch. Usually, contact becomes less and less frequent with the passage of time. An exchange that must be planned or routed through a letter or phone call is more difficult to effect than one that can occur within the context of face-to-face informal contact.

In many cases, persons who can repopulate clients' support systems will be readily available in the new setting. Additionally, if our clients possess the social skills required to make contact and establish relationships with new supporters, the disruption caused by a move is apt to be relatively transitory. As much as Joan (presented in Chapter 2) missed the circle of friends she had left behind, she came to her new situation optimistic that there were people who could fill similar places in her life. She also had the social skills required to locate and establish contact with such people. As a result, she had a new set of friends within a year of her move. The phone calls and letters back to her former acquaintances became less frequent, and she drifted out of contact with some members of her former support system. Their places had been filled by persons in her new setting.

Though Joan's transition was a relatively smooth one, observation and the professional literature indicate that relocations are often problematic. For example, Evans and Mobberly (1974), studying the postservice experience of a group of Vietnam veterans applying for service-related assistance, found that all subjects demonstrated a pattern of frequent moves. Moreover, the researchers found that these moves resulted in disruption to their access to family-based support resources.

At each of three levels (particular others, informal network, and society), how do the factors identified in Table 6.1 operate to reduce the social support available to individuals who experience separation?

Separation from Particular Others

It is not uncommon to find clients, whose need for either specific types of social support (e.g., physical intimacy, companionship, material assistance) or support in general, focuses on a particular person. This may occur even when there are other equally viable (at least from an objective point of view) sources of that assistance. Elderly persons who dismiss the relevance of companionship from anyone other than their children (Chapman & Pancoast, 1985) or adolescents who consider themselves to be totally alone without the affection of a particular boyfriend or girlfriend stand as examples of this pattern.

If the preferred/required individual is available, capable, and willing to provide the needed supportive resources, clients are apt to feel their needs are being recognized and met, and typically no difficulty arises.

However, if the individual is separated from this uniquely preferred supporter, the feeling of deprivation can be overwhelming, even if (as we have noted) there are other equally adequate sources of the needed resources (Gottlieb, 1988). For example, Ben (whom we met in Chapter 2) described himself as a "one-woman man." That view of himself acted as a barrier to his establishing relationships that might have met his need for intimacy and companionship. Although he was generally comfortable with his decision to continue as a single person and enjoyed sharing activities with his brother's family, sometimes he also had strong feelings of loneliness and emptiness.

The disruptive effects of physical separation from a particularly prized other can be heightened when additional client- and/or other-based barriers are operating. Occasional visits, phone calls, or letters, cards, or gifts sent by mail, though usually lacking the vigor of face-to-face contact, can provide individuals with a clear sense of being supported. If clients do not make their needs known, it is understandable that supporters might not reach out to them through visits, phone calls, or letters. However, if the supporters are preoccupied with their own concerns, are angry or disapproving, or believe that it's time for the clients in question to "stand on their own," assistance may be withheld, in spite of awareness of need.

Separation from the Informal Network

Ben and Arlene's sense of being unsupported focused on one person. In contrast, Joan's experience centered on her separation from a circle of friends and co-workers. Initially it might seem that being separated from many of one's supporters rather than just one would present a more formidable problem to adjustment. However, as we have seen, if the one person is uniquely preferred, the impact of that single separation can, subjectively, negate the support provided by others. As Gottlieb (1988) noted, "Different relationships confer special significance and relevance on the supportive provisions they bring to bear" (p. 16).

It is important to recognize that separation from a uniquely preferred supporter and from the system often occur in tandem. The same relocations that take clients away from parents or lovers can separate them from their broader family and/or circle of friends. Often the loss of a uniquely valued supporter is so compelling to clients that they fail to recognize the accompanying negative impact of the absence of other supporters.

The ease with which clients are able to fill the vacuum created by physical separation from a formerly responsive informal support system is greatly dependent on their possession of the skills needed to replenish such a system, and on their willingness to use those skills. Also, the characteristics of the new setting can exert a strong influence on the reestablishment process. Persons moving to locations where there are few people have limited opportunities for coming into contact with new supporters.

Prejudice or fear of outsiders can also make the reconstitution of an informal support system problematic if clients happen to fit into a category that persons in the new setting fear or devalue. In such situations it may be difficult for a newcomer to break out of isolation even if there are many persons with whom (objectively) mutually beneficial support relations might be formed.

Finally, the characteristics of preexisting support systems themselves may affect the extent to which they are, or are not, easily replaced. Wilcox (1981) found the degree of success experienced by his female subjects in adjusting to divorce was negatively related to the density of their informal support system. In other words, the *less* persons making up their systems knew and interacted with one another, the *more* the women were apt to cope effectively with the divorce.

The negative association of system density with successful resolution of separation issues may result from characteristics of the separated individuals and/or the persons making up the systems. Though dense systems are not necessarily family-dominated systems, family-dominated systems are typically dense since there is usually interaction among relatives. A dense system may be an indication of difficulty in establishing support relationships; since the individuals have difficulty developing new relationships, they depend primarily on relationships that are "inherited" rather than achieved. If such is the case, the observed density will typically be the result of one or more of the client-based barriers examined in Chapter 4.

However, the presence of a dense system can also reflect the operation of family norms and attitudes that discourage the development of supportive relationships with nonfamily (Hirsch, 1981). In that case, clients may have difficulty responding to separation from their informal system because dense, family-dominated systems create covert and explicit barriers to expansion of their support systems.

Separation from the Broader Social Context

A relatively common situation that comes close to the idea of separation from society at large is that encountered by persons who move from one culture or subculture to another that is very different. Immigrants, missionaries, military and business personnel assigned to posts abroad, and scholars doing fieldwork in a distant location are examples of this phenomenon.

In many instances, individuals do not make such a move alone—family or a group of co-workers accompanies them. Also, many persons separated from their cultural or subcultural group are able to find small groups or communities of culture-mates in the new setting. The presence of family or a community of other expatriates may help to offset the loss of social support that otherwise might have accompanied the move. However, consider the situation of persons who make the move alone and/or arrive in a setting in which such factors as the absence of culture-mates, prejudice against their group, or lack of facility in the language of the new setting exist.

Such immigrants are apt to find themselves cut off from emotional, material, appraisal, and informational support. They may be faced with severe other-based barriers to establishing a new informal network. The personal and family disruption often experienced by persons in such situations can (at least in part) be understood in terms of the impact of other-based barriers to social support (Stroller & Krupinski, 1969). Even when the impact of relocation does not reach pathological levels (perhaps because of the presence of "back home" people or a particularly high level of personal adaptability), the immigrants may be characterized by a longing for the people and things of "their" homeland.

Focusing on another type of separation, House (1981) has commented on how the structure of some occupations causes work-related isolation. He cited research indicating that

> factory workers in highly individuated and demanding jobs experienced markedly lower levels of coworker support. But such conditions of physical isolation are not unique to factories. They also characterize many craft and service workers (repairers who work alone, lone police officers in patrol cars), sales and clerical workers (traveling salespeople, isolated clerks), and even high level professionals such as many physicians and dentists in solo practice. (1981, p. 124)

Such workers may be able to counterbalance work isolation by free-time contact with family and friends. However, if their families are impaired in terms of their ability/and or willingness to be supportive or if the workers are deficient in their general ability to form relationships, the isolation the workers experience in the work situation may just be one element of a broader separation from supportive relationships.

Limited Resources
(Cells 2, 5, and 8 of Table 6.1)

Froland et al. (1979) noted that persons are often unsupported because their past or potential supporters refuse to provide additional assistance. Such "moving against others" client behaviors as exploitation or aggressiveness can quickly alienate others in the natural system and even strain the responsiveness of formal helpers. It should come as no surprise, therefore, when we find that the social networks of our narcissistic, abusive, or exploitive clients are peopled with individuals who withhold assistance because they are angry, alienated, and/or burned out.

On the other hand, we also may encounter situations in which our clients lack support from their natural systems because the potential supporters lack the material and/or emotional resources to be of assistance, even though they are willing to do so (Dunkel-Schetter & Wortman, 1981).

Limited Resources of Particular Others and the Natural System

Precisely because they are part of a network, our clients and the persons in their informal support networks are apt to be exposed to the same stressors (Eckenrode & Gore, 1981). The potential negative effect of this sharing of context on the exchange of support has been noted by Vaux (1985):

> For the very reason that they share certain problems, members of some groups (e.g., the poor or the young) may also lack the resources of money, information, or esteem necessary to provide others with support. Such resources may be in short supply within a group because all members are exposed to similar demands. (p. 90)

Consider the impact of an industrial plant's closing on a worker whose natural system is composed primarily of immediate family and former co-workers. The economic stress precipitated by the loss of employment not only affects the now-unemployed person, but can be expected to have a negative impact on the immediate family as well. A spouse, who might otherwise be a source of emotional support, may become preoccupied with anxiety or resentment at having to lower economic expectations or at having to take a part-time job to tide the family over. If members of the extended family have also been directly or indirectly negatively affected by the same economic misfortune, they are apt to be as limited in their material or emotional resources as the client. Even in situations in which the informal network enters a period of unemployment with considerable strength and mutual support, the passage of time may find that relationships become overtaxed and the exchange of support declines (Liem & Liem, 1979).

In the midst of this rather pessimistic discussion of the ability of persons who are in the same boat to be supportive of one another, we must also note the existence of opposite patterns. Group work generally, and mutual support groups specifically, is built on the assumption that persons experiencing the same or similar life concerns can be of help to each other (Pearson, 1986). Literature and direct experience provide us with examples of families and other groups who have faced common threats with solidarity and mutual aid and encouragement. However, these instances are apt to be important to counselors as positive exemplars, rather than as representative of their clientele. Strong, resourceful networks will usually be able to fashion some solution to problems stressing the entire group. Those clients whose networks have preexisting flaws (perhaps hitherto undetected) are those who, when they encounter difficulty, are faced with the necessity of reaching beyond that network for assistance. They often become our clients or those of other human service providers.

Limited Societal Resources

The recurring "guns or butter" debate that surfaces at each consideration of the federal budget illustrates the reality that, even in good economic times, the actual availability of revenues interacts with issues of ideology and group interest to influence the setting of priorities. Such priority setting inevitably results in decisions that can affect the amount of social support available to individuals from formal and informal sources. Reductions in federal, state, and local human service programs translate quickly into fewer services being available to many of the clients who come through our doors (Vaux, 1985).

Often the impact of limited societal resources is direct. When health care programs, job retraining programs, nutritional programs, or academic enrichment programs are cut back or eliminated, the persons who have been their direct beneficiaries are often left with nowhere to go or are faced with the reality that the limited services remaining are insufficient to cover their needs. For example, an elderly person may still receive social security benefits, but may find that more and more of those benefits must be paid back in the form of higher contributions to rent or medical coverage.

The impact of limited societal resources can also be felt indirectly. Clients themselves may not be participating in government-supported programs and therefore are not directly affected by the cutting back of a job retraining program. However, if the primary wage earner(s) of a family cannot gain access to retraining, the psychological and material status of other family members may be markedly affected as unemployment or underemployment continues.

In our work, we often find ourselves saying, "If only this or that service were available, the chances of progress would be much greater for my client." If adequate day-care services were available for the isolated single parent, the possibility of additional training or education would be enhanced. If family intervention services were more available, perhaps we could soften the price in pain and suffering paid by the current and future generations of a family pummeled by the effects of addiction and/or abuse.

Recognition of how a shortage of societal resources often has negative impact on our clients presents us with personal and professional choices. On the one hand, it may be helpful to focus our efforts on helping clients develop and maintain personal resources and resiliency. For example, we might encourage them to maintain their morale in the face of limited options. We might also help them mobilize their own self-help resources and aid them in "doing more with less." However, we will often recognize that clients' lack of support, even in situations of broader societal economic difficulties, flows from the low priority attached to programs that could respond to their needs. This awareness confronts us with the necessity of action that might change those priorities by affecting the perceptions, knowledge, and values of persons who set those priorities. The target of such interventions (to be examined in Chapter 7) is not our clients; rather, it is those persons who are in a position to influence the formation and implementation of policies affecting human services.

Others' Attitudes and Behaviors
as Barriers to Social Support
(Cells 3, 6, and 9 of Table 6.1)

In Chapter 4, extensive consideration was given to how clients' withdrawal, social ineptness, and moving against others act as barriers to the reception of social support from others. The same three factors, when they characterize clients' supporters, can operate as other-based barriers. The following discussion examines the particular features these barriers display when operating as other-based barriers. Case examples will be presented.

Withdrawal of Others

We have seen that past and potential supporters may withdraw when clients move against them. In other cases, however, supporters' withdrawal may be more the result of their own perceptions, beliefs, needs, or experience than a consequence of clients' characteristics or behavior. In such instances, an other-based barrier to the flow of social support is operating. Withdrawal of others can operate at two of the three levels previously defined: particular others and the informal network.

Withdrawal of particular others. To illustrate how clients' access to social support can be affected by the withdrawal of a particular other, consider the experience of Claudia. Claudia was devastated when the man with whom she had an intimate relationship for over two years suddenly told her that he was feeling hemmed in and needed to stop seeing her. He indicated that while he loved her and found a great deal in their relationship that was satisfying, he didn't feel that he was ready to make a commitment to anyone and therefore wanted to let things cool off between them.

Although events in the course of any relationship can be expected to reflect the influence of characteristics and actions of both partners, the withdrawal of Claudia's fiancé apparently stemmed from his deeply ambivalent feelings about making the commitment that marriage represents. Claudia reported that he had been married previously. That relationship had ended in a divorce that was deeply humiliating and hurtful to him. Although he had proposed marriage, Claudia believed that almost as soon as he had done so, he become tense and uncomfortable in his interaction with her.

Claudia's experience illustrates how the actions of a particularly significant person can cut off social support that may be difficult to replace quickly, if at all. Of the many types of support Claudia had received from her fiancé, she particularly found herself missing the emotionally focused elements of love, physical intimacy, and companionship that he had increasingly provided.

Fear may lead others to withdraw from relationships in an unwarranted or irresponsible fashion. This can confront clients with a marked and often unexpected loss of support over which they have little control. Even if clients go to great lengths to demonstrate that the concerns are unfounded or attempt to meet the concerns of others, they may find that they cannot reassure the supporter. Coming to terms with the loss of a relationship is often made easier when the client can recognize that the departure was due primarily to the concerns and beliefs of the other person, and not the result of anything about the client.

Withdrawal of the informal network. It is clear that families and informal networks can be disrupted by the presence of such difficulties as addiction or sexual abuse. We can see that such dysfunctionality has a marked affect on the amount and type of social support received by network members considered to be deviant (Fisher et al., 1988). For example, while some others in the family or network may withdraw support from the abuser, others may worsen the situation of the addict by offering well-intentioned but ultimately unhelpful enabling behavior. That such disruptive conditions as addiction or sexual abuse can have a dramatic effect on the flow of support to and from persons other than the problem person is often less recognized.

As individuals struggle to cope with the negative impact of disruption of the natural system, they often channel their already-overtaxed material and psychic resources into self-survival. They withdraw from the problem person and (perhaps) from other network members as well. This focusing on self-survival by erstwhile supporters may be the system "burnout" that Turkat (1980) and others noted. Family members neither give nor expect much support from one another, as each is too busy nursing personal hurts or conserving personal resources.

In an alcoholic family, some members disengage, spending as little time and investing as few psychic resources as possible at home. Eventually, a spouse may detach emotionally and physically from the relationship with the addict, recognizing that previous attempts to be supportive have actually been counterproductive. Children may become heavily involved in school activities and form supportive relationships with peers and responsive adults outside the informal system. As each member moves to establish relationships in less conflicted contexts, the family group becomes less cohesive. It develops into a place where no one, not just the problem member, is supported.

Disengagement from a disrupted family or network can be a functional response to a negative interpersonal situation. Indeed, the encouragement of such disengagement may be a central counseling strategy with clients enmeshed in disrupted systems. However, we should recognize that the support loss caused by the flight of nonconflicted family members from the family is apt to affect everyone, not just the problem member. While it may be appropriate for us to reinforce disengagement from a conflicted family, in many instances it will also be useful to help clients explore how they can balance the need to protect themselves with the need of other family members for their support.

Ineptness of Others
(Cells 2, 5, and 8 of Table 6.1)

The fact that supporters are willing to be of assistance is no guarantee that clients will actually be supported. A number of other-based factors clustering under the general heading of "others' ineptness" can prevent clients from receiving intended support. Supporters may

- lack the ability to recognize that clients need to be supported;
- not be able to identify the particular type of supportive response appropriate to the situation at hand; and/or
- not possess the attitudinal disposition and/or behavioral skills required to implement the appropriate supportive response.

Ineptness of Particular Others and the Informal System

Particular others, and perhaps even segments of the informal system, may have difficulty being of assistance to clients because (good intentions and a willingness to help notwithstanding) they lack the particular skills required to make needed support available. Their attempts to be supportive may prove misdirected, insufficient, or bungling (Chesler & Barbarin, 1984; House, 1981).

Informal systems that are peopled with individuals who lack the skills on which social acceptance and integration depend are not apt to provide good contexts for clients to develop effective social skills. Commenting on the characteristics of back wards of mental institutions, Christoff and Kelly (1985) noted:

The social environment of certain patients (especially those patients on institution [sic] "back" wards, or those living in socially impoverished settings within the community), provided little opportunity to use, practice, and be reinforced for socially skilled behavior. (p. 366)

With less impaired, noninstitutionalized populations, we may observe similar effects. For example, parents who are themselves shy and fearful may find that they do not have the social facility to help one of their children acquire social skills needed for effective nonfamily interaction. The learning environment provided by family interaction is, in actuality, a place in which social ineptness is modeled, if not encouraged.

Supporters who have difficulties identifying and responding to individual differences may attempt to use a helping approach that, while sometimes beneficial, is ineffective (perhaps even detrimental) to a particular person in need of support. For example, some very dependent clients may be aided when supporters strongly refuse to provide further assistance. While such actions seem nonsupportive, they may actually be very helpful in prompting some clients to develop their own personal resources. However, a parent or family group may rigidly apply a "sink or swim" approach to all requests for assistance. Such rigidity may result from a strict family ideology or from the inability to differentiate between valid and invalid requests for assistance. The indiscriminate application of a sometimes-appropriate helping strategy can result in some clients being overwhelmed and defeated, rather than boosted and prompted to success.

In families of limited means, we may find that the informal network is very restricted in material resources that can be made available to clients. However, in spite of limited material resources, those supporters may be very skilled in providing emotional, informational, and appraisal support. For clients needing emotional support, such a family can be a very rich source — material limitations notwithstanding.

In contrast, consider a college student who is very well provided with material resources but lacks the emotional support he needs because the persons in his informal network are unable to express love, acceptance, or comfort except through a very indirect giving of "things." The inability of supporters to relate at an emotional level results in a deficiency of the particular type of support most important to the student. He may come away from contact with his family feeling very well provided for, but unloved.

Societal Ineptness

The same lack of awareness and skill that can prevent particularly significant persons and others in the informal support system from supporting clients can also operate at the level of the broader social context. If people in general cannot "see" that individuals or groups are in need of support, they will not be supportive. Even if there is a general awareness of the need for support, there may be a lack of understanding about the particular type of response that is most appropriate and/or the ability to implement those responses.

If an individual or a group of individuals do not fit prevailing societal patterns, other people may have difficulty recognizing the need for social support and may not be able to determine the type of response that is appropriate. Persons who march to the beat of a different drummer or come from a generally unfamiliar culture or subculture pose problems for potential supporters.

Individuals' idiosyncrasies and cultural differences may make it difficult to identify when support is needed and to determine the particular responses that will be received as support. Widespread lack of awareness and understanding of "different" individuals and groups can cause assistance to be offered when none is required and support to be withheld when it is needed. Also, in attempting to support persons whom we do not understand, we run the risk of offering a form of assistance that is irrelevant, ineffective, or (in the worst case) noxious.

Others' Moving Against Clients
(Cells 3, 6, and 9 of Table 6.1)

Unlike other-based ineptness that may be accompanied by (at least) some concern, clients who lack social support because others are "moving against" them are, by definition, faced with others' antipathy. Feelings of anger and hatred can cause others to withdraw from, reject, or verbally and/or physically attack clients who could benefit from their assistance.

While clients' own hostile behavior may lead others to move against them, our focus at the moment is on those situations in which it is the supporters' difficulties (e.g., intolerance, fear, stress) that cause antipathy. Supporters' negative feelings can be expressed in a variety of ways. Others' moving against our clients can take two broad forms: rejection and aggression.

Rejection

The hallmarks of rejection are disapproval and disdain. Rejected clients are told, directly or indirectly, that they are unacceptable. Since they do not meet others' standards, they are ignored or criticized. More actively, rejected clients may be abandoned or driven away.

The basis of others' rejection is usually the belief that the client is in some respect (e.g., belief, attitude, behavior) unacceptable. Sometimes the objectionable characteristic or behavior is something over which the client has little or no control. We can see this type of rejection operating in racial prejudice or the negative stereotyping often applied to physically handicapped persons.

Other times, rejection stems from the fact that the client has "become" something disapproved of by a particular other or the informal network. Arlene, whom we met in Chapter 2, is an example of a person who experienced a loss of support because she had become someone (i.e., a person who had married interracially) disapproved of by an important supporter (her father). He refused to see her and attempted (though unsuccessfully) to have other family members cut off contact with her.

Hirsch's (1979) notion of "new identities" is useful in discussing the situation of clients' lacking support because they have become something unacceptable to others. Although the formation of new identities can be a useful strategy in opening up additional sources of support to clients, Hirsch notes that the informal network often resists such actions. Family members, friends, or co-workers may fear that new undertakings will lead the individual away from their influence and from identification with them. Supporters may discourage or even prohibit the development of new identities; thus, the establishment of new relationships that could be associated with those new ventures is inhibited.

The influence (either encouraging or discouraging) exerted by particular others and the informal network when clients reach out to obtain social support from others is part of what is called the "gatekeeping" function (McKinlay, 1973). If family, intimates, or friends oppose or otherwise discourage clients from seeking assistance from outsiders, such help-seeking becomes more problematic. Parents may forbid their children to talk about family problems with the school counselor; spouses may ridicule their partners' intention to seek psychological assistance for depression or feelings of lack of fulfillment. If individuals ignore these directives, they may be punished or ostracized. Awareness of the effects of gatekeeping can help counselors understand why particular clients, or groups of clients, do not seek outside assistance, resist such help when it is offered, and/or are rejected by their network when they disregard network norms to seek or accept outside assistance.

Examining the impact of rejection at a broader societal level, we can note that support deficiency resulting from ostracism by society at large is rare. In a small, isolated, hunting and foraging society, we could imagine a person being taken to the outermost edge of the group's territory, banished, and forbidden to return. The "shunning" used to discourage nonconformity in some communal religious groups is a contemporary example of groupwide ostracism.

Although less total, perhaps something approaching that circumstance occurs with the more stringent forms of incarceration — individuals are forcibly separated from their informal support systems and their ability to associate with others is restricted. From fiction, we can recall Phillip Nolan in E. E. Hale's short story, "The Man Without a Country." Nolan was banished, condemned to a life of exile, and passed from ship to ship as a way of separating him from his loved ones and his native land.

In real life, although the form of involuntary separation may be less dramatic than that of Phillip Nolan, formal societal rejection in the form of incarceration clearly can disrupt the flow of support to an individual from a preexisting informal support system. It can also limit the development of new support relationships. However, all but the most extreme forms of imprisonment allow for some interaction with others. Such interaction opens up the possibility of developing informal and formal relationships that can counterbalance the formal rejection of the broader society.

A final observation can be made concerning the impact of rejection, whether that rejection comes from a particular other or from the informal system in general — a separation of a few miles can be as impactive as that of a much greater distance. Even a small separation, if accompanied by disapproval and rejection on the part of the others, can cut off virtually all contact and exchange. Arlene is a case in point. Though she passed within sight of her parents' home almost daily, and often spoke with other members of her family, the impact of her father's withdrawal from her was as profound as it would have been had they been separated by thousands of miles.

Aggression from Others

We have seen that others may act on their disapproval by withdrawing from, or rejecting, clients. It is also possible that disapproval will be expressed more actively through exploitation or punishment. Aggression lacks the concern for individuals that sometimes accompanies supporters' withdrawal and ineptness. Aggression moves beyond disapproval to devalue the significance, worth, and rights of others. They (in this case, our clients), become reasonable targets for aggression through a process of dehumanization.

While close relationships and family interaction can be the source of considerable support, they can also be contexts within which people are emotionally and physically abused. The antithesis of the positive power of social support is seen in the destructive effects of child abuse, abuse of elders by their children, and spousal abuse.

If clients have other support alternatives and possess the inclination and/or ability to seek out others, they will disengage from the aggressive person. However, if clients are unable or unwilling to go elsewhere for support, or if the aggression is intermittent, they may cling to a relationship in which the balance of "support-to-stress" is weighted in a negative direction (Gottlieb, 1983, p. 112). Children are locked into abusive families by their real lack of self-sufficiency and mobility. Also, their lack of experience and perspective may make it difficult for them to realize that their situation is unusual. In cases of wife abuse, low self-esteem or the acceptance of husband-to-wife violence as normal (perhaps because of a family background where such violence was common) may lead the victim to not question the aggressor's assertion that the abuse is deserved.

Aggression from particular others, and from the informal network more generally, is often resistant to influences from inside and outside the network. Gottlieb (1983), citing work by Browne (1982) and Hilberman and Munson (1977-78), noted the operation of several causative factors for this resistance. First, abused persons fail to seek support from others because of embarrassment or fear. Second, the abusers often impose isolation from potential supporters on their victims. Finally, even if abused persons reveal their plight, others are apt to be hesitant to respond, believing that such private matters are beyond their proper concern.

The impact of aggression from particular others and the informal network on the flow of social support is also multifaceted. First of all, the abused individual is deprived of the support that might otherwise have come from the aggressor. Moreover, beyond the lack of support, there is the matter of the victim's being saddled with additional difficulties, further exacerbating their need for assistance.

At a broader societal level, prejudice, negative stereotyping, and the devaluation of individuals and groups also can be expressed through exploitation and aggression. In the extreme, devaluation of individuals and groups can lead to warfare, subjugation, and genocide. Though less extreme, the cumulative effect of discrimination and exploitation can be crippling. Groups that are sensitive and generous in providing emotional, material, and informational resources to "their own" may be ruthless in denying those resources to others. As individuals and groups, excluded persons may thus be denied the benefit of assistance that would help them grow materially and intellectually.

Interaction of Self- and Other-Based Barriers

Often, though other-based factors are operating, we can also identify client-based factors that contribute to the disruption of the flow of support. For example, Joan had made a decision to move, and Arlene had taken an action to which she knew her father was deeply opposed. In practice, unidimensional situations, vis-à-vis the interruption of social support, are not often encountered. However, for descriptive and heuristic purposes, it is possible to identify situations in which support deficiencies stem primarily from the perceptions, attitudes, and responses of others or from the influence of features of the physical environment over which the client has little or no control.

Barriers to Social Support
Located in the Physical Environment

The requirements of Section 504 of the Rehabilitation Act of 1973 that focus on making public facilities accessible to physically handicapped persons reflect a recognition of the manner in which the design and furbishing of buildings can reduce access to people and places. Requiring that buildings be accessible to persons with physical limitations, previously impossible (or at least problematic), opens up new options for support from formal and informal sources. Along similar lines, observers have noted that the physical layout of neighborhoods

(Carp, 1975; Festinger, Schachter, & Back, 1950) or the design of apartments or dormitories (Holohan, 1982) can raise barriers to the establishment and maintenance of supportive relationships, even among persons with good physical health and social skills. Even more broadly, the lack of public transportation, such as that characterizing most rural areas, can erect barriers to the initiation of contact with informal and formal supporters. The absence of public transportation coupled with few, poorly maintained roads also can make it difficult for helpers from formal and informal systems to reach out to those same rural persons. It may very well be that the traditional, fiercely independent attitudes of some isolated persons make them resistant to the help of would-be supporters (Rathbone-McCuan & Hashimi, 1982). However, if it is difficult or impossible for any contact to take place, the process of developing trust and/or fashioning an intervention that will be palatable to the values and needs of isolated individuals may never begin.

Conclusion

We have seen a variety of ways in which aspects of the social and physical contexts can act as barriers to our clients' receiving the amount and/or type of social support they need. While withdrawal, exploitiveness, or aggression may occur as a response to clients' noxious attitudes or actions, such negativism can also be the result of others' beliefs, needs, and decisions. Determining whether clients' support deficiencies result from the operation of one or more of the externally based barriers discussed above or flow from the impact of the client-based barriers examined in Chapter 4 is an important step in developing a counseling strategy to increase the support available to our clients. We have considered strategies and interventions for removing client-based barriers in Chapter 5. Chapter 8 turns to a examination of strategies and interventions that can alleviate or remove externally based barriers to the reception of social support.

Chapter Seven

Externally Focused Support Interventions

When we find that clients lack the amount and/or type of social support they need, there are a number of reasons why we might focus our counseling interventions on the social and physical contexts rather than on the clients themselves. The primary reason for doing so is that, in many cases, that is where the barriers to the flow of social support are located. By addressing the external factors directly, we go to where the problem is, in the hope that the result will be that our efforts become more focused and effective. Additionally, we avoid the error of "blaming the victim," that is, holding clients responsible for deficiency and ineffectiveness when, in fact, the fault lies elsewhere in the social or physical context.

Beyond the recognition that particular clients lack support because of factors external to themselves, some theorists and practitioners generally conceptualize social support as an environmental variable (Shumaker & Brownell, 1985). This view holds that contextual issues and factors, rather than characteristics of clients' functioning, cause support deficits. Even if clients show attitudes or behaviors that act as barriers to their reception of social support, those characteristics are considered to be the result of such external influences as social injustice, neighborhood decay, or family dysfunction. The environmental perspective is reflected in those therapeutic approaches that focus on the significant others, families, extended families, social networks, neighborhoods, work settings, communities, or broader societies of clients.

The same "causes" (i.e., separation, lack of resources, dysfunctional attitudes and beliefs) and "levels" (i.e., particular other, informal network, broader social context, the physical context) that were used as an organizational framework in Chapter 6 can be employed in conceptualizing and designing counseling interventions aimed at increasing the availability and/or quality of social support to clients by removing or ameliorating barriers in the broader social and physical context.

Table 7.1 (an expanded version of Table 6.1) presents categories of interventions defined by the interaction of two dimensions: type of barrier and intervention target. Note that two of the target levels (society, physical environment) that were separated in Chapter 5 have been collapsed here. This has been done because the elimination or modification of barriers located in the physical environment (e.g., building or upgrading roads, making public facilities more accessible to persons of limited mobility) typically rests on effecting change in the attitudes and behaviors of the same persons in the social context (e.g., the public, and/or business or government policymakers).

Most of these cells (especially cells 1, 2, and 3) delimit the same types of interventions described in Chapter 5 (e.g., the elimination of dysfunctional behavior or the use of shaping to establish effective behavior). However, in the present discussion, such interventions are aimed at our clients' actual or potential supporters rather than at the clients themselves.

Issues Relating to
Externally Focused Support Interventions

There are a number of considerations that cut across the design and implementation of externally focused support interventions. In general, these are strategic issues. For example, what is the likelihood that our intervention will prove disruptive, rather than beneficial, to the current or future ability of supporters to be of assistance? Also, is it better (easier, more effective) to repair or replace a relationship that is delivering little, low-quality, or inappropriate support? There are also broad considerations of counselor role, theoretical orientation, and skill repertoire that can exert an important influence on counselors' willingness

Table 7.1.   Interventions Focused on the Removal/Reduction of External
              Barriers

Barrier

Target		Separation	Lack of Resources	Dysfunctional Attitudes and Behaviors
	Particular Other	Informing Contact-encouragement 1	Provision of resources Encouragement of resource-seeking Enhancing ability to seek, develop resources 2	Informing Corrective experience Confrontation of dysfunctional beliefs 3
	Informal Network	Network-oriented intervention (e.g., informing, healing) 4	Network-oriented intervention (e.g., co-ordination, informing, fostering network's communication) 5	Network-oriented intervention (e.g., healing, informing, fostering communication among network 6
	Broader Social and Physical Contexts	Informing to raise others' awareness 7	Community development Political action 8	Presentations, media campaigns to change perceptions and attitudes 9

or ability to initiate externally focused interventions. Finally, in our
contact with clients' supporters do we think of ourselves as working
with those persons as individuals, or do we focus on them through the
social groupings (e.g., peer groups, families, work groups) to which
they and our clients belong?

To Intervene or Not?

Gottlieb (1981) called attention to the possibility that the efforts of formal helpers to strengthen the effectiveness of natural support systems may be unwarranted or even detrimental. He suggested that "benign nonintervention" should often be the preferred stance of human service workers toward natural systems for several reasons (1980, p. 476). He noted that the apparent inadequacy of supporters with reference to the needs of clients may only be temporary. Supporters may not have fully focused on the situation of the client; when they eventually do, the network will mobilize and provide the needed assistance.

What the counselor interprets as lack of help or nonhelp on the part of supporters, though very different from the strategy or actions that a trained helper would employ, may actually be viewed and experienced as helpful by clients. Through narrowness of perspective or arrogance, trained helpers may assume that their way is better. In attempting to "upgrade" the operation of supporters, we may end up encouraging professional styles of helping that, at best, are viewed as irrelevant by supporters. At worst, such attempts may actually deflect or destroy the effectiveness of the natural system. If formal diagnoses are made, the imposition of diagnostic frameworks by professional helpers may frighten supporters away from clients and/or cause them to be stigmatized by the persons in their natural systems.

In sum, an incautious intervention based on incomplete or inaccurate understanding of the natural system's resources and style may disrupt the ability or willingness of supporters to provide the assistance of which they are capable. Clients and their supporters may become estranged, leaving the client with less assistance and (perhaps) more dependent on formal support sources than necessary.

Repair or Replace?

If it is true that many of the persons who finally seek assistance from counselors and other mental health practitioners do so because their natural sources of assistance have, to some degree, proven unresponsive or ineffective, then replacement of those supporters with others would seem to be an appropriate strategy to use as the basis for counseling intervention. Tolsdorf (1976) spoke from this perspective in observing that when clients were rejected by their natural networks, or those networks were distant, ineffective, or unresponsive, it would often be necessary to devise networks to provide needed social support.

Gottlieb's (1988) term "grafted tie" also focuses on the broad strategy of providing new supporters who can plug gaps in the resources of individuals' existing support persons (p. 19). When we encourage a client to develop a new intimate relationship or circle of friends or we refer another client to a support group, we are implementing an "if it's not working, get a new one" strategy.

Nonetheless, however strong the rationale on which they are founded, replacement-based interventions are not always easy to carry out. First of all, what makes perfect sense from the counselor's objective perspective may be unacceptable from a client's point of view. Battered wives and abused children often show vigorous resistance to efforts to encourage their physical or emotional distancing from a noxious relationship. Clients' fear of retribution, feelings of loyalty or obligation, and even simple inertia can lead them to cling to relationships that are, to varying degrees, dysfunctional in their ability to provide various types of support. These factors may even operate when relationships are actively harmful. Given such resistance, it will often be necessary to deal with the attitudes that lead clients to persist in dysfunctional or destructive relationships before a replacement-based intervention can be implemented.

Another factor that can make it difficult for clients to replace supporters who are not delivering adequate support is that new persons with the resources and/or inclination to fill the gap are simply not available. For example, it may be difficult to find someone who will be equally available if the sometimes helpful, but often exploitive, relative of a rural elderly person is excluded. In the abstract, it is easy enough to say, "Get new friends" or "Don't have anything to do with your family"; however, even when such recommendations are appropriate, they may not be followed because (good social skills and willingness to comply notwithstanding) some clients will be in situations where persons to replace those friends and family are scarce and/or not inclined to be responsive.

Besides the issues of client resistance and supporter availability, there is at least one other reason a replacement strategy might not be pursued when we find that clients are lodged in deficient support relationships. If the effect of our intervention were to be that clients became more dependent on formal sources of social support (e.g., counseling, social welfare agencies), we might actually be creating additional difficulties for them. Assistance from informal sources tends to be more readily available to individuals than that from formal support systems. Family, friends, and co-workers are part of individuals' daily life situations; thus no special efforts or arrangements need be made to gain access to these people.

Also, there is generally less stigma attached to seeking or receiving assistance from kith and kin than from formal sources. By strengthening individuals' ability to elicit and receive support from the natural system, we also reduce the likelihood that they will be adversely labeled by themselves or their significant others (Gottlieb & Schroter, 1978). As mentioned earlier, such stigmatizing (which may be exacerbated by the imposition of the clinician's diagnostic labels on the functioning of clients) can result in the withdrawal of supporters from clients.

Finally, an important strength of assistance from the natural system is that it is apt to be presented in a language and a form familiar to individuals. This may be an especially important consideration when clients come from cultural or subcultural groups holding different views regarding the substance and form of what is helpful from those held by the counselor (Pearson, 1985).

Although the replacement of dysfunctional support relationships may initially seem an attractive alternative to counselors, in practice there are a number of considerations that make it problematic. These difficulties may move us in the direction of using replacement-based interventions as only part of an overall strategy (e.g., leaving contact with most of a client's family intact, but urging that a particularly punitive sibling be avoided) or of persisting in the effort to reform what initially seems an unpromising natural network. Chapman and Pancoast (1985), for example, reported that agency staff working with elderly clients in both the United States and Canada have "found it easier at times to intervene to change a negative relationship than to foster new positive relationships" (p. 58).

Direct or Indirect Intervention with Supporters?

Network-focused interventions (examined later in this chapter) involve direct contact between the counselor and the persons making up clients' informal networks. For example, when we convene a family session or go into a client's classroom to ask fellow students to be sensitive to the impact of a handicapping condition, we expand the boundaries of the helping relationship to include the persons whose characteristics and actions we would otherwise only hear about through clients' statements. Pattison (1973) has noted that while it often makes a great deal of sense to intervene directly with the persons who are at the heart of what is best and worst about clients' situations, doing so puts many individually oriented practitioners on unfamiliar ground. As multifaceted as the content and process of one-to-one counseling are, the convening of clients' networks adds greatly to the complexity of intervening. Without mastery of the techniques and understanding provided by training in small group, family counseling, and network-intervention procedures, the counselor may find the prospect of direct intervention overwhelming and may thus avoid it.

While the avoidance of contact with clients' informal networks stems from counselors' limited training and experience, it may also be the result of a realistic assessment that clients either have or can be helped to acquire the resources to effect change in the natural system themselves. For example, supporters sometimes offer a well-intentioned, but inappropriate, form of assistance. Seeing this, we might judge that encouraging clients to give clear, timely feedback to supporters about why the intended help is not supportive and helping them to communicate what they would prefer would be possible, beneficial for the client, and contributive to the supporters' effectiveness.

Strengthening clients' ability to effect their own changes with particular persons or the network more generally may be less disruptive to the operation of the informal system than intervention from outside. Less resistance to change may be precipitated because no outsider is stepping in. Moreover, intervention initiated from the outside that focuses on the difficulties and needs of a network member runs the risk of stigmatizing that person to the others in the network. The client is no longer "just cousin Sally," but someone who is so bad off that she needs a helping professional to look after her. Working to strengthen clients' ability to manage their informal relationships reduces the likelihood of further identifying them as sick, inadequate persons in the eyes of their family and friends. It also can equip clients with interpersonal skills that may prove helpful in future interaction with those persons.

The issue of network resistance to the direct intervention of an outside helper focuses our attention on another reason why we might find such approaches problematic. Mostwin (1972) described the resistance of many Eastern European ethnic groups to outside intervention. However, such resistance is clearly not limited to particular nationality groups. Discussing the hesitancy of many families to become involved in a network-mobilizing treatment approach, Rueveni (1979) noted that "unless the crisis reaches unmanageable proportions, most families will insist on delaying their decision for mobilizing their network" (p. 86). Widely held norms concerning the desirability of handling problems within the group, while strengthening group solidarity and contributing to the mobilization of group assistance, can also serve to make it difficult for outside resources to penetrate the group's boundaries, even when those resources could be beneficial. In the face of active resistance by clients' informal networks, the indirect strategy of strengthening the clients' own ability to cope more effectively with an unresponsive or noxious system may be a preferred counseling strategy.

Another important indirect strategy for effecting change in clients' natural systems is to work through a person who, while not of the network itself, is acceptable to and influential with it. Clergy, neighborhood persons, or folk healers may have sufficient influence with the natural system either to move it toward a more beneficial manner of interacting with the client or toward greater openness for collaboration with the counselor.

Focusing on Individuals or the Group?

One approach to altering the network's affect on clients is to focus on changing supporters (whether individual supporters or several supporters) as individuals, then assume that such change will result in an increase in the amount and/or quality of the support available to our clients. Another strategy is to focus on the supporters as members of an interconnected system. Coming to the task of increasing the amount/quality of the social support provided to clients, our interventions can be guided by the recognition that changes in the functioning of a supporter may be affected not only by altering the beliefs and behaviors of that supporter, but also by changing the content and process of network interaction. Indeed, context-oriented theorists and practitioners hold that since individual dysfunction is usually the result of systemic factors, the cure of that dysfunction is achieved most effectively by interventions that focus on changing the social network.

Interventions Focused on the Informal Network

There are many situations in which our major strategy will be to focus on effecting some sort of change in supporters (whether they be particular others or the network generally) rather than in our clients. We do this in an effort to increase their willingness to be supportive to clients. The decision to pursue a strategy that focuses on supporters can be based on a number of factors:

- We judge that, in fact, the causes of a client's not receiving support from others lies more with those others than with the client (e.g., the supporters are unreasonably angry at the client or are rejecting the client because of misinformation).

- We judge that, while the supporters' negative reactions are justified, the supporters have greater personal resources for change than does the client. We may judge that the supporters have greater emotional stability or more flexible value systems than the client and thus are more apt to be able to accept the client's negative behavior than the client is likely to be able to change that behavior.

- The others, while not specifically exerting a negative influence with regard to the availability or quality of the client's support resources, are judged to be persons who could exert positive influence on others who are exerting such negative influence.

Whatever the basis for our movement toward an other-focused strategy, our approach is to identify the barrier and initiate an intervention appropriate to its removal. As we have seen, such strategies and their derivative interventions can be viewed as falling into two broad clusters: those in which the focus is on supporters as individuals and those in which supporters are viewed as components of a system whose functioning and impact is broader than the sum of the constituent parts.

Increasing Clients' Support
by Changing Supporters as Individuals

There are several reasons why a counselor might move toward a strategy that engages clients' supporters individually rather than working with them as a group. We have already noted that some counselors are more accustomed to working in a one-to-one format than in a small group situation. Additionally, we might choose an individual-focused intervention because of the preferences of the supporters in question. Networks characterized by conflict or mutual mistrust may display powerful resistance to the convening of the entire network or even its subsets. In such instances, counselors may have only two choices:

working with the network members on their terms or not working with them at all.

Sometimes we may determine that there are just one or two persons who, because of their influence, central location in the network, or unique resources, are key figures in determining the response of the network to a client. If such persons are open to contact by the counselor, it may be maximally effective to focus our intervention on them. In doing so we will be on familiar ground—working with individuals to change perceptions, attitudes, and behaviors that are dysfunctional. In these situations, however, our clients stand as a target beyond the supporter with whom we are working. That is, if we can remove or reduce the effect of the other-based barrier operating in our clients' supporters, we will increase the amount and/or quality of the social support that is available to those clients as they deal with their life concerns.

The interventions we initiate to pursue removing the other-based barriers characterizing particular supporters can include (a) provision of information, (b) corrective experience, (c) confrontation of irrational beliefs, (d) fostering the development of insight, and (e) skill training. These are the stock-in-trade of one-to-one practice. The specific intervention (or combination of interventions) used will vary as a function of counselor and client variables, as was discussed in Chapter 5.

If, in addition to working with single supporters, we bring together two or three individuals who may share a common location, resource, or concern (e.g., all are classmates or co-workers, or have access to the information needed by our client), the use of small group management skills will be useful. In such instances, we are not moving into a network-focused intervention; rather, we are pursuing a relatively circumscribed effort to affect a few individuals who, as individuals, can be affected in a way that increases the flow of support to the client.

Network-Focused Interventions
(Cells 4, 5, and 6 of Table 7.1)

In most counseling settings, clients present themselves (or are presented by others) as individuals who have concerns or problems that need to be reduced or ameliorated. Pattison (1973) noted that there are two, quite divergent, stances that can be taken in understanding and working with clients. The first stance (which he called the "closed" model) assumes that problems "belong" to clients and that their resolution can be best effected by focusing our attention on clients as separate individuals. This is the model that dominates the work of counselors, psychotherapists, and caseworkers who close themselves into an office and, following a variety of strategies, intervene to foster change in the client. The second stance (the "open" model) proceeds from the assumption that while a problem may present itself to us housed in a particular person, the genesis and/or cure of that problem inevitably involves the social network of which the client is a part. This is the model that underlies the work of practitioners who view the immediate or extended family, or even the informal network more broadly, as the target of treatment. Following a variety of formats, these practitioners include clients' significant others in the treatment process.

Pattison (1973) noted that the open approach to treating individuals' problems dominates the healing practices of traditional societies: "It is the model of the shaman, the primitive healer, the folk healer" (p. 403). In stressing the continuing validity and potency of the open model, Pattison and other network-oriented writers (e.g., Attneave, 1969, 1976; Erickson, 1975; Garrison, 1974; Rueveni, 1979; Speck & Attneave, 1979) call attention to the reality that even in contemporary life much of individuals' experience (for better or worse) is affected by the actions and attitudes of the persons around them.

When we find clients attempting to cope with life concerns in the apparent absence of adequate social support from their informal system, a central issue is how potential supporters can be changed into actual supporters (Eckenrode & Gore, 1981). Counseling interventions that focus on network involvement can, ultimately, be conceptualized as efforts to reduce or remove the person- and context-based barriers operating to reduce the flow of social support to our clients.

Involvement of clients' informal network can proceed from one of three assessments of the cause and cure of the problems presented to us at the beginning of counseling:

- Clients' problems are a direct consequence of network deficiencies and conflicts, and the client (while a separate individual) can be viewed as the expression of the dysfunctionality of the entire network.
- While clients' problems are, to some degree, the consequence of network deficiencies or dysfunctionality, there are also positive network resources that can be mobilized in resolving those problems.
- The network apparently has had little or no role in the development of clients' difficulties; rather, it can be viewed as a reservoir of resources

useful in the resolution of those difficulties even though (for some reason) they are not flowing to the clients.

Attneave (1969) noted that "natural clans and networks, like other human institutions, can focus energies in healthy or pathological directions" (p. 193). Whether we view the natural network as a chronic source of negative influence or as a continuing, readily available source of social support should vary with the particular client and network with which we are working. When there is a strong, functional system present, our strategy will typically center on engaging supporters whose resources, for some reason, have been blocked. When there are system-based dysfunctionalities that have had a negative affect on clients, strategies of replacing or healing the network will get our attention.

The Network as Problem

In this situation it becomes apparent that while there is an identified client, the problems of that client are a reflection of the dysfunctionality of the broader natural system. We may find, for example, that in trying to understand the academic difficulties of a college student, we quickly are presented with the fact that he comes from a family that is ripped apart by the continuing substance abuse of a parent. If the student has served the role of mediator and peacemaker, he may be feeling deep ambivalence about having "abandoned" the family to go to college. He may also be under direct pressure from other family members (expressed through frequent phone calls and requests that he return home) to maintain his accustomed role. Because of his ambivalence about being away from home, he may lack the motivation to put in the time and effort required to excel in his courses.

Although a dysfunctional system may provide some types of social support (for example, material support) to the client, we may find that it is beyond our ability to effect any remedial changes in it. In such a situation, we are likely to retreat from a system-focused strategy and follow some variant or combination of supporting clients' ability to separate themselves physically and/or psychologically from the demands and impact of the disrupted system and helping them replace the dysfunctional system with a healthier one. Our hope would be that a new or expanded system might be able to provide needed social support without also generating difficulties.

The perceptual, attitudinal, and behavioral changes required to effect client movement away from a preexisting support system have already been discussed in the examination of interventions aimed at reducing client-based barriers (Chapter 5) and thus will not be considered here. We can simply note that the success of a strategy of replacing a dysfunctional support system (either in part or in whole) derives from the fact that it not only terminates or reduces the noxious impact of others on clients, it can also reduce the density of clients' systems through the addition of new people not embroiled in family difficulties. These new "outsiders" are in a position to provide the emotional and appraisal support that stressed family members cannot.

Network as Cause and Cure

It is probably most often true that the informal network's affect on clients is a mixed one; that is, the network not only causes them difficulties, it also contributes positively to their functioning. For example, Wilcox's (1981) research into the role played by social support in women's coping with the consequences of divorce found that the social support offered by the families of the "poorly adjusted" sample had both negative and positive consequences:

> Many women noted that relationships with family members were at once the most supportive and the most stress-producing. Even though they frequently offered high degrees of emotional sustenance, family members were more likely to be judgmental than non-kin. (p. 109)

Given this mixed effect, an important focus in our attempts to get a picture of the role that the natural network might play in our work with clients is the determination of what Gottlieb (1983) called the "balance of support-to-stress." When stress caused by interaction with supporters greatly overshadows support received, we may conclude that some variant of a replacement strategy is most reasonable. When the stress generated by the network at least comes close to being balanced by positive network resources, consideration of strategies involving network intervention become more reasonable.

The determination of where a particular client's network stands with reference to the balance of support and stress rests on gathering data (from the client and others) about the nature of the exchange between clients and their supporters. Gottlieb (1983) suggested that such data can be gained through a two stage process: (a) asking the client to indicate how often each network member has interacted to provide emotional support, cognitive guidance, companionship, environmental management, and material aid and services; (b) asking the client to provide global judgments with reference to each member concerning whether or not more of the various types of support are desired from each member, and if the overall relationship with each supporter is more stressful than supportive (pp. 112-113).

The Network as Cure

When the network does not seem to be providing its existing supportive resources, even though there is no apparent systemic dysfunction, it may be useful for the counselor to determine the effectiveness of the network's communication. One of the values of convening networks is that doing so allows members to combine information and thereby build a more complete picture of a client's situation than any member (or subset of members) had held before. This communication also allows members to find out where other persons in the network stand concerning their view of, and reactions to, the client's problem. Also, better information about past helping efforts and future alternatives can be shared.

Pooling of such information may be enough to stimulate the system into effective action. Essentially, members say, "Now that I know what the situation is, I'll be glad to help." This increases the likelihood that existing lines of communication and influence can be put to work in making decisions and initiating action. In this situation, the counselor's activity centers on what Rueveni (1979) called the role of "network convener" (pp. 73-76). The network is called together, put into contact and, through interaction and exchange, its curative resources enhanced.

Elements of Network Intervention

A number of practitioners have developed and described formats that network-oriented interventions can take. Rueveni's (1979) network intervention approach, for example, consisted of six phases, which he described as retribalization, polarization, mobilization, depression, breakthrough, and exhaustion-elation (pp. 33-36). Garrison (1974) developed a network-focused intervention for persons experiencing acute or chronic crises. Based on a model developed by Hansell (1970), the "screening, linking, planning" approach described by Garrison emphasizes (a) action that is initiated as close to the crisis as possible; (b) conducting the intervention in settings that are a natural part of the patient's life — home, school, workplace; (c) participation by the individual's natural system; and (d) a focus on returning the individual to, or maintaining the individual in, the community.

Whatever the specific format, there seem to be a number of elements that, in various combinations, make up network-involving interventions. These are as follows:

- the decision that a network-involving intervention is appropriate;
- the decision as to which network members will be asked to participate;
- assessment of the strengths and limitations of the network;
- convening the network;
- fostering a sense of group purpose and commonality;
- ameliorating such systemic dysfunctions as rivalry or unresolved resentments;
- opening up communication and exchange among members;
- fostering problem solving and coordination of effort;
- carrying out skill training and other behaviorally oriented activities to enhance network resources; and
- developing resources needed for ensuring continuity and follow-up to the intervention.

Each of these elements will be considered briefly as a means of suggesting the building blocks a counselor might use in developing a framework for a particular network-involving intervention.

Is a Network-Involving Intervention Appropriate?

The decision that an intervention focused on the informal network is appropriate might be made primarily on ideological bases. A strong theme running through the literature (e.g., Attneave, 1976) is the desirability of contributing to the effectiveness of the informal social contexts in which individuals spend so much of their time. Natural support systems built on kin and affective relationships can be viewed as the ground on which personal effectiveness is built and maintained. In an era of growing depersonalization and professionalization of helping exchanges, persons who stress the importance of fostering informal, face-to-face relationships may reach out to system-focused interventions as a way of keeping the ethos of the close, extended family, the village, or the tightly knit neighborhood alive in the experience of contemporary individuals.

Beyond ideological issues, the decision that a system-involving intervention strategy is appropriate will also involve a consideration of system resources and liabilities. Does an assessment of the exchange between clients and their supporters indicate a pattern of both beneficial and detrimental elements? The more the balance favors benefit, the more reasonable it is to assume that the network can be engaged in a way that will result in an increase of the support flowing to clients. In cases of an extreme imbalance in the direction of high stress, a strategy of replacement is apt to deserve our attention.

Also, in considering the appropriateness of a system-involving strategy, attention should be turned to determining the feasibility of such an approach. The resistance of many network members to opening individual and systemic deficiencies to public view has been noted. Rueveni (1979) cautioned that many members will only consent to an intervention involving the broad network when all else has failed. Because of such resistance, convening the network for a helping intervention may be a good idea but an impossible one to implement.

Finally, the fact that important segments of the network are inaccessible because of physical distance, lack of travel resources, or physical mobility difficulties may make it difficult or impossible to actually bring the network together.

Whom to Include?

When working with a couple, a nuclear family, or even an extended family, the boundaries of the treatment unit are fairly apparent. When we move to a concern for engaging the informal social support system or the informal network in our intervention we move into an area where such boundaries are less discrete. This lack of clear boundaries stems from the fact that individuals do not have a support system, but rather have a number of overlapping groups of supporters whose specific composition differs as a function of the specific issue at hand. House's (1981) call for a differentiated research approach allowing for the specification of "*who* gets *how much* of *what kinds* of support *from whom* regarding *which* problems" reflects the recognition that individuals go to different persons for different sorts of assistance with differing concerns (p. 39).

Most theorists and practitioners begin the process of defining the limits of a network-focused intervention by falling back on a determination of the persons who are exerting (or might exert) an important influence in a client's difficulty. For example, Hurd, Pattison, and Llamas (1981) took the following position in identifying the scope of the network on which intervention will focus:

> For most clinical purposes, the *a priori* defining assumption is the ego-centered social network of the identified patient. And more specifically,

[is] the relatively circumscribed "closer" affective and instrumental persons immediately linked through personal contact with the patient. (p. 247)

In most cases, the determination of those persons who fall within such a definition will have to be arrived at through collaboration with the client and other informants. Movement from a consideration of who might be included in the actual intervention to the determination of who will be included can be problematic. At one extreme, the approach of including every relevant network member can be adopted. Trimble (1981) noted that such a stance can result in a gathering ranging "in size from 20 to 80 or more participants" (p. 269). Such full-scale interventions present the convener with challenges: finding a place big enough to accommodate everyone; locating and securing cooperation of possible participants; and developing a treatment team large enough to coordinate both full-group and subgroup activities.

In addition to such mechanical issues, members and subgroups of the system will often disagree about who should be included in the meeting. Attneave (1976) pointed out that parents will often want to exclude some of their teenager's friends, and that the same issue often arises between spouses or siblings. She noted that in such an impasse, some form of negotiation will be necessary. Negotiation failing, counselors may have to make arbitrary decisions, relying on their own judgment as to the possible contributions all persons might make.

Identifying Network Resources and Deficiencies

Most advocates of network-involving interventions recommend some effort be spent on developing a concrete delineation of the structure and resources of the support network relevant to the issue at hand. These data can be useful in deciding whom to include in the intervention. Attneave (1976) described a process of developing a "network map" (pp. 223-224) that results in a graphic representation of the relationships of various sorts of persons (e.g., household members, emotionally significant persons, persons who are causally or functionally related to the concern at hand, distant or marginally involved persons). Her approach to constructing the network map engages the client and other network members. She cautioned that the mapping process inevitably raises strong feelings and should be carried out only with the assistance of a nonnetwork person who can make sure that such feelings are properly discussed.

Not only can the process of mapping the network focus on determining the limits of the intervention and specifying lines of communication and influence, it can also be used to locate trouble spots and resources that bear an important relationship to clients' concerns. For example, the graphic representation of who knows, or interacts with, whom can reveal schisms based on antipathy, or simple lack of contact. Moreover, members' discussions of who to include in or exclude from the intervention can be translated into a graphic presentation of factors that can contribute to the resolution of clients concerns and those that may act as barriers to effective network response.

The process of developing a picture of structure and resources can contribute to both procedural effectiveness and group solidarity. A knowledge of the resources at hand and an understanding of existing lines of communication and influence can be an aid in decision making, assignment of responsibility, or troubleshooting. Such activities as defining the membership of the group, clarifying its strengths and resources, and honestly confronting its limitations can foster the building of group identity and commitment.

Convening the Network

The convening process can vary in difficulty and complexity, depending on the size and nature of the group identified. Attneave (1969) noted that "the energy required to organize a network and be clinically effective as well may dampen the ardor of many therapists. . . . It also probably accounts for the comparatively short life of most urban therapy networks" (p. 207). Even when network members can assume task responsibility, locating individuals, assuring their attendance, and coordinating the availability of many people can place enormous demands on staff time and resources. It is little wonder that (whatever their conceptual attractiveness) network-oriented interventions are often quite restricted in the proportion of possible participants actually included.

Assuming the logistics of convening are successfully developed and implemented, some attention needs to be focused on psychological dimensions of the assembly process. Rueveni (1979) has described a planning meeting, called a "home visit," used to involve network members in the design of the intervention right from the beginning. Conducting the meeting at the family home is an important consideration for Rueveni:

The home is the preferable location, since it is the prime natural habitat of most family systems. Meeting at home reinforces the team expectations that preference is given to the home as a place where their friends and relatives may be called to convene if necessary. The home meeting is, for many families, a convenient, less stigmatized place to convene than, for example, a psychiatric facility. (1979, p. 27)

The positive psychological value of convening meetings in the natural settings of members (e.g., homes, schools, workplaces) has also been stressed by Hansell (1970) and Garrison (1974).

Fostering Commonality and Purpose

The frequency with which the terms *tribe* and *clan* are used in describing the gathering in network-involving interventions gives some hint of the psychological impact that such an assembly typically has on participants. Trimble (1981), in his synthesis of several network intervention approaches, described an initial "retribalization" stage "in which the network affirms ties and recognizes itself as a social collectivity" (p. 269). This initial sense of solidarity and group belonging is often quickly disturbed by what Trimble (1981) and Rueveni (1979) called the "polarization" stage. Nonetheless, the initial sense of group identity continues to underlie the network's movement toward providing assistance, however halting and fractious that movement might be.

Opening Up Communication

One of the unique strengths of network-involving interventions is that they represent a powerful vehicle for airing the differing perceptions of network members. This disclosure takes place within a context that allows members the opportunity to receive and react to one another's presentations. Such airing and exchange can be especially important in situations characterized by little exchange among members generally or those in which subgroups are cut off from the usual exchange of information and opinion.

The very factor that leads network members to resist network-involving interventions (that is, the fear that "dirty laundry" will be hung out in public) can cause convening the network to be an efficient modality for helping the network discover and coordinate its resources for the benefit of the client. Assuming that the apprehensions, hidden agendas, and residual resentments of members can be brought to light and (at least) minimally resolved, the flow of communication among members can allow a relatively full picture of clients' situations to emerge. Network members who had only been marginally aware of the client's total situation can now fully appreciate what the problems are. Individuals who had been unaware of negative feelings or expectations that had been blocking others' willingness to provide support, can turn their attention to resolving those negative factors. Finally, through the group's consideration of the problem, and its examination of alternatives for its resolution, previously unrecognized emotional, informational, material, and appraisal supportive resources can come to light.

In a relatively intact, unconflicted network, the counselor's role with regard to opening up communication may be largely that of a procedural technician. With deeply divided groups, a great deal of time may have to be devoted to tending to the resolution of resentments, lack of trust, and unresolved conflicts before the open exchange of information will occur.

Remediating the Network

As the level of network dysfunctionality increases, it is also increasingly necessary for the counselor to focus on remediation when developing a network intervention. Eckenrode and Gore (1981) noted that as networks become more stressed, the likelihood that the members of those networks will obtain support from the network decreases. Therefore, increasing the supportiveness potential of their support systems to our clients will often depend on the reduction of intra- and extranetwork stressors affecting members.

In ameliorating intragroup stressors (e.g., conflict, schisms, negative attributions), counselors can draw heavily from the theory and practice of group and family counseling approaches as a basis for their work. The power of catharsis in reducing intensity of feeling, the development of insight into the presence and impact of members' and subgroup alliances, and the use of psychodramatic techniques in the resolution of past misunderstandings are examples of the manner in which concepts and procedures from other therapeutic domains can be extrapolated to the network intervention situation.

When alleviating extragroup stressors as a means of increasing the supportive potential of the network, counselor role can center on such activities as referral to outside resources, or advocating the network's interests with outside persons or agencies that may have been unresponsive or acted in a fashion inconsistent with the members' needs.

Fostering Problem Solving and Coordination of Effort

Froland et al. (1979) suggested that an important aspect of the helper's role in network-involving interventions centers on the coordination and integration of supportive resources from different segments of the network. In a similar (though more impressionistic) vein, Attneave (1969) described the role of the helper in network interventions as similar to that of an orchestra leader. Even if networks are not seriously fragmented, the necessity of persons working together when many of them are (to varying degrees) unknown to one another can create difficulties in establishing effective communication and maintaining procedural coherence. Here, the counselor's function may focus less on the healing of dysfunctionality and more on serving as a resource for coordinating and managing the group's interaction.

If the network has self-management resources within itself, it may only be necessary for the counselor to sanction their emergence by involving members in the development of ground rules and procedures. In situations in which distrust and/or fear color group interaction, the counselor may continue to be looked to as a procedural chair, in spite of the fact that members possess high quality group management skills.

Whatever the situation, the counselor will probably be seen as a valuable resource both in the adoption of a problem-solving stance by network members and in the application of that stance to alleviate clients' difficulties. The counselor can reinforce problem-centered comments and efforts, suggest alternatives of which the group may not be aware, and bring internal and external resources that had not been considered to the groups' attention. In the management of problem-solving interaction, the counselor can present information and model behavior that networks can apply to their individual functioning and future network interaction.

Skill Development

Attention has already been called to the reality that in many situations it will be necessary for the counselor to focus on healing emotional pain and conflict in the network before newly developed or existing resources can become available to clients. In addition to emotional issues that feed network dysfunctionality, lack of group interaction skills can make effective network response to clients problematic. Unger and Powell (1980) suggested that one of the ways of enhancing a system's ability to be supportive is for the counselor to stress the development of interpersonal skills, including "listening, respecting another's opinions, cooperation, reciprocity, and the value of mutual help" (p. 572). Such skills can foster collaboration and the development of harmony in a system, especially if dysfunctionality is not deeply set. However, lack of disruption and conflict does not ensure that clients will be supported. Heller (1979) noted that while it is clear that different kinds of supportive action have differing effects, supporters are often not very skilled in determining the particular types of support that are needed. In many instances, therefore, skill training with supporters may profitably focus on helping them to develop the ability to "read" clients more effectively. Such training might focus on developing listening skills or establishing the ability of supporters to make opening, non-judgmental responses that will encourage others to talk. The goal of such training in effective communication is to make it more likely that supporters will have accurate data about clients' needs on which to base their supportive responses. However, once they have determined what is needed, they may lack the specific behavioral skills required to deliver that support. Focused training in the ability to carry out such actions as setting limits, fostering independence, advocating, stress reduction, or decision making may help supporters become more effective in implementing their judgments of how to support clients.

Providing for Continuity and Follow-Through

The reality that most network-involving interventions are difficult to organize and implement (Attneave, 1969; Rueveni, 1979) typically results in their lasting only a few sessions. While it may be possible to have numerous sessions with a small, easily assembled network (as is typically the case in family counseling), large, far-flung, or contentious networks will usually have to be approached with the idea of maximizing impact in one or two sessions. Mechanisms should be built into the intervention to ensure follow-through of the intentions and commitments arrived at in the network assembly. In Rueveni's (1979) network intervention, "support groups" represent such a vehicle for follow-through.

> Support group members make arrangements for future meetings and keep telephone contacts with the family members, with each other, and, if necessary, with the team. Their function is to discuss, plan, and help carry out additional alternatives. . . . Support group members are usually those network activists who are willing to mobilize their own resources in a collaborative effort. (p. 37)

Usually these support groups (there may be several formed from a network) are organized around a task or issue related to the provision of assistance to clients. For example, one support group might focus on developing child care for a client needing that assistance. Another might take on the responsibility of making frequent contact with an isolated individual whose depression seemed to be directly related to loneliness.

The central functions of Rueveni's support group mechanisms (i.e., specification of tasks to be accomplished, allocation of responsibility for those tasks, communication among members with regard to progress, convening the group or subgroups as needed) can be met through other vehicles. In small networks, tasks cited for future work might be pursued by an individual. Subsets of the network (for example, "activists" who have been working on particular tasks) might meet on a regular basis under the auspices of an influential network member or those of the counselor. The form of the mechanism used to ensure continuity and follow-through is probably less important than its compatibility with network style and expectations.

Follow-through can provide the counselor with an opportunity to strengthen the network in its continuing ability to be supportive. The same problem identification, goal setting, communication, and assignment of responsibility that are useful in resolving the present difficulty can be viewed as continuing resources of the group, ready to be activated and drawn on as future needs dictate. Rather than assuming network members will come to this realization, the counselor may wish to spend time sharpening their awareness of how they can nurture and strengthen the understandings and skills that are being (or have been) honed in dealing with the situation at hand.

Broader Societal Contexts as Barriers

The network-involving interventions discussed above — even those involving large numbers of people — deal with persons who have some fairly direct ties to the client. As relatives, co-workers, friends, or friends of friends, the client is a real, distinct individual to them. Focusing on support as a contextual variable (Rook & Dooley, 1985) leads quickly to the recognition that while the personal network is a central factor in determining the amount and quality of clients' social support resources, there are also individuals and systems beyond clients' informal networks whose views and actions can profoundly influence the availability of social support.

A decision of a city council or the U.S. Congress to expand or retract support for child care, health services, worker retraining, or public transportation can have a rapid and marked impact on the resources available to individuals as they deal with ordinary and extraordinary life concerns. More generally, the attitudes and beliefs of "the public," when they are expressed in such forms as ageism, sexism, racial, ethnic or religious prejudice, or social Darwinism, can affect the degree to which individuals' needs for social support are recognized, confirmed as valid, and responded to (Vaux, 1985).

Strategies for Removing Barriers
Located in Broader Social Contexts

Recognizing that the attitudes and actions of individuals and systems beyond clients' personal networks can play an important part in the generation and amelioration of barriers to the flow of social support to our clients, we are faced with the question, "If that's where the action is, what do we do about it?" Of course, one answer is "Nothing!" Like Candide, we can focus our attention on our own garden, our own immediate, face-to-face contacts with clients and their significant others. Certainly, there is much good work to be done there, and the need for it is as apparent as full appointment schedules or long waiting lists for counseling services.

Another response to the question is to begin the process of identifying, mastering, and implementing the strategies and interventions that can be useful in eliminating or reducing the impact of those barriers to the flow of social support located in individuals and systems that lie beyond our garden. Conyne (1987) has pointed out that the use of system-focused strategies and interventions to improve the status (material, psychological, social) of clients

> is based on the assumption that human problems result from oppressive social conditions rather than from individual or interpersonal deficits. Thus both community development and social and political action approaches are used to alter the basic social, economic, and political conditions of society that are thought to strongly influence human health or misery. (p. 149)

We do not have to embrace the view that the social context is the exclusive source of individuals' difficulties to recognize the importance of contextual factors in affecting the degree to which clients are or are not supported. Behaviorally oriented interventions with clients may have to contend with societal factors that reinforce dysfunctionality. Similarly, while initiating an individually focused, dynamically oriented program to raise a client's self-esteem, we may also recognize that prevailing negative stereotypes were a contributing factor in the development of poor self-image.

Direct and Indirect Strategies Focused on the Broader Context

Just as network-focused interventions can be conceptualized as direct or indirect, depending on whether the counselor establishes face-to-face interaction with the network or works through other persons (e.g., the client) to effect change in it, so too may interventions designed to modify persons, groups, or institutions in broader social contexts.

Indirect strategies for effecting change in barriers lying outside the network itself focus primarily on efforts to strengthen the network's ability to carry out change on its own. This is the strategy of empowerment. Direct strategies are involved when counselors assume responsibility for bringing a wide range of actions directly to bear on the persons, groups, or institutions in the broader social context whose characteristics or actions create barriers to the flow of social support to our clients and others who make up their social networks.

Empowering Clients and Their Supporters

Throughout this chapter, the desirability of intervening with clients' informal support systems in a way that strengthens their continuing viability and effectiveness has been stressed. To this point, the focus of that strengthening has been on contributing to the systems' ability to provide needed social support directly to clients. We have discussed the strategy of healing systems in order to remove emotional barriers that reduce the flow of support. The use of skill training approaches to increase supporters' ability to recognize the specifically relevant supportive response has also been considered. In one sense, such interventions can be considered efforts to "empower" the system — methods of providing the people in those systems with the understandings and tools needed to gain greater control over, and effectiveness in, maintaining the groups' integrity and pursuing its interests.

There is another focus that empowering clients' support systems can take. This alternative flows from the recognition that important factors influencing the amount and quality of assistance received by individuals are housed in the broader social context (institutions, community, nation), beyond clients and their natural support systems. Just as it is possible for counselors to empower systems by helping them gain better control over the ability to provide support directly to clients, so is it possible for us to strengthen those systems by increasing their ability to influence those broad contextual factors that can exert control over the social support flowing to clients.

Some empowerment may result just from the act of convening the network. Simply being together and experiencing themselves as a group can foster group solidarity. When members of the system piece together the far-ranging effects of clients' concerns (the scope of which no one of them had been entirely aware) it may be possible for them also to get a picture of how contextual factors (e.g., the unresponsiveness of a work situation, the operation of sexism) have been operating to exacerbate clients' difficulties. Consensual validation of the presence and impact of these negative contextual factors can develop into a commitment to doing something about them. Resource-rich systems, possessed of a sense of their own potency, may need little help from the counselor in developing strategies and interventions to neutralize or modify negative contextual factors that operate to clients' detriment.

Networks possessing fewer resources, having more limited understanding of ways or the uses of group power, and less confidence in their ability to effect change present the counselor with the opportunity/necessity of playing an empowering role. We can help the network develop the awareness and skills required to confront and influence barriers located in the social environments beyond the world of their immediate, face-to-face functioning. The focus of these interventions can be viewed as

- raising the group's awareness of its own boundaries, needs, and rights (consciousness-raising);
- providing the group with resources that will contribute to members' understanding of the situations they face and the alternatives available to them; and
- helping the group acquire the skills on which effective confrontation of external barriers rests (consultation).

Consciousness-raising. Effective network action to eliminate or ameliorate the effect of external barriers often requires the realization that the difficulties experienced by the client are the result of outside factors whose operation in some way infringes on the rights of the group. The fragmentation of understanding that often precedes the convening of a network may be dispelled when members come together to combine and compare information about what the client's situation actually is and the factors that led to the difficulty. However, it will often be true that members have attitudinal or experiential blinders that prevent them from even recognizing that an inequity exists. In networks generally characterized by naiveté or a fatalistic acceptance of authority, there may be a tendency to view action aimed at removing barriers as impossible, unnecessary, or doomed to failure.

A number of researchers (e.g., Rotter, 1966) have noted that the tendency to view life as being controlled by factors beyond one's control (e.g., fate, "the system") tends to be positively associated with lower socioeconomic status. The various "power" movements of the last three decades can be viewed as attempts by groups of persons (previously cut off from the power to control important aspects of their lives) to confirm their significance as human beings and to claim their rights. An important part of the empowerment process is raising individuals' self-worth as a basis for insisting that their rights and interests be recognized.

Similarly, counselors can contribute to the potency of clients' informal networks by helping to raise members' awareness of how individuals or institutions in the broader social context are (through ignorance or ineptitude, or by conscious design) acting against their interests. It may be difficult for supporters to recognize that clients' rights are being ignored by school or workplace policies and procedures. It is often even more difficult for supporters to develop enough of a sense of power and hope to believe that it is worthwhile to confront the operation of those policies and procedures.

Consultation to networks. Conyne (1987), drawing on a wide body of literature, describes consultation as a three-way process through which an individual, group, or broader system is helped to deal more effectively with a particular situation by drawing on the assistance of an expert. This tripartite conceptualization (expert, consultee, problem situation) adapts easily to the role that counselors can play in empowering clients' support systems. Through consultation, supporters can gain understanding of situations that bear importantly on the development and remediation of clients' difficulties. Moreover, the counselor as consultant can help the system recognize existing resources and develop additional resources needed for acting on objectives set by the group.

Of the several consultation models described by Conyne (1987), the "mental health" model, based on the work of Caplan (1970), seems most directly applicable to the process of empowering clients' informal systems to deal with barriers to social support existing in the broader social context. This model focuses on the knowledge and skills of consultees (in this case, clients' supporters).

> Here, the "spread of effect" concept is critically important. That is, the professional counselor, through consultation, enables the consultee to gain greater competencies so that, in turn, the consultee becomes better able to help his/her clients. (Conyne, 1987, p. 176)

By acting as a resource for information and skills acquisition, the counselor helps supporters orient themselves to the realities of the situation at hand. Alternatives for action and the resources for such action become known to the group. Skill training to help network members become more effective in dealing with external persons and systems might focus on such areas as decision making, confrontation, mediation, and networking.

Intervening Directly to Affect the Broader Social Context (Cells 7, 8, and 9 of Table 7.1)

Recognizing that clients' social support resources can be strongly influenced by the operation of such contextual variables as institutional practices or government policies leads logically (though not easily or even necessarily) to a consideration of interventions that directly seek to ameliorate the impact of those factors. We may have the repeated experience of seeing clients whose difficulties are caused, or contributed to, by such factors as societal insensitivity or discrimination and whose supporters are themselves hampered by similar stressors. For many counselors, such experience becomes a springboard for direct involvement in attempts to modify those factors. One might move to these direct interventions as an expression of personal ideology or simply as a strategy to reduce the negative impact of the social environment.

The roles of advocate, raiser of public awareness, or activist will be unaccustomed ones for many counselors whose training and satisfactions tend to focus on offering direct service to individuals. As unfamiliar and unaccustomed as these activities might be, they often will be precisely the roles that can increase the availability of support from formal and informal sources when broad issues of societal priorities and resource allocation act as barriers (Lanoil, 1976).

Beyond issues of training, experience and accustomed routine, there are other problems awaiting counselors who would move to an integration of these direct modes of affecting the social context into their activities. The traditional counselor role highlighting scheduled contacts with individuals and small groups in an office, within the agency or school, is reasonably neat, discrete, and predictable. Interventions that seek to influence the social environment directly take counselors out of the office and the agency to deal with intervention targets not part of our typical way of "doing business."

How does a counseling program organized around traditional assumptions accommodate the flexibility of schedule, location, and activity that is unavoidably required by, for example, community development and activism? Particularly, how can these essentially preventive interventions be supported when the ongoing remedial activities on which the counseling service has typically been built remain? These are substantial problems requiring extensive individual and institutional commitment for their resolution. In the face of such problems, some counselors and institutions will opt to institute only limited forays into the realm of directly modifying broader social contexts, and will support them through "out of the hide" and "on one's own time" methods.

However difficult it may be for a counselor or counseling service to move toward greater involvement with interventions aimed at altering pathological factors housed in the broad social context, their potential to contribute to the welfare of our clients should be recognized. Conyne (1987), discussing primary prevention-oriented interventions, suggested that the strategy of directly confronting contextually based barriers can include such activities as education, community development, and social and political action. These activities, though seemingly far removed from the face-to-face focus of traditional counseling interventions, can (when successful) improve the supportiveness of the contexts within which clients and their supporters operate.

Education. A wide range of educational interventions can be focused on the social context at several levels. The common element behind such interventions is that they involve efforts (using a variety of vehicles and formats) to provide individuals with information and perspectives that can raise awareness, correct misinformation, alter attitudes, and change behavior.

Education can take many forms. When counselors speak to local service organizations about the importance of respite care alternatives for the families of individuals requiring extensive care, a process is begun that, ultimately, can lead to the greater availability of resources capable of reducing the burnout of natural support systems. The awareness and beliefs of lawmakers and administrators can be affected through testimony presented to governmental bodies at local, state, and national levels. Talk shows or panels on community access television channels can serve as vehicles for educating local audiences about the existence and impact of situations that have negative effects on the ability of clients' supporters to be of assistance.

Educational interventions can call the public's attention to the corrosive effect of such factors as discrimination, the absence of worker retraining programs, lack of home health care alternatives, or insufficient services for supporting and strengthening families. Education can increase general support for resources that strengthen clients' informal support networks by reducing the stressors affecting them and by increasing the resources to which supporters have access. Conyne (1987) pointed out that the counselor's stance in educational interventions can range from that of a neutral, objective disseminator of research to an "activist collaborator" who, in an attempt to shape awareness and attitudes, "steps aside from a position of value neutrality to espouse and press for the adoption of particular points of view or courses of action that can result in social policy" (p. 132).

Community development. Community development work can be conceptualized as the result of shifting the focus of empowerment-focused interventions from clients' natural support networks to the broader community. Thus it represents a cluster of activities aimed at helping members of a community develop the awareness, group solidarity, and skills required to initiate action designed to effect changes that are in their interest. Lippitt (1985) asserted that "one of the great gains for basic democracy is the discovery of the great resources of operating in heterogeneous groups and utilizing the great resources of pluralism of the community." His suggestions for effective community development work place emphasis on (a) involvement of a wide variety of community persons, (b) the importance of ongoing technical consultation to participants, (c) the cooperation of the media, (d) the training of skilled group leaders who will provide continuing leadership, and (e) continuing linkages between those involved in the intervention and members of established community structures.

Social and political action. Interventions that implement educational and community development strategies often have political bodies (and/or their constituent members) as their focus. This targeting of politicians is a recognition of their affect on many aspects of individuals' lives. Politicians are often able to act positively or negatively to affect factors that, in turn, affect the ability of clients' supporters to be of assistance. For example, the insensitivity of elected officials to the corrosive impact of inequity on workers' aspirations and self-esteem can help to perpetuate situations that are deleterious not only to the workers involved, but also to other individuals for whom these workers are a source of emotional and material support.

Conyne (1987) noted that action to change the operation of political systems can range from the confrontational, conflict-centered approach of Saul Alinsky (1972) to quieter strategies that stress active participation in the political system. If one is dissatisfied with the responsiveness of a school system's adult basic education program to the needs of immigrant or single parents, running for the school board or supporting sympathetic candidates might contribute to a beneficial change in policy and practice. More confrontationally, the same goal might be pursued by organizing public demonstrations (e.g., staging a sit-in at the board's office or picketing the homes of board members). Rather than waiting to be invited to present testimony to legislators, counselors can actively seek out key office holders and administrators to lobby for programs that will strengthen the ability of natural systems to provide social support for their members.

Professional organizations are another vehicle for political action-minded counselors. The American Association for Counseling and Development (AACD) and the American Psychological Association (APA), as well as many of their state and local affiliates, have political action arms. Both organizations also have a structure of divisions and task forces that focus their energies on identifying action needed to further the interests of client groups. The political action channels available through AACD, APA, and other organizations (e.g., the League of Women Voters) typically are hungry for the energy and efforts of committed persons. By contributing to them, counselors have the opportunity to pool their efforts with like-minded persons in working for objectives of benefit to the persons who make up our clients' natural support systems.

Interventions Focused on the Physical Context
(Cells 7, 8, and 9 of Table 7.1)

In Chapter 6, it was noted that the physical environment can present barriers to the flow of social support to individuals. The role of such environmentally based barriers as physical distance or the lack of roads or public transportation alternatives are apparent. Perhaps less apparent are the effects of building design and community layout on the ease with which persons can come into contact with one another. While discussing how human service professionals can contribute to the enhancement of physical contexts vis-à-vis the facilitation of supportive exchanges among residents, Gottlieb and Schroter (1978) suggested that input by human service workers into housing design and community development processes can result in greater attention being given to the ability of persons in those contexts to interact and form groupings. Awareness of the role of the physical context in fostering or discouraging supportive exchange is also reflected in Gottlieb's (1979) suggestion that human service workers be actively involved in working with community people to "arrest physical planning projects that threaten to destroy existing and viable neighborhood-based support systems" (p. 477).

The form of Gottlieb's suggestion (i.e., that we work in concert with local resources) points to the fact that interventions initiated to ameliorate barriers resulting from characteristics of the physical environment take the same form as those used to address barriers lodged in broader social contexts; that is, education, community development, and social and political action. While it is true that individuals are not the cause of the rough terrain, bad weather, or physical distance that can negatively affect the availability of social support from natural and formal sources, individuals and groups of individuals do have influence on decisions about whether or not roads are built and maintained or if convenient, affordable public transportation exists.

In seeking to overcome the negative impact of the physical environment on persons' ability to form and maintain supportive relationships, our targets, then, are the same persons and institutions on which our efforts to reduce or eliminate barriers in social context were focused. The same member of Congress or state legislator who is influential in the area of funding for worker retraining, may also be involved in decisions about public transportation, urban planning, or housing for the elderly. In either case, education, lobbying, or political pressure can raise awareness of how public policy and programs can aid or restrict the ability of individuals to be supportive to one another.

Conclusion

This discussion of interventions that focus on the removal or amelioration of barriers to the exchange of social support housed in the broader social and physical contexts has led us far away from the usually quiet, circumscribed world of traditional one-to-one and small group counseling formats. The suggestion is that there is a big world out there beyond the walls of our offices and our institutions. It is a world where decisions made by individuals and groups often have immediate positive or negative affect on the supportive resources of natural and formal support systems available to our clients and their supporters.

Interventions that focus on networks and broader social contexts are, likely, not for everyone. The decision about whether or not one moves into the hurly-burly they represent is most apt to be based on factors of individual predilection and institutional expectation. Some strong advocates of the expansion of traditional counselor role (Conyne, 1987, among them) hold that we ignore the broader world of the social realities only at the risk of eventual ineffectiveness or irrelevance. We risk ineffectiveness because our "closed" interventions (Pattison, 1973) heal and nurture clients only to have them reenter the same contexts that contributed to their difficulties in the first place. We may become irrelevant because we are so few and the sources of dysfunctionality so pervasive that there will never be enough of us to go around; thus many needy persons will be left with the necessity of latching on to other vehicles for personal and situational change. Although these options (e.g., extremism, substance abuse) may eventually be selfdestructive, to the unserved they seem to hold out a way of actually doing something about the noxious life contexts in which they live.

Of course, there is a middle ground. Those of us who are more comfortable in the traditional roles of counseling can at least be supportive of colleagues and programs that focus on broader contexts. Collaboration and team-focused efforts can address both individual and contextually based barriers to support. Counselors who have skills across a range of support-focused interventions may spend most of their time pursuing traditional strategies, but they follow their clients' needs into broader context-focused approaches when appropriate. We may not convene all (or even parts) of clients' networks in every instance, but do so on those occasions when it is apparent that the network is central to the cause and/or cure of the observed difficulties. Finally, if the strategies of political and social action are not our style, we can contribute to such activities through our membership in and support of professional and cause-focused organizations.

Chapter Eight

Ansel: A Case Study

To illustrate how social support perspectives and procedures can be incorporated into counseling practice, consider the counseling experience of a client named Ansel.

Ansel, a 22-year-old single man, sought counseling for a range of personal concerns summarized in the following statement:

> I'm really lonely. I don't have any real friends, just people I say hi to at work. I get up in the morning, have a cup of coffee, go to work, come home, fix something for my dad and I to eat for supper, go up to my room, clap on the headset, listen to music until I fall asleep, get up the next morning, and start it all again. My life is going nowhere, my job is minimum wage, I got no friends, I got no girlfriend. I think I'm getting as weird as my dad.

Excerpts from sessions will demonstrate how social support issues can be clarified and counseling strategies initiated in assisting clients to move toward access to the types of social support most relevant to their life concerns.

Background

Ansel was adopted as an infant. He had no recollection of, and almost no information about, his biological parents. His adoptive parents were divorced when he was 16. His mother was awarded custody of him, but he saw his father most weekends and sometimes during the week. Prior to the divorce and in the year thereafter, there was a great deal of conflict (mostly verbal, but sometimes physical) between his parents. Arguments centered on financial problems and mutual recriminations about past infidelities. Ansel described himself as "stuck in the middle" of this conflict, running back and forth between his parents, trying to straighten things out.

A year after the divorce his mother moved in with a man with whom she had had a relationship for several years. This man, also divorced, had three children. When it became apparent that there was not enough room in the boyfriend's rented house for everyone, Ansel was "shipped back" to his father, somewhat against the preferences of both the boy and the father. A year later (when Ansel was 18, four years prior to the beginning of counseling), his mother and her boyfriend moved to a distant state. Ansel asked to go along with them, but was refused, so he continued to live with his father. After graduation, he took a job as a cook's helper in a small, center city restaurant.

Ansel said that his mother's original moving out, and the changes of neighborhood and school it involved, disrupted the friendships he had developed during middle school and the first years of high school. He had no close friends after that move, although there were a few guys with whom he would get high several times a week. After he graduated from high school his drug use stopped, mainly because he no longer spent time with his former friends. Ansel indicated that other than occasionally going out with his father for a few beers, he no longer was substance involved.

Ansel's Situation as Counseling Began

Ansel described his interaction with his father as very limited. Typically, they saw each other briefly in the morning and then again at suppertime. In the evening, the older man would either fall asleep in front of the television or go to a nearby tavern and drink. As Ansel talked about their relationship, it seemed more empty than harsh. He had the opinion that his father was a difficult person to get along with, offering as evidence the fact that although the older man had dated several women after his divorce, none of those relationships had worked out.

The interaction between father and son was superficial, consisting mainly of leaving each other alone. However, Ansel indicated that his father had been disparaging of some recent attempts at self-improvement that Ansel had considered taking. When he mentioned he wanted to get his driver's license, his father's response was that it wouldn't do Ansel any good since he couldn't afford a car and he wasn't going to let Ansel ruin his. To Ansel's statement that he was thinking about taking some courses at the local community college, his father said, "Why do you want to do that? It will cost you money and get you nowhere." Ansel viewed his father as a lonely, bitter, socially inept man who was stuck in a dead-end janitor's job. His deepest worry was that he might be growing more and more like his father as time passed.

Though he had a circle of people with whom he came into contact at the restaurant, Ansel felt that he had no friends. While he exchanged pleasantries with them and responded to their chitchat, he believed that he didn't know how to carry on a conversation; therefore, he avoided talking with them as much as possible lest he look stupid. When he first started work, co-workers had invited him to parties and picnics, and he had been asked to go out after work for a drink. He always refused, finding some excuse why he couldn't go. Soon, he was no longer asked.

Although Ansel was neatly, though simply, dressed, well groomed, and at least average in personal attractiveness, he indicated that he considered himself ugly, citing gaps between his teeth and pimples on his face as particularly offensive features. Neither of these were markedly noticeable to casual observation and, even when noticed, generally would not be the basis for criticism or rejection. Ansel desperately wanted a girlfriend, but he felt that no girl would ever be attracted to a "loser" like him. The fact that he did not date led him to fear that other people would think he was "queer." This fear was another factor that contributed to his distancing himself from people at work.

Ansel's Support Resources and Deficiencies

When it became clear that Ansel's relative isolation from supportive relationships was an important part of the concerns that brought him to counseling, he was asked to complete the Personal Support System Survey (P3S) described in Chapter 3. While the data provided by the

P3S will be used to describe and analyze Ansel's situation and interpersonal functioning, it should be remembered that much of the same information could be gathered using less structured, conversation-based approaches. Moreover, in the theoretical and research literature of social support, there are, as has been noted, a number of other social support assessment instruments that can be used to gather information about individuals' support networks. These, to some extent, parallel the P3S in their form and data they yield.

Perhaps the best place to start in developing an understanding of an individual's status with reference to social support is to get a picture of the specific types of support that person considers most important and then to determine his or her level of satisfaction vis-à-vis those specific support types. This provides a reading of social support status specific to the particular individual with whom we are working, rather than a view based on patterns generalized from empirical or logical analysis. The Likert scales found on pages 3 to 5 of the P3S (see Appendix A) require that respondents indicate the level of importance attached to each of the 13 support areas and also the extent to which they are or are not satisfied with the availability of that support in their lives. Logically, the most important support areas to consider are those that individuals describe as important (i.e., rated 1 or 2 on the satisfaction scale) and for which they also describe a low level of satisfaction (i.e., rated 4 or 5 on the satisfaction scale) concerning their availability.

Examining Ansel's ratings (see Appendix C), we can observe that four scales (Love, Physical Intimacy, Companionship, and Acceptance) fall into the pattern of being rated high in importance and low in satisfaction. We can also note that all of these scales fall into what House (1981) identified as emotional support. Though at some point Ansel might have found it helpful to receive information about educational alternatives (informational support), to get feedback about how other people actually perceived his appearance (appraisal support) or to have had someone offer to take him out to renew his driving skills (material support), it was clear at the beginning of counseling that his strongest experienced support needs were those associated with close, caring interpersonal relationships. It was the absence of friends, especially a girlfriend, that brought Ansel to the point of seeking assistance.

Counselor: I think it might be useful to begin by looking at your relationships with people by seeing what it is that you really want to get from them, but aren't. All right?

Ansel: Okay.

Counselor: Look down through your ratings on these scales [pointing to the scales on pages 3 to 5 of the P3S] and see if there were any you rated toward the "very important" end of the scale on the first scale, and toward the "very dissatisfied" end of the second scale. Are there any like that?

Ansel: I'm not sure exactly what you mean.

Counselor: Well, look at the "love" scale. Your check mark is in the first space, indicating that it is very important to you to receive caring, affection, and warmth from others. On the other hand, your check on the "satisfaction" scale is in the last space, indicating that you are very dissatisfied with the amount of love you are receiving.

Ansel: I see.

Counselor: Are there any other scales that combine a rating in the first or second space on the "importance" scale with a rating in the fourth or fifth space on the "satisfaction" scale?

Ansel: Well, here's physical intimacy . . . and companionship . . . encouragement [turns page] . . . acceptance . . . and . . . that's all.

Counselor: Right. Love, physical intimacy, companionship, encouragement, and acceptance are the sorts of things that you consider to be important to get from other people, but you have a strong feeling of dissatisfaction with regard to what you actually are receiving. What do you make of that?

Ansel: Well, there's nobody I'm close to. I don't date.

Counselor: It looks as if you feel that nobody really cares about you, that you're isolated both from the close feelings and physical sharing that you might have with a girlfriend, and that you don't have other friends that you could do things with.

Ansel: That's about it.

Counselor: So, in other words, if you could change your life, it would be to have closer relationships with people, relationships where you would receive love and caring, as opposed to some of these other things, like "guidance" or "knowledge" or "help."

Ansel: Right. I can take care of myself, but I'm really lonely.

Ansel's experienced deficiency with regard to emotional support provided the primary focus of the early stages of counseling. While an ultimate goal was to help him identify the barriers that were reducing his access to emotional support and to assist him in removing those barriers, I believed that the counseling relationship itself could serve an important (albeit temporary) role in providing him with a source of caring and acceptance.

Structural Characteristics of Ansel's Support System

By examining Ansel's P3S data, shown in Appendix C, we can focus on the structural features of his support system. First we notice that it is a relatively small system — five persons. In and of itself, the fact that it is small (Esperon, 1985/1986, for example found that the mean system size of a male undergraduate sample was 7.71) is probably not too significant. As indicated in Chapter 3, the research literature does not point to a strong pattern of association between system size and health status or reported satisfaction with support resources.

Family proportion (.40) is similar to what Esperon (1985/1986) found in his sample of male students (.46). The proportion of the system made up of co-workers (.40) seems large. For example, data gathered by the author for another population of employed, young adult males found a mean co-worker proportion of .18. Whether Ansel's reliance on the work situation represents the operation of a good coping strategy or is an indication of ineffectiveness in forming relationships in more informal social situations would be a useful issue to be explored when presenting and discussing these results with Ansel.

It may also be observed that the "same age" cohort proportion (.40) of Ansel's system is somewhat below those found by Esperon (.61) for his undergraduate male sample. Given the general importance of peer group relationships to persons at this life stage, we might have expected a higher proportion of the informal system to be composed of age peers. These results provide another focus for inquiry and discussion: Why doesn't Ansel have more people of his own age in his system?

Counselor: Let's examine the people you listed as making up your natural support system to see if there are any patterns that might shed some light on your feelings of isolation and loneliness. First, we can talk about the size of your system, then there are several questions I'd like to ask about the people you've listed; for example, how many are family? How many are of your own age group? How many are men; how many women? Sometimes by looking at these questions, we can discover not only what your relationships are like, but also get an idea of why they are what they are, as well as how we might go about making some desirable changes. Okay?

Ansel: Sure.

Counselor: You listed five people in your support system: Dad, Mom, Bill, Terry, and Gladys. One thing that is important to remember is that there are no good or bad numbers in and of themselves. People can be, and often are, satisfied with support systems that vary widely in their size and in kinds of people who are in them. Different people can also be satisfied or dissatisfied with very similar systems. One person might be happy at having 10 supporters who are mainly all family members, while another might feel that was too few or feel that they are too dependent on their family. The thing I want us to look at is how you feel about your support system, and to examine the consequences of the way your system is and how you feel about those consequences. Okay?

Ansel: I think so.

Counselor: First of all, you've listed 5 people. That's really not too unusual in terms of other people your age — some people might list more, others fewer. Do you have any feelings about the size of your support system?

Ansel: Not really. I guess I could use a few more people, but I've never been real popular, and that's okay if I just knew how to feel more comfortable with people and wasn't afraid to talk to them and get to know them.

Counselor: So it's not so much that you want a lot more people, but rather that you would like to be able to relate differently to the people you do have.

Ansel: And maybe some different kinds of people, or different people.

Counselor: Like who?

Ansel: Well, like Bill. I call him my friend, but I haven't really talked to him in four or five years. In junior high school I used to go over to his house a lot; his mom was really nice to me. But after my mom moved out and I lived with her that year, he got tight with some other friends and we never hung around together, even after I moved back with my dad.

Counselor: So Bill is a friend in the sense that he's someone you were once close to, but you actually don't do things with him anymore.

Ansel: Right.

Counselor: And you'd like to have at least a few friends that you could see regularly, do things with, and be close to.

Ansel: That's true.

Counselor: Okay, well that idea of how frequently you actually see people in your support system is something we'll return to in a bit, but for now let's just say that you're not as much concerned about the size of your system as you are about the kind of people and how you interact with them. Now let's look at who it is that you did list. The first thing that catches my eye is that two out of the five, your mom and dad, are family members. Let me ask, is that all the family you have — any grandparents, uncles, aunts, or cousins?

Ansel: My dad has a brother who lives on the north side, but they don't get along at all. His father died when I was little, and my grandma lives with my aunt somewhere in Pennsylvania. They never come up here . . . sometimes my grandma calls up, but that's all. My mom's family is from up near Merina (a small city about 80 miles distant). I have two uncles and an aunt. We used to go up there in the summer to visit my grandmother on that side, but since my folks split they haven't had anything to do with us. They never did like my father anyway.

Counselor: Any cousins?

Ansel: Ya, a couple up north, but I haven't seen them in a long time.

Counselor: Do you ever think about making contact with your mother's family again?

Ansel: Not really; my dad would have a fit.

Counselor: And what about his family?

Ansel: I don't know what the point would be. We don't care about each other, so we leave well enough alone.

Counselor: Well, maybe that's something we can return to later on, but for now let's just note that you do have more family than you've listed here.

Ansel: That's true.

Counselor: Another thing, how many of these people are of your own age?

Ansel: Two — Bill and Terry.

Counselor: Less than half. Do you have any feelings about that?

Ansel: What do you mean?

Counselor: Well, most of the people you've listed in your support system are older — right?

Ansel: Ya.

Counselor: Well, if you had your preference, would you like to have a larger or smaller proportion of people your own age — or would you keep it about the same?

Ansel: I'd like to have more people my own age.

Counselor: More — or a larger proportion?

Ansel: I can't see that it matters as long as I had more friends my own age.

Counselor: So you wouldn't mind more older people, but what's most important is friends your own age.

Ansel: Right.

Counselor: I also see that there are somewhat more males than females on your list. Any feelings about that?

Ansel: Just that I wish I had a girlfriend.

Counselor: So when you said before that you'd like more friends your own age, you're particularly interested in having one of those be a woman you could date and be close to.

Ansel: Ya.

Counselor: One final thing on this part of the survey that we might talk about is that I notice that almost half of the people you listed are people you work with. It looks as if the restaurant is a major source of your contact with people.

Ansel: Well, I see Terry and Gladys every day I go to work.

Counselor: Do you consider them close friends?

Ansel: Maybe more acquaintances. I don't get out into the dining area much, and they don't come into the kitchen too much, but we say hi and talk about stuff.

Counselor: So you're really not close.

Ansel: Not really. Terry is into sports, so we talk about basketball and stuff.

Counselor: And what about Gladys? What's she like?

Ansel: Gladys is the cashier. Sometimes I think she thinks she's my mother — tells me to stand up straight, smile. She's nice, I guess, but she can be a pain sometimes too.

Counselor: How so?

Ansel: Well, she's always inviting me to come have dinner with her and her family on the weekend.

Counselor: Sounds as if that makes you uncomfortable.

Ansel: I'm nervous around people I don't know.

Counselor: Is there anything about Gladys and her family that makes you particularly uncomfortable?

Ansel: No. Just that they would probably think I'm weird.

Counselor: Why is that?

Ansel: I wouldn't know what to say. I can see me sitting there like a dummy, looking like a tongue-tied fool.

Counselor: So you avoid meeting Gladys' family because you're afraid that you wouldn't know what to say and that they would judge you.

Ansel: That, and also because her daughter thinks I'm a jerk.

Counselor: Tell me about that.

Ansel: She comes to pick up Gladys. I've seen her a couple of times.

Counselor: And?

Ansel: And, she's really nice looking and probably thinks I'm goofy looking.

Counselor: How do you know that?

Ansel: I can just tell.

Interactive Characteristics

The foregoing session segment illustrates how data concerning the structure of a client's natural support system can be summarized and interpreted to the client. We also see how the data can form a basis for helping the client consider how present interpersonal concerns may have their basis in that structure. Another broad area of consideration that often is useful in uncovering barriers to the flow of social support is to examine how the natural support system operates.

Information generated by posing the following questions will often yield insights into the manner in which our clients themselves diminish the amount of assistance that comes to them from family, friends, and co-workers:

- How stable is the informal system?
- How frequently is contact made with supporters?
- How many of the supporters know, and have contact with, each other?
- How reciprocal are the relationships the client has with the persons in the informal system?
- If there are nonreciprocal relationships, what is the specific form that lack of reciprocity takes? For example, is support given by the client to supporters without being returned? Is support received by the client without it being returned to the supporters?

If we determine that a client has very infrequent contact with most of the people in his support system, it becomes apparent that information concerning the causes of that infrequent contact (e.g., moving or withdrawal because of fear of rejection) may have important implications for the counseling interventions we develop.

Interactive Characteristics of Ansel's System

At first glance, the information relating to the operation of Ansel's support system seems to present a favorable picture. The data indicate a mix of longtime and recently acquired supporters, and it appears Ansel can maintain continuing support relationships as well as forging supportive contacts with new people. Vicarious support (that is, support derived from persons with whom interaction does not actually take place) is a minor element of his resources. However, despite these appearances, we've heard Ansel describe himself as a person who has little close contact with others, who feels lonely, and views others as critical and rejecting. The person he lists as a friend is someone with whom he has had no actual contact for several years. His contact with the mother who rejected him is limited to an occasional phone call. He and his father live in the same house, but they have little emotional contact. He distances himself from the two co-workers listed because he fears that closer contact would result in rejection.

Ansel's subjective experience is perhaps more clearly reflected in his description of his relationships in terms of the reciprocity and density of his system. He identifies only one reciprocal relationship—that with his father. But what, exactly, does this great preponderance of nonreciprocal support relationships suggest? Is Ansel a person who "bleeds others dry" through demands for assistance while giving little in return? From what we've learned of him so far, he is not. In fact, he seems to run away from others when they offer the support of companionship and attention. Nor does it appear that the lack of reciprocity Ansel describes follows a pattern of his "giving and giving" while receiving little in return from his network. Rather, Ansel presents himself to us as a young man who believes that most of the people from whom he gets some vague sense of belonging (for that is all that he seems to be able to identify as support received from others) hardly know he exists.

Counselor: You've indicated that your father is the only person who you think considers you as a supporter.

Ansel: I'm not much, but I guess he depends on me to help keep the house picked up, and we do talk and do stuff together once in awhile.

Counselor: But why is that? Don't you think your mother or the people at work depend on you for at least such simple things as someone they like being with, or maybe the feeling that it's nice knowing someone likes and thinks well of them? I mean, even if you're not their closest friend or do lots of favors for them, don't you think they feel that they're glad that you're around?

Ansel: I don't think anyone really cares whether I'm around or not. They put up with me.

Counselor: So, it sounds to me as if you feel really isolated and lonely, but also trapped. You want to be close to people, to have friends—especially a girlfriend—but don't really believe that you're the kind of person that other people want to get close to.

Ansel: I don't know how to talk to people. Everyone else seems to know what to say. I just go blank and stand there like a fool or say something dumb.

Counselor: Is that true when you talk with your father?

Ansel: No, I guess not.

Counselor: So what's the difference?

Ansel: Well, he's my father. I know him.

Counselor: And what's so scary about people you don't know?

Ansel: It's not scary really — well, maybe kinda — just that it kills me to have someone laugh at me or put me down.

Counselor: Sounds as if that's happened a lot.

Ansel: When I was in school. Not so much anymore.

Counselor: I would guess you don't let yourself get in a situation where that might happen.

Ansel: What do you mean?

Counselor: The picture I get is that even if someone tries to get to know you, like Gladys and Terry at the restaurant, you run the other way for fear that you might get hurt — that they might put you down.

Ansel: I guess that's about it.

Counselor: And what's the result?

Ansel: The result is that I don't have any real friends — that I'm lonely.

Counselor: And what it all seems to come down to is that because you feel that you're such a loser, you expect that no one else could like you.

Ansel: Because I *am* such a loser.

The density of Ansel's system is low. Applying the formula for determining density described in Chapter 3 to the "who knows whom" data results in a density figure of 0.10. That is, out of a possible ten pairings of individuals who could know and have frequent contact with each other, only one pair (Gladys and Terry) actually do. This is a very "thin" system; while Hirsch (1981) noted that such systems can contribute to effective coping (mainly because people who do not have contact with one another are less apt to overlap in terms of information and other support resources), such does not seem to be the case with Ansel. It seems that the low density of his system does not result from forming supportive relationships in many different areas. Rather, the reality seems to be that Ansel is so socially inhibited that the only relationships he has are those he inherits by birth or those that are thrust on him simply by his having to be in a given situation (work, for example).

In summary, what does an examination of the interactive characteristics of Ansel's informal system tell us about the causes of the support deficiencies he experiences? The answer to that question is, at once, "not much" and "a great deal." The direct/vicarious ratio and frequency of contact data wave no red flags. However, the marked lack of reciprocal support relationships suggests something is seriously amiss. The information that comes from face-to-face interaction with Ansel clarifies the specific form this lack of reciprocity takes and suggests its cause. While Ansel views himself as receiving a thin sort of companionship and attention from others, his father is the only one to whom he believes he contributes any sort of support.

It seems clear that Ansel distances himself from others, fearing that close contact will result in rejection. We can speculate that the rejection represented by his mother's sending him back to his father, along with her subsequent move and refusal to allow him to go along, played an important part in the formation of his expectation of hurt at the hands of others. Beyond the more recent rejection by his adoptive mother, we can ponder the possibility that the earlier abandonment by his biological parents also played a part in Ansel's deep-seated expectation that others would find him wanting. He touched on his adoption only two or three times over the entire course of counseling, and consistently rejected my observation that being given up by his biological parents may have left an impact on his expectations of others. His typical response to such observations was some variant of "They must have had a good reason."

Whatever its genesis, it is clear that Ansel's lack of a rich supportive network stemmed from his withdrawal from any significant contact with others. It is also clear that his lack of self-esteem was a central feature of the situation. Believing himself to be a loser, he expected rejection and criticism and avoided it by simply not giving anyone the opportunity to get close enough to have a chance to target him.

The awkwardness and hesitancy that Ansel showed in the face-to-face counseling situation is not communicated very well in a printed protocol. Though able to capture and articulate very subtle facets of his experience, he spoke softly and haltingly. He made very little eye contact and generally presented the picture of someone who wanted to attract as little notice as possible. In addition to some very self-defeating attitudes about himself and others, it was very clear that Ansel also had severe social skill deficits. These deficits served to reinforce and compound his fears of others.

Barriers to the Reception of Social Support

Of the four levels at which barriers to the flow of social support can operate (i.e., the client, the natural network, the broader social context, the physical environment), client-based barriers seemed to be the most significant determinant of the amount and quality of assistance Ansel received. Certainly it would have been helpful if his parents were more active in recognizing and responding to his needs, and in a better world more awareness of, and outreach to, underemployed, "lost" young adults would characterize the broader social context. However, even in his less-than-perfect situation it seemed that many more supportive resources were available than Ansel was developing and using.

At the informal level, at least two of his co-workers apparently were willing to relate to him more extensively than he was willing to allow. In the community, there were still former schoolmates and neighbors who probably could have been contacted. In terms of formal support resources, there were church groups, activityfocused clubs, and volunteer programs that might have served as entry points to supportive relationships.

There were, then, at least adequate informal and formal support sources available to Ansel. However, his fear of negative judgment and consequent rejection kept him on the fringes of his social world — close enough to be a part of it, but removed enough to keep himself out of the view and attention of most other people around him.

My almost exclusive focus on client-based support barriers with Ansel had another determinant — his consistent resistance to the involvement of his significant others in the counseling process. Even though he came to counseling regularly for over a year, he did not tell his father, mother, or co-workers that he did so. Though he reached out to counseling as a way of breaking the impasse he was experiencing in his life, he expected that other people would criticize or think less of him if they knew he was seeing a "shrink." In light of his fear of, and resistance to, network-involving interventions, focus remained on help-

ing Ansel become more effective in establishing and maintaining interpersonal relationships. Any attempt to modify the informal network was
done indirectly, by working with Ansel to help him develop the skills
for enhancing others' awareness of, and inclination to respond to, his
needs for emotional, material, informational, or appraisal support.

Ansel's Dysfunctional Beliefs and Their Consequences

Ansel's low level of self-esteem was readily apparent early in the
counseling process. He used such adjectives as "ugly," "weird," and
"dumb" to describe himself. He also referred to himself as a "burnout"
and a "loser." In turn, his poor opinion of himself led him to believe
that others disliked him and wouldn't want to have anything to do with
him. He expected rejection and punishment from others because he
considered himself worthy of rejection and punishment. Thus others
were viewed as likely sources of pain and hurt, and (within his logic)
best avoided.

Another aspect of Ansel's self-view that seemed to reinforce his
avoidance of others was his belief that he was a fragile person. Early in
the counseling process, he often responded to encouragements to try out
one strategy or another to make contact with potential supporters with
variant of "I couldn't take it if they laughed at me or told me to get lost."
Because he thought of himself as weak and easily overwhelmed, he
couldn't risk rejection because he believed that the consequences would
be devastating.

In sum, we can see Ansel as a young man loaded down with a number
of beliefs about himself and others that prompted fearful, anxious
feelings when he had to deal with people. Even the anticipation of
interacting with all but the most trusted persons precipitated fear.
Clearly Ansel felt that others were best avoided by "a person like me,"
and he had moved toward building a life-style in which he had emotional intimacy with no one and ongoing social contact with only a few
persons.

Interventions Focused on Ansel's Dysfunctional Beliefs

At the beginning of counseling I spent much of our time together
simply listening to Ansel's outpouring of unhappiness and fear in an
attentive, caring way. If Ansel was fearful of interpersonal closeness, it
seemed apparent to me that a relationship of trust had to be established

between us. At first, he was nervous and cautious. Gradually, he became more comfortable and disclosing in his interaction with me. This emphasis on relationship building can be considered to have served two functions.

First, I expected that reducing the amount of anxiety Ansel experienced in his interaction with me would make it easier for him to begin considering his views of, and beliefs about, himself and others in a more differentiated, flexible manner. I believed that with a greater sense of psychological safety, Ansel would be able to attend to new data from his own experience, and to perspectives and information provided by me. Indeed, as time went on, he was able to back off from his blanket condemnation of himself as a "burnout" and recognize that while there were certainly aspects of his life situation that warranted change, there were others (e.g., successful employment, good grooming) of which he could be proud. As time went on, he began to recognize that much of the condemnation he saw in others was based on his assumption that others would not like him because he did not like himself.

Second, as Ansel's level of trust and comfort increased, he became more robust in his ability to be open when I confronted his assumptions and beliefs. As time went on, he came to be able to catch his own unwarranted generalizations. At one point he said, "I know, I know, you don't have to say it. Not everyone in the world is looking at me and judging me!" Our own interaction provided Ansel with experience that, implicitly and explicitly, forced him to question his preexisting assumptions about himself and others.

Our interaction can also be conceptualized as "direct experience" that provided Ansel with new information he could use in thinking about himself and others. Our exchange provided Ansel with firsthand experience about how he was seen by at least one other person. Although, as a counselor, I did not represent the typical person he might meet, our interaction did provide him with continuing experience that called into question his assumption that others were critical and disposed to be hurtful.

From my perspective, one of the most significant events in working with Ansel occurred rather late in the counseling process, after he we had completed many of the cognitive and behaviorally oriented interventions aimed at making it easier for him to establish and expand supportive relationships. From the beginning, it was my belief that there was a strong connection between his mother's abandonment a few years before and Ansel's withdrawal from others. I raised this possibility with

him several times, but his early response was to minimize the importance of this event. He didn't blame his mother, he said; he just wished
she lived closer. He attributed his current lack of friends to the impact
of moving and graduation from high school rather than stemming from
a relatively focused decline in his willingness to get close to others after
his mother moved away.

After nearly a year of counseling, when he had markedly altered his
views of, and behavior toward, others, Ansel returned to a discussion
of the impact of his mother's rejection of him.

Ansel: You know, what I'm learning is that most people aren't so bad, and
that even if someone mocks you out or doesn't like you, it's not the end
of the world.

Counselor: I guess you haven't always felt that way.

Ansel: Well, I used to. When I was growing up I had friends I hung around
with. You know, I wasn't class president or anything, but I had friends —
wasn't someone who had to run away whenever anyone came close.

Counselor: Then it changed.

Ansel: Yeah, it changed. I guess it was my mom. If my own mother didn't
want me, if her boyfriend and his kids were more important to her than
me, who could you trust?

Counselor: So you decided not to let anybody get close enough to hurt
you like that again.

Ansel: I'm not sure I decided that, but I sure got scared of people. It was
weird.

This insight, coming as it did toward the end of the counseling
process, seemed to represent a circling back by Ansel to tie up some
loose emotional strands. He had made considerable progress in moving
toward being able to establish and maintain relationships with persons
who could meet his support needs and for whom he could also be a
source of support. Now he seemed able to look squarely at the pain
caused by his mother's rejection and to follow the trail of its affect on
his relationships with others. On the other hand, he continued to dismiss
the original abandonment by his biological parents as having any
connection to his uneasiness with people. He may have been right, and
certainly his progress in developing and maintaining interpersonal

relationships suggests that even if there were unresolved issues, he was nevertheless able to experience considerable growth.

I believe the establishment of a relationship of trust, based on Carl Rogers's (1962) core relationship conditions (empathic understanding, acceptance, counselor authenticity), produced positive results in and of themselves in the form of increased perceptual and cognitive flexibility. Moreover, the trust Ansel had in our relationship provided a foundation for the behaviorally focused interventions that dominated the latter portion of my work with him.

Ansel's Dysfunctional Behavior and Behavioral Gaps

Ansel's life was controlled by his withdrawal from others. While he went to work regularly, he hung on the fringes of the work situation. He seldom initiated contact with others, except as a direct requirement of doing his job. He engaged in conversation with Gladys and Terry, but seldom did so unless they initiated the interaction. We've also seen that Ansel had very little interaction with his father. Apparently, while he did not actively avoid his father, he also did not go out of his way to interact with him.

Beyond work and home, Ansel had only the most superficial contact with others. He took public transportation to and from work, but he reported that he seldom talked to anyone. What friends he said he had were, in actuality, persons with whom he had once interacted, but had not seen in several years.

Ansel expressed his avoidance directly and indirectly. In addition to not seeking contact with others, his whole demeanor communicated that he wanted to keep his distance. He generally avoided making eye contact. Also, he spoke quietly, with the direction of his speech projected downward or to one side as a consequence of avoiding direct eye contact.

In addition to the things that Ansel did to avoid or minimize significant social exchange with others, his lack of social skill served to make the development of supportive relationships problematic. One of his chief concerns was that he didn't know what to say to other people. He described himself as "tongue-tied," and he thought that other people found him stupid because he didn't know what to say.

As Ansel became more comfortable in the counseling situation, it became clear that his conversational difficulties resulted more from the inhibitory effects of anxiety than from any real intellectual or mechanical deficit. However, Ansel did seem to be rather restricted in terms of his knowledge of and/or ability to use a range of "gimmicks" that facilitate conversation (e.g., asking questions about topics or events that are known to be of interest to the other person). If he ever had developed a rich repertoire of conversational skills, it was clear that his isolation from others had given him little opportunity to polish and maintain them. His isolation had also cut him off from developing a body of information about verbal and nonverbal cues that can be used to gauge the progress of a conversation with another.

Interventions Focused on Ansel's Behavioral Barriers

In a broad sense, the relationship establishment activities previously described can be viewed as extinguishing the anxiety that Ansel experienced in social interaction. There was no gain to avoidance in the counseling situation. My acceptance of him held whether he was being direct (with reference to both the content and process of his conversation) with me or was protecting himself with quietness or obliqueness. The implicit message of my acceptant stance was clear: "Ansel, in this situation, no one is going to do the things you fear so much."

Desensitization

While there were many things about relationship formation and maintenance that Ansel could learn in the counseling situation itself, it was also true that a greater willingness to open himself to more extensive interaction with others would provide an even wider, more varied learning context. With this in mind, about a month into our working together, I suggested a desensitization intervention to Ansel, pointing out that it would be a way of making it easier for him to start making contact with new people, as well as allowing him to deepen his relationships with people he already knew.

Ansel was given training in relaxation in the counseling situation. Also, I provided him with an audiotape that he used at home to practice until he could quickly move himself into a deeply relaxed state. Incidentally, the utility of this relaxation training extended far beyond its specific use in the desensitization process. Ansel quickly found that he could (as he put it) "talk himself down" in advance of situations he believed would otherwise be stressful. This proved a very versatile resource in helping him extend the specific gains that were established in our work together.

Following the typical desensitization process, Ansel and I put together a list of stressful events involving contact with others. These situations ranged from incidental contact with his father (least stressful) to asking Gladys's daughter for a date (most stressful). It took many weeks for us to work through the hierarchy. Ansel showed much of the same hesitance and lack of ease in this work that he experienced in his everyday functioning. Our typical procedure was to spend some time at the beginning and end of each session simply talking; in between, the desensitization procedure was carried out.

Throughout the process, I prompted Ansel to begin trying out, in "real life," the sorts of actions he was beginning to be able to visualize comfortably in counseling. Pointing out to him that nothing succeeds like success, I suggested that he be conservative in determining the situations for which he was ready. Increasingly, as we proceeded, Ansel reported he was talking to the people who were a part of his usual comings and goings. He also found that he was able to stay in interactions longer, rather than simply saying a few things and retreating, as had been his usual way. Even without any specific training in relationship initiation and maintenance skills, Ansel found if he just relaxed and didn't run away, conversations were not as difficult as he had feared. Also, he was taking note of how others handled interaction. For example, he noticed that Gladys typically began her conversations with people by inquiring about their families, complimenting them on their appearance, or commenting on something that had been on television recently.

Conversational Skill Training

Although Ansel quickly began using his greater interpersonal comfort to identify, then try, the conversational strategies of others around him, we also spent some of our time in a systematic effort to help him acquire greater skill in conversing with others. His fear about not knowing what to say when talking with others was one of the major barriers to interacting with others at the beginning of counseling.

The starting point for enhancing Ansel's ability to engage in conversation was determining what his existing skills and deficits were in this domain. Consistent with the procedure suggested by Kelly (1982), a relatively informal, unstructured assessment procedure was followed. First, I drew on my own (by now) extensive interaction with Ansel as a basis for getting a picture of his conversational skills. Second, as we formally moved into a skill training format, I asked Ansel to role-play several conversations that he had recently had with others. Ansel enacted one fairly extended conversation (centered on keeping the house picked up) he had had with his father. The other conversation he portrayed was a brief interaction he had recently had with his co-worker Terry about a televised college basketball game.

It seemed to me that Ansel's primary skill deficiencies lay in several of the areas identified by Christoff and Kelly (1985) as those most typically focused on in the skill training literature. Specifically, Ansel's ability to initiate and sustain verbal interaction suffered from weaknesses with regard to:

- making self-disclosing statements;
- offering positive opinion statements;
- reinforcing or acknowledging others;
- maintaining appropriate voice level; and
- maintaining an appropriate nonverbal dimension to verbal communication (e.g., smiling, maintaining eye contact, holding a comfortable and open posture).

Some of these skill areas had already begun to improve. In our interaction, Ansel displayed an increasing amount of eye contact and his voice level became stronger. Generally, his nonverbal presentation came to be more relaxed and reflected a greater openness. He reported that the effects of the desensitization training made it easier for him to relax around other people. With this increased comfort came a more direct, pleasing appearance in terms of his nonverbal self-presentation.

The training process focusing on improving Ansel's conversational skill consisted primarily of (a) providing him with a description of the skill, (b) demonstrating it for him, (c) asking him to demonstrate it for me, (d) coaching him concerning inaccuracies or errors he showed in his presentation, (e) discussing with him the things that made it easy or difficult for him to use the skill, and (f) setting up a homework task for him to carry out during the ensuing week.

At the next session, we would usually review his progress (or lack thereof) during the past week. If he had encountered difficulty, we would discuss the nature of the problem and often move to a role-played enactment of the situation in which he had had that difficulty. The role playing helped to provide me with a basis for identifying the specific nature of the difficulty. Further use of role playing for modeling and practice purposes would follow.

Conclusion

Ansel is a good example of a person whose lack of skill in interpersonal relations stems from the inhibiting effect of anxiety rather than from serious lack of skill. The acceptance of the counseling relationship and the greater relaxation resulting from the desensitization intervention allowed Ansel to bring forth those responses of which he was capable but had feared to make. Also, the disconfirmation and modification of many of his beliefs about the hurtfulness of others eliminated much of the apprehension he had attached to social exchange. Increasingly, it became possible for him to approach and stay with people. More and more, he was able to use those social skills that he had long possessed, as well as those acquired in, or enhanced by, the skill training we did.

This is not to say that Ansel suddenly blossomed into a confident, socially skillful person. At the end of my regular contact with him he could still be called a quiet, shy person. However, previously he had been painfully shy; now he was cautious rather than fearful. He was not nearly as boxed-in by his withdrawal, and he was able to pursue his personal goals, even when that involved meeting new people and engaging in something more than superficial exchange.

One of the first self-enhancement actions that Ansel took was to get his driver's license. He enrolled in a private driver instruction program and quickly acquired the information and skill required to pass both written and performance tests. Though initially his lack of access to a car prevented him from using his license, the simple fact that he had one seemed to boost his self-esteem greatly. Eventually, his father relented and allowed him to use the car. The older man would sometimes ask Ansel to run errands in the car, and occasionally would even ask if his son wanted to use it to go to the movies or a ball game. Buying his own car was one of Ansel's top priorities.

With regard to his work, he reported that he was more comfortable and outgoing. The preexisting relationships with Terry and Gladys were expanded. Terry, though not a close friend, became someone with whom he would go to sports events, and occasionally go out drinking. Terry had even tried to fix him up with a date. Ansel backed away from that offer, but he was interested and felt that sooner or later he would ask Terry to set him up again. He got to know more of his co-workers and was included in the periodic away-from-work socializing that took place. His acceptance of invitations established him as "one of the crowd" and reversed several co-workers' views of him as an odd person who didn't want to be included.

As much as his comfort with the interpersonal dimensions of work increased, Ansel continued to believe that his job did not have the potential to allow him to achieve what he might. He believed that he had technical abilities and interests that would go unfulfilled if he stayed in the food service field. I supported his ideas about pursuing some course work at the local community college. While in my office, he called the counseling service at the college to set up an appointment for information about course offerings and program alternatives and requirements. We spent part of a session role playing a discussion with the counselor to help Ansel clarify his own questions and needs and to aid him in making his expectations about the counselor more concrete and realistic. At the end of our regular sessions, Ansel had enrolled in an introductory electronics course to explore his interest in that field.

The one area that seemed most resistant to any observable progress was the development of heterosexual relationships. Ansel came to counseling stating that having a girlfriend was his greatest need. We had focused on his concerns in our discussions and in the desensitization intervention. While he was more comfortable around women (even women of his own age whom he found attractive) he found it difficult to move beyond quiet friendliness to develop and expand his relationships with them. He was, however, not uncomfortable with his relative backwardness in this area. Just the ability to look at and talk to women was great progress, he believed. He was sure that when the time was right he would begin dating. Terry had offered his help, and he saw taking courses as opening up the possibility of meeting a whole new group of people — especially women.

In summary, Ansel was on his way. The self-based barriers that had separated him from others were substantially reduced. Increasingly, he was able to approach and maintain contact with others. This expanded social interaction opened up previously absent resources of emotional, material, informational, and appraisal support. These resources made his day-to-day functioning more rewarding and meaningful. They also eased the tasks of beginning college, developing an intimate relationship, and setting a new career direction.

Chapter Nine

Other Directions

In the previous chapters, it has been difficult to keep from dashing off in a number of different directions while discussing how the lives and experiences of clients are affected by social support issues. Consideration of the application of support-related concepts and procedures to counseling practice presents us with many possible avenues for exploration and discussion. How could it be otherwise? As we have seen, social support is a process basic to the development of humanness itself. Its presence or absence bears heavily on the development and maintenance of personal effectiveness. Therefore, we should expect to find support-related issues and events surfacing in almost any area of human endeavor.

In this last chapter, I would like explore a few of these avenues. While ultimately related to, and having implications for, counseling practice, they may be somewhat away from the direct, online work of many counselors. Most of these directions (e.g., conceptualizations of human effectiveness) have a long-standing presence in counseling and counseling-related literature. Others (e.g., cross-cultural applications and support groups) have a more contemporary ring to them.

This final chapter is designed, then, to round out a consideration of how the construct of social support can inform counseling theory and practice. The construct will be used as a springboard to pursue issues and activities somewhat beyond the range of previous chapters.

The Effective Person

One reading of this book is that it has stressed the importance of individuals' being willing, and having the skills, to make contact with others in order to gain the resources (emotional, material, informational, appraisal) needed to cope with life's demands. In Chapter 4, we considered how client-based dysfunctionality of attitude and behavior can interfere with individuals' reception of social support. In Chapter 5, we examined counseling strategies and interventions for removing these barriers. The message behind those chapters is that if clients can be helped to become more self-confident, "nicer" to others, and more socially facile, their chances of getting the assistance they need increase.

On the one hand, the assertion that people need people is obvious and incontestable. However, it is difficult to push this perspective very far without also feeling the need to raise some qualifications. Certainly, everyone needs help sometimes, but it is also important to be able to stand on one's own, right? It is nice to have family and friends to depend on, but one should not be too dependent or one loses their respect, true? Clearly, there is a deep ambivalence held by many of us with regard to needing and receiving assistance from others. In the extreme, to need help is to be viewed as ineffective, incompetent, and childish. This would seem to be particularly true for persons who use traditional sex role formulations as a basis for judging their acceptability as well as that of others. Stereotypically, to be a man is to stand tall and alone, to function independently, and to be self-sufficient. While dependency and lack of self-sufficiency may be somewhat more acceptable in traditional formulations of the female role and behavior, even here there are limits beyond which a woman goes only at the risk of being viewed as an unwarranted drain on others.

Yet, recognition of the importance of mutual assistance also runs very deep in human affairs. Barkow (1977) and other psychobiological theorists asserted that altruism and individual-to-individual aid is the foundation on which successful groups and species are based. There is an apparent sense to the view that successful individual and group development is furthered by an arrangement in which individuals lacking the material or nonmaterial resources for dealing with general or specific life demands are assisted by others who have a sufficiency of such resources. Moreover, unless we conceptualize individuals as absolutely falling into one of two groups (the haves and have-nots) with regard to the possession of resources needed for effective functioning, the ability to be both giver and receiver of assistance would seem to be a valuable attribute. The demands of life are complex, the personal resources of individuals limited, and persons who never find themselves in the position of needing help are either operating in very tightly controlled contexts or kidding themselves.

Also, we can note that various models of human effectiveness are on both sides of the dependence/independence issue. Most such statements (e.g., Allport, 1963; Heath, 1980; Maslow, 1954; Rogers, 1962; Shoben, 1957) focus on the importance of autonomy, selfdirection, and independence. However, they also highlight the centrality of ties to others in the attention they pay to the importance of identifying one's own welfare with that of others, and deep relationships with at least a few persons.

Traveling alone, standing on one's own, supports our notions of individualism and allows us, as the adage "one travels fastest by traveling alone" points out, to pursue our individual goals of achievement and identity (apparently) most efficiently. However, the image of the rugged, self-sufficient individual who needs nothing from anyone is, I believe, not only a distortion of reality, but the source of great mischief in the functioning of individuals and groups. Individualism is, of course, a relative concept. Our humanness is based on a process of socialization through which the physical care of others—their direct and implicit teaching—shapes us into individuals who can exist within, and contribute to the life of, the immediate and extended human groups that make up our social context. Continually, the efforts of others, seen and unseen, realized and unrealized, support us. If we strive and accomplish, that is made possible by the fact that there is a foundation of material and nonmaterial culture, not of our own making, on which we build.

While there may be variation among groups and subgroups with regard to their specific formulation of the proper balance between individual autonomy and obligation to the collective, any successful group must have mechanisms that provide for an exchange of resources between those who (either in general or at any particular time) are sufficient and those who are not. Clearly, such exchange works to the benefit of the individuals who are assisted in dealing with situations that otherwise would be overwhelming. The exchange also benefits the group by increasing the likelihood that the overall health of its membership will be maintained.

However, such exchange can operate effectively only if (a) there is a sufficient pool of resources to be drawn on (that is, there are, at any point in time, enough members who are functioning well enough to provide the needed resources), (b) the "sufficient" members are willing to extend the needed resources, and (c) the "insufficient" members are willing to ask for and/or receive the resources they need. Simply, this boils down to an assertion that both group and individual welfare are served by individuals who are (at least sometimes and in some respects) competent enough to be able to assist others, altruistic enough to be willing to help, secure enough in their own worth to be able to ask for assistance when they need it, and/or accept it when it's offered. How does this assertion translate into a formulation of the effective person, and what are the implications of that formulation for our goals and activities in working with clients?

First of all, it seems that however great clients' needs for assistance may be at any particular point in time, and however appropriate it may be for them to receive assistance from others, we also need to be concerned about helping them maintain and/or develop resources and competencies that will allow them to look after themselves and to be of assistance (perhaps at another time) to others. As the research of Froland et al. (1979) suggested, supporters can be depleted and become disaffected. Persons who can use help from others as an element in strengthening their personal competence (thus moderating their subsequent need for assistance) reduce the likelihood that their supporters will be drained dry. However, increased competence of clients has broader implications than just reducing the burnout of supporters. Stronger, more competent clients have more resources from which to draw in offering support. Clearly, the offering of such support to others (perhaps even former supporters) not only benefits the receivers, it also enhances the self-esteem of the now-supporter, strengthens the bond between the persons involved, and (by extension) strengthens the broader group.

Beyond the issue of helping clients develop the skills and competence needed to maintain themselves in ongoing reciprocal relationships, we also need to consider the attitudinal sets that underlie the ability to be both supporter and support recipient. Easy exchange of supportive resources requires that supporters be sufficiently empathic to be able to recognize others' needs and altruistic enough to care about alleviating those needs. As we have seen, narcissism can lead people to be insensitive to and/or uncaring of others. In such cases competence is "kept home," and a family member, co-worker, neighbor, or friend, now in need of assistance but potentially a supporter, is not served. This may be disadvantageous to the person needing help and (at some point in the future) to the nonsupporter.

Another facet of this discussion of the role of attitudes in the flow or blockage of social support is a consideration of those attitudes that affect clients' comfort or discomfort with receiving support. I believe that one of the factors that allows people to accept help with grace and appropriate gratitude is the ability to recognize that needing help with regard to a particular situation is only a part of who they are; there are other strengths and competencies that continue concurrently with the need for assistance. Certainly, clients who can preserve a continuing sense of worth are more apt to be able to look back to the times when they have filled the role of supporter and to believe that they continue to have resources that will make it possible to do so again.

Fisher and his colleagues (1988) pointed out that it is usually easier for persons to accept help from members of their natural network than from strangers because natural networks have norms that do not demand immediate reciprocation of assistance from kith and kin. While we feel obligated to return a gift from a stranger quickly (and hence we tend refuse the gift if we are not in a position to reciprocate), we can be more relaxed with a friend. Perhaps, within the network, any given exchange of support takes place in the context of past and anticipated exchanges. These recollections and anticipations counterbalance asymmetry that may exist at any given moment.

In sum, a social support-oriented perspective on the issue of personal effectiveness highlights the importance of reciprocity in relationships. Reciprocity, as we saw in Chapter 5, also emerges as an important issue in the support-related conceptual and empirical literature. The centrality of reciprocity focuses our attention on the importance of helping clients develop personal competence to enhance their self-esteem, reduce the likelihood of supporter depletion, strengthen the continuing viability of clients' support system, and (most generally) contribute to the effectiveness of the immediate and more extensive social groupings of which these clients are a part.

Primary Prevention

A recent television advertisement for motor oil traces the hazards of not keeping a regular car maintenance schedule. Having just informed a car owner that major engine repair could have been avoided with frequent oil changes, the solemn mechanic turns to the camera and says something like "It's your choice — you can pay me now or pay me later." The message is one that underlies primary prevention efforts in the medical and mental health fields — factors that can lead to the development of human dysfunction, if ignored, will eventually cause trouble. Often the trouble will be greater than that involved in attending to possible difficulties while things are still working well. The primary prevention approach thus runs contrary to another bit of folk wisdom also relating to mechanical contrivances — "If it ain't broken, don't fix it."

Another primary prevention-relevant message (this one seen on a bumper sticker) tells us, "If you think education is expensive, try ignorance!" This admonition, similar to the message of the motor oil commercial, bases its appeal for preventive intervention on economics — it's cheaper to prevent a crisis than to remedy one. In a society focused on material gain, where the economic "bottom line" is often the primary basis on which decisions are made, it should not surprise us that financial rather than humanitarian values should be put forward to support the importance of education. But perhaps that is being ungracious — the economic base for primary prevention is a real and a valid one, provides a selling point, and certainly warrants our attention.

Conyne (1987) made a carefully constructed and impassioned case for the relevance of primary prevention to the counseling field. He suggested that primary prevention can provide a conceptual base that is coherent, consistent with our historical roots, and capable of serving as a rich source of strategies and interventions. If, indeed, the focus on essentially normal individuals, health, and the development of competence in our literature is something more than rhetoric (Hansen, 1981), then the growing attention now being focused on relating primary prevention to counseling theory and practice is long overdue and represents a logical focus for strengthening (some would say, at last developing) a clear professional identity.

Though primary prevention is interesting, perhaps even an issue about which to become enthusiastic, what does it have to do with social support-oriented perspectives and practices in counseling? As Conyne pointed out in his synthesis of varying formulations of primary prevention, a central element of such definitions is that primary prevention is a proactive, before-the-fact approach to dysfunctionality; that is, it attempts to prevent the occurrence of dysfunctionality rather than focusing on remedying what is already in place. Given this focus, it is logical that those contexts typically playing an important role in the development of personal effectiveness or ineffectiveness would receive particular attention in primary prevention-focused efforts. Conyne (1987) noted that such contexts can be conceptualized as broadly as "society" itself, and doing so can lead the primary prevention-oriented mental health worker to focus on the remediation of such macrosystem causes of individual dysfunctionality as racism, sexism, or exploitive economic practices (pp. 129-130).

My concern with the impact of personal support systems leads me to focus on those social contexts that are closer to individuals (closer in the sense that the people are known to one another as individuals and typically have frequent, direct contact) as the contexts within which to apply the concepts and approaches of primary prevention. Conyne (1987) suggested that interventions aimed at these immediate, personal social contexts involve "microsocial change" efforts (pp. 133-134). The family, peer group, and work group are examples of such social contexts. They often play a powerful role in the development and maintenance of personal effectiveness. Conversely, they may contribute to the onset and continuance of dysfunctionality.

In Chapter 1, I noted that House (1981) cited three different effects of social support: (a) improving the context to reduce or eliminate or reduce the presence of potentially harmful factors, (b) strengthening individuals as a means of reducing their vulnerability to future stressors, and (c) buffering individuals against the harmful effects of stressors currently being experienced. As House noted, the first two effects (which are, in measurement terms, main effects) operate before the onset of stress and thus could be considered primary preventive in nature (pp. 30-40). In contrast, the "buffering effect" (i.e., the ability of social support to help individuals cope with the negative impact of stressors as those stressors are experienced) would relate to secondary prevention (i.e., efforts that serve to limit or reduce the impact of dysfunctionality that has already become established).

When counselors intervene with such microsystems as families, informal peer groups, or work groups to increase the flow of social support (perhaps by initiating such activities as skill training or raising awareness of available alternatives for action), we strengthen the groups' ability to help their members deal with the onset of future stressors. Supportive microsystems can "troubleshoot" for members, steering them away from pathogenic factors, thereby helping them maintain health. Supportive microsystems can also help their members develop higher levels of robustness than might otherwise be true and thus be more resistant to the negative impact of stressors they subsequently encounter. People spend much of their time within the context of the natural network; thus they are readily available, accepted places of attention and influence.

Some of the strategies identified by Conyne (1987) for increasing the primary prevention potential of microsystems (all of which fall under a broad strategy of education) are "focused information dissemination," "competency training," and "training of care givers" (pp. 135-141). When we contribute to members' ability and willingness to be supportive, we enrich the potential of these groups, and, thus, we are carrying out primary prevention. In turn, we strengthen the systems' ability to act as agents of primary prevention. By initiating such competency-enhancing programs as communication skills training for workers and supervisors or offering parenting classes for parents-to-be, we are, in effect, making an investment in the future — spending relatively few of our resources now in order to avoid a much costlier bill later. We strengthen people to reduce the likelihood of future damage.

Support Groups

If, with regard to group work, the 1960s were the decade of the encounter group, the 1980s must be the decade of the support group. The form and focus of support groups vary widely. Free-standing and under the aegis of parent programs and institutions, they can be found in a wide range of locations and contexts.

While it may be true, as Killilea (1976) noted, that often an important element in their formation is the rejection of professional help in favor of peer help, we can also note that support groups seem quite compatible to use by professional mental health workers. The particular form such use takes varies. The professional can be the initiator, the continuing formal leader, an occasional provider of needed information, a process consultant, or a combination of any of these roles.

As a counseling practitioner with a particular interest in group work, I have logged many hours in a wide range of group procedures. These experiences have ranged from information-focused group orientation procedures to highly personal, group counseling sessions where self-disclosure and personal risk taking were highlighted. One focus of my interest in support groups has been to determine how, if at all, they differ from other group modalities traditionally used by counselors and other helping professionals.

It is my belief that any group procedure that is genuinely a *group* procedure centers on mutual help (or self-help, if the self is defined as a group of persons facing similar difficulties). Thus the presence of mutual help or peer-based assistance, contrary to Levine's (1988) view, does not provide a unique characteristic of such groups. Also, if support is viewed as a multifaceted phenomenon that includes such disparate activities as information giving, material assistance, provision of feedback, and offering of comfort, any effective group, whether or not it is conducted by a counselor, will be a group in which support is exchanged.

It seems to me that if there is something unique about support groups, it lies not in the fact that their members share a common concern in the basic therapeutic mechanisms (Yalom, 1975) they employ, or whether they have peer or professional leadership. Rather, elsewhere I have suggested that the matter of why the members lack the social support needed to deal with their concerns can provide a conceptually coherent and practically useful basis for delineating what is, and is not, a support group (Pearson, 1983).

My view is that support groups should be considered surrogate support systems, provided or sought out when individuals lack support primarily because of factors not having to do with their own characteristics or actions. Such non-client-based factors may relate to features of their physical situation (e.g., isolation), or those of their existing natural system (e.g., familial rejection, supporters' lack of needed resources).

The introduction of a surrogate system to replace, or supplement absent or deficient social support stands in contrast to an intervention (even a group intervention) aimed at being of assistance to persons who lack sufficient or appropriate social support because their attitudes and behaviors act as barriers to the flow of social support. I believe that helping people establish or reestablish supportive relationships with the functional systems from which they have become estranged because of their (the clients') dysfunctional attitudes and behaviors is the arena of counseling or psychotherapy.

If support groups are defined as "groups created by professional mental health workers, or by 'peers' to fill the support needs of persons whose social support deficiencies result from factors having to do with the physical environment, natural system, or broader social context," then many groups currently labeled support groups would be called something else. In many cases, they would be considered counseling or psychotherapy groups since (whether a professional or a peer serves as the leader) they seek to remedy such negative, client-based factors as those discussed in Chapter 4 (e.g., shyness, lack of social skill, aggressiveness toward others) that reduce support availability.

I believe such narrowing of the use of the "support group" label would be of benefit to both initiators and participants in mental health-oriented groups of whatever name or form. I have suggested that many of the groups currently passing under the label of support group would have been called something else (e.g., encounter group, group psychotherapy) a decade ago (Pearson, 1983). The support group designation is one that seems to be less threatening to many people than many of the more long-standing labels (e.g., a counseling group for students with college adjustment difficulties or a psychotherapy group for persons with substance abuse problems). Making assistance more palatable to persons who would otherwise avoid it is a reasonable concern; however, to mask the fact that the changes on which the group focuses may be quite basic and extensive can be of disservice to both the leadership and members.

My intent here is not to assert that counseling and psychotherapy done within a peer group model is never appropriate. The apparent effectiveness of the Alcoholics Anonymous format for treating many varieties of substance abuse suggests that the peer-centered model can be a powerful stimulant to fundamental attitudinal and behavioral changes in persons resistant to other treatment modalities. Rather, my plea is simply that when a label is used, it should provide useful information. I believe the view of support groups I have put forth provides a definite enough set of referents to allow reliable decisions to be made about what is or is not a support group. This enhanced reliability would benefit persons needing to make decisions about the relevance, possible impact, and demands on leaders and members of a group they might be considering leading or joining.

Finally, beyond the issue of developing a more precise use of the label "support group," what are the other implications of the point of view I am suggesting? Perhaps one of the most obvious is that when we work with clients who seem to be dealing with life concerns in the absence (relative or absolute) of social support from their natural system, we would want to examine why that deficiency exists. If we found that a young man's social isolation (and consequent difficulty adjusting to a new work situation) resulted from a long-standing fear of people, we would view him as appropriately served by a counseling or psychotherapy group. If his isolation resulted simply from the fact that his new job site is two thousand miles away from his home and he was having more difficulty expanding his natural system than would be the case if he were closer to home, a support group (a surrogate natural system that would serve as a transitional resource until a new system is established) would be appropriate.

Finally, as counselors whose training and role focus on assistance to essentially normal individuals dealing with life concerns appropriate to their developmental status, what are the sorts of support groups we might sponsor or encourage? Applying my views of both support groups and counseling, it seems to me that the groups of most relevance to our work would be those focused on meeting the needs of persons coping with normal life transitions that separate them from their preexisting natural systems and/or confront them with needs and demands to which their preexisting system is not equipped to respond.

The young man just discussed exemplifies the first situation; that is, his transition (moving to a new work situation) was complicated by physical separation from the natural system within which he operated before the move. What would be an example of a client who experiences difficulties because of the natural system's limitations vis-à-vis the amount or type of social support needed? Consider a woman, dealing with the disruptive impact of divorce, whose natural system has had little or no contact with the realities of divorce and single parenthood. While her preexisting system might be quite effective in responding to her needs for material assistance, its resources for providing informational or appraisal support could be limited. If her natural system is limited in the ability to provide information or appraisal, participation in a support group for divorced persons could serve as an effective means of filling the gaps of her still available, but limited, natural system.

This view of support groups as surrogate systems that fill support gaps resulting from non-client-based barriers is consistent with Gottlieb's (1986) formulation of when their use is appropriate:

A support group approach is warranted when individuals are in stressful circumstances requiring the learning of new social norms, the acquisition of a new social identity, access to information (about thoughts, feelings, and behaviors) that is consensually validated, and opportunities to practice social skills and to establish new social ties with similar peers who may become members of the participants' social network.

If we wanted to take the additional step of considering how we could use support groups as a primary prevention strategy for our counseling clients, we would try to identify persons among our clientele who are at risk of experiencing difficulties with upcoming life transitions because they were separated from their natural support system or who have systems that might reasonably be expected not to possess resources sufficient or appropriate to the clients' needs. In general, natural systems that are already stressed with regard to the needed resources (e.g., a family that has long-standing financial difficulties), even if inclined to be of assistance, might have difficulty offering material support. Similarly, systems composed of persons whose life experience has given them little exposure to the changes required by clients' upcoming transitions will often be limited in their ability to provide relevant information. By identifying clients who are at risk because of such system-based factors, counselors can, either through referral or by creating a support group, provide linkages with surrogate systems that will be in place as the life transitions are encountered. In this manner, the transition can be eased and the likelihood of subsequent dysfunctionality reduced.

Cross-Cultural Counseling

Stepping back and viewing humanity as a whole, it is apparent, as Wohl (1981) and others noted, that counseling and psychotherapy are helping/healing procedures embraced by only a relatively few cultural groups. Because of our own cultural encapsulation (Kagan, 1964; Wren, 1962), we may be tempted to consider our views of psychological health and dysfunction and the processes through which they are established and restored are universal. However, we need only to turn to an extensive body of theoretical and applied literature (e.g., Beauvais, 1977; Cole & Bruner, 1972; Pedersen, 1979; Shweder & Bourne, 1982; Sue, 1978; Triandis, 1985) to be reminded that conceptualizations of such constructs as "psychological health," "personal effectiveness," and "help" vary greatly among cultural groups.

House (1981) has stressed the importance of carrying out research centered on specifying what types of social support have what sort of effect on health in what situations (p. 83). While he did not focus specifically on culture as a dimension of situational variation, doing so is certainly consistent with his views. Proceeding in this direction would lead us to examine whether or not there are particular types of assistance coming from particular sources that are differentially desired by, and/or effective with, persons from specific cultural groups. Extending our inquiry even further, we would concern ourselves with searching for intragroup variation in patterns associated with such subgroup variables as sex and age that further elaborate the question, "What sort of help, from whom, for what difficulties?"

Centering our consideration of cross-cultural issues on the role and operation of natural support systems, it should come as no surprise that while help from kith and kin is a basic feature of human functioning (Barkow, 1977; Kropotkin, 1972), there is considerable variation in the form and content that such help takes among cultural groups. For counselors whose practice touches on cross-cultural contexts and clientele, a recognition and understanding of the norms guiding the goals and operation of clients' natural systems can be a matter that is crucial to effectiveness.

Our attempt to gain such awareness and understanding can be guided by several questions:

- How does this group (or subgroup) define the proper balance between individual autonomy and responsibility to the group?
- How do members of the group define personal effectiveness and dysfunctionality?
- What does the group view as helpful, and what are the processes and actions through which it is provided to members?
- What are the most appropriate/effective ways of working with the natural support systems of clients belonging to this group?

Pursuing such questions can provide counselors with information that helps to make otherwise puzzling attitudes and behaviors of clients and their kith and kin more understandable. We may come to understand that a client's resistance to approaching his parents for assistance does not indicate fear or distrust of them, but simply represents his group's prescribed way of getting help in such situations (wait quietly until your need is noticed and it will be responded to). We may also arrive at a realization that actions and attitudes that are, to us, ineffective or unhelpful actually embody the group's best efforts to be of assistance. What we view as cold indifference is perhaps understood by both helpers and help receivers as a statement of respect and faith in the person's ultimate competence.

Finally, a willingness to enter into the perspectives and experience of others may provide strategies for gaining credibility with the persons who make up our clients' natural support systems (Sue, 1978). We may come to realize, for example, that before we will be viewed as an acceptable source of assistance, we will have to receive the informal approval of an influential religious or political figure in the community. The anthropologist's or qualitative researcher's notion of "gaining access" to the group (Bogdan & Bicklen, 1982) may be useful to counselors seeking to gain credibility with clients and their natural system.

Establishing entry to, and credibility with, the natural system are important in light of the system's influence in encouraging or discouraging clients to seek assistance from mental health workers (McKinlay, 1972). In exercising a "gatekeeping" function, kith and kin can prompt potential clients to seek out, and persist in, treatment. In contrast, influential system members can, through their opposition, make it difficult or impossible for contact to be made with outside helpers.

As difficult as it may be to gain data for answering the questions posed above, I believe that the biggest barrier generally lies in the willingness to pursue the questions rather than in our ability to do so. Pedersen (1981) noted that most people have a tendency to assume their views of the world absolutely reflect what is true and real. Such an assumption can lead to dismissing the significance of the worldviews of persons from other cultural groups. In the extreme, we may not see any need to pose such questions. With regard to natural support systems, we assume that our notions about the ways and circumstances in which kith and kin provide assistance hold for everyone. Therefore, we are convinced that we already understand what is, and ought to be, going on between clients and their families when support is given and received.

At a less extreme level of self-preoccupation, we may be aware of the fact that differences exist among cultural groups but consider such difference an annoyance, or, in Pedersen's (1981) words, "an enemy to be opposed and ultimately defeated" (p. 31). For example, a counselor may recognize that the family or peer group expects a client to defer to its preferences in making career decisions. If the counselor believes such decisions should be made by individuals themselves, free of pressure from others, clients may be encouraged to distance themselves from the influence of the informal system in order to "get the family off this kid's back!" To counselors who reject the importance and validity of cultural variation because of personal insecurity, interpersonal insensitivity, or deeply held ethnocentrism, empathic understanding becomes at best irrelevant and at worst a threat to what is good and true.

The argument over the validity of cultural relativism has undoubtedly been with humanity as long as the ability to be aware of intergroup differences. The presence of referenda recently put before voters in several states to establish English as the official state language is only one indication that profound disagreements about the value of cultural differences continue. While there are many ideological bases for recognizing cultural variation as a fact and possible source of benefit, let me suggest that there is also a very good pragmatic reason for doing so — they constitute the "ground" of persons' identity and provide the framework that provides meaning to their spiritual, social, and physical experience.

To the extent we dismiss the importance of the cultural context, we separate ourselves from data that can be extremely useful in understanding and working with clients; specifically, our assessment of the strengths, deficiencies, and operation of natural systems are apt to be incomplete and/or inaccurate. Without a clear understanding of the features and significance of clients' natural systems, the likelihood of viewing families and peer groups as the source of pathology increases (Pattison, 1973). This is true even if those groups are actually providing extensive assistance, albeit in a form and for goals that may not be viewed as important or acceptable by the counselor.

By pushing procedures and goals on clients and their supporters with little consideration of their views, values, and customs, we are apt to heighten defensiveness and fear and exacerbate any "us versus them" feeling that may already exist. Thus the task of establishing credibility with the clients and their significant others is impaired, and the likelihood of their being willing to sanction and cooperate with our interventions is reduced (Sue, 1978). That is not a very good way to build a relationship, especially if that relationship is one we hope will eventually open clients and their supporters to a wider range of views, beliefs, and behaviors.

I believe that the tendency to view differences (at both the individual and group levels) as troublesome and dangerous is a very deeply entrenched human characteristic. When it leads us to devalue and oppose the culture of our clients summarily, we are apt to strengthen the very processes in them that drives our own intolerance. My experience suggests that individuals are generally reality oriented enough to be able to adapt effectively to situations and events that challenge their cultural assumptions. However, when individuals and groups experience coercion (whether that coercion is deliberate or results from insensitivity), the issues of functionality and coping become mixed up with the need to defend personal and group integrity — old gods must then do battle with the new. If we are not willing to enter the experience of others, to present our views and ways as alternatives that may or may not have relevance to them, we run the risk of reducing the likelihood that the changes we would prompt will actually occur (Lewin & Grabbe, 1948).

Counselor Education

Interventions designed to remove client-based barriers to the flow of social support were presented and discussed in Chapter 5. These interventions should be comfortable turf for most counselors. Working with individuals in one-to-one and small group settings to modify or eliminate attitudes and/or behaviors that reduce the flow of social support is an extension of our typical client-focused routines. The interventions discussed in Chapter 7 that have clients' contexts as their target are apt to be less familiar ground. These approaches lead us to intervene with the people, groups, and physical settings that make up the contexts within which our clients live.

That we are less familiar (and usually less comfortable) with dealing with "contexts" than with clients themselves probably reflects the content and process of the programs in which we receive our training. In general, counselor education has been based on theoretical models of health, dysfunction, and change that center on intraindividual dynamics and processes. Typically, these models are drawn or extrapolated from individual-focused psychological perspectives rather than from the more group-related perspectives of sociology and anthropology. While marriage and family counseling and community counseling are specialties in which an appreciation for the importance of context is found, top to bottom counseling is a field in which the individual as an autonomous, deciding, acting entity is the central focus (Lewis & Lewis, 1983). If clients' contexts are considered, it is usually only to generate information on which client-focused interventions can be based. For example, we might examine the characteristic values, dynamics, and operations of clients' families or peer groups to increase our effectiveness in helping them resist or circumvent social influences that we/they judge to be harmful or ineffective.

By definition, social support involves other people. It is also a construct centered on the way others contribute to the establishment (in some cases, reestablishment) and maintenance of personal effectiveness. The very term *support system* focuses our attention on the interrelatedness of people and on the benefits that can, and often do, flow from this interrelatedness. We do not have to deny the reality of family dysfunction or harmful peer influence to take the position that the natural system is the most readily available, and preferred, source of assistance for most people. Also, we do not have to move to focusing exclusively on clients' social contexts as the targets of our interventions to assert that the ability to recognize, understand, and interface with natural systems are competencies that most counselors should possess.

As a matter of fact, there is no lack of recognition of the importance of context-focused understanding and skill in guidelines for counselor education promulgated by our professional associations. For example, the Council for the Accreditation of Counseling and Related Educational Programs (CACREP, 1987) requires (in its guidelines relating to the examination of "helping relationships") studies focused on "factors, other than participants, that influence helping processes including environmental and social factors, [and] relationships external to the helping process" (p. 26). Similarly, among the outcomes of the Third National Conference for Counseling Psychology (Gazda, Rude, Weissberg, 1988) were recommendations for the inclusion of internship experiences allowing students to develop competencies in carrying out interventions focused on systems and environments. Also, the necessity of stressing "the importance of observing and influencing human environments and activities in order to take a proactive stance toward prevention of such problems" was recommended (p. 363).

The relative lack of emphasis on the development of contextfocused understanding and skills is apparently less a matter of professional association awareness of their importance than of counselor educators' ability, or will, actually to do something about designing program components that foster their acquisition by students. Assuming that at least some of the understandings and skills needed for effectively working with natural support systems are apt not to be part of counselors' native (i.e., the consequence of everyday experience) resources, and that such behaviors are not apt to spring, full blown, without some assistance, what might be done to help counselors and counselors-to-be develop those competencies in preparation and continuing education programs?

Perhaps the first place to start is by systematically emphasizing the E (environment) in Kurt Lewin's (1951) classic assertion that behavior (B) is a function of the person (P) in interaction with the environment (E). "Context" has been defined by Eckenrode and Gore (1981) as "the embeddedness of life events within temporal, psychological and social situation that determine both the meaning of events and the individual and group capacities for dealing with them" (p. 46). The ability to focus on context ought to be a more central focus in preparing counselors to understand clients, develop helping interventions, and put those interventions into operation. Most counselor educators are products of Western cultures in which individuality and independence are stressed. Because of this, they may find it difficult to shift and broaden their perspectives to recognize the pervasive influence of the social and physical context.

Blocher's (1987) "developmental human ecology" represents just such an effort to put a focus on context at the center of the counseling process. Blocher indicates that the perspective of developmental human ecology is based on the following position:

> Rather than studying or intervening with the individual in isolation, we can take as a unit for analysis the "ecosystem," that is the person in context. An ecosystem is the immediate physical, social and psychological context of transaction between the individual and the environment. When we use the ecosystem as our unit of analysis, we begin to focus on, rather than to ignore or obscure the context within which behavior occurs. (1987, pp. 66-67)

Pushed by a heightened attention to the role of context in clients' development and change, counselor educators would find it reasonable and important to explore how ecological issues and events could be considered in the various components of their programs. For example, we might expect that counseling theory courses would give extensive consideration to theories that highlight contextual influences on individual behavior; for example, the work of Lewin (1951) or the sociologist Durkheim (1951). We might also expect that perspectives and concepts from such social science fields as social psychology and anthropology would be integrated into the material of counseling theory courses more than is currently the case.

Greater attention to contextual issues would also have an affect on the content and process of courses that focus on helping counselor education students develop intervention skills. For example, group procedures courses are a natural place for students to develop the skills needed to convene and interface with those coherent natural groups that are such an important part of clients' social context. Many group management and facilitation skills currently taught in group procedures courses can be transferred directly to family and peer groups. Students can be helped to see that convening clients' natural groups in order to enhance or create the supportive resources needed by clients can be an effective adjunct, or alternative, to formal helping activities. Broadly speaking, the point can be made that group facilitation and management skills can be aimed at targets other than just clients themselves.

Testing and assessment courses are another area of counselor education that has greater potential for contributing to counseling students' ability to recognize and act on contextual issues than is typically realized in current preparation programs. There is an extensive literature (e.g., Astin & Holland, 1961; Huebner & Corazzini, 1984; Moos, 1976; Stern, 1970) that examines the interplay between individuals and their physical and social contexts. This literature can provide counselors with general assessment approaches, and specific instruments useful in developing interventions to increase the supportiveness of the formal and informal contexts where our clients operate. Finally, as we have seen in Chapter 3, there are a number of research and clinical instruments that can be used to generate information about clients' support needs and resources.

The Third National Conference on Counseling Psychology (Gazda, Rude, & Weissberg, 1988) has recommended that practica and internships be designed to include opportunities for students to participate in context-focused interventions. The conference proceedings pointed out that the experience of assessing and working to modify detrimental environments can provide students with models and skills on which to build future context-focused interventions.

Finally, we can note the following as examples of how the examination of support as a contextual variable might find its way into the content and activities of other aspects of counselor education:

- consideration of the role of social support (e.g., information, appraisal, material assistance) from the family, peer group, or subgroup may play in vocational choice and career development;
- examination of how counseling services can be designed and implemented in ways that recognize and capitalize on the contributions of social support from natural systems;
- development of awareness of the manner in which the perspectives and style of clients' natural support systems can affect their expectations for, and evaluation of, counselors' helping efforts; and
- exploration of how the helping style and activities of peer groups and subgroups can be adapted to formal helping efforts.

Greater attention in counselor education programs to contextual factors generally and to social support variables more specifically should help to prepare counselors whose ability to understand clients and whose range of counseling strategies is broader than is generally now the case. I believe these outcomes would be beneficial because a broadened repertoire of understanding and activity is apt to result in more varied, individual-specific practice.

However, moving toward a greater focus on social support and natural systems in counselor education is apt to present problems as well. I've already noted that placing greater attention on contextual variables is likely to lead to a reexaminination (and perhaps broadening) of the constructs and models on which many counselor education programs are based. For many educators this is apt to require more than just a minor shifting or expansion of subject matter. Individuals' views of psychological health and personal effectiveness are heavily value laden. To accept that some clients will place responsibility to the group ahead of their own personal needs, preferences, and characteristics in selecting an occupation may require a leap toward cultural relativism that some counselor educators will have difficulty making. Some will not be willing to make it at all. The same issues of value orientation and willingness to broaden or change one's perspective also apply to broadening one's view of such basic constructs as "help," "change," "growth," and "happiness."

Finally, and perhaps even more fundamentally, a greater focus on the role and impact of natural support systems also requires at least a partial reformulation of counselor role. We will be obliged to move away from considering the counseling relationship (individual or small group) as a quiet oasis, insulated from the complicated, often conflicted, interactions and relationships of clients' lives. Often, the counselor's function will be to develop a detailed understanding of the structure and resources of those relationships. Then, armed with that understanding, we will move on to identify and carry out interventions that establish (sometimes, reestablish) the supportiveness of clients' natural systems.

Again, this will probably run against the grain of the established preferences and styles of many people who currently prepare counselors and other helping professionals. Those who derive satisfaction from being the primary source of help, rather than the facilitator of natural systems, are apt to find such a reconceptualization of the counselor role of little interest. Others will consider the shift to a greater emphasis of contextual factors to be a threat to the integrity and coherence of counseling itself.

Not to worry; there will always be instances where the lack of social support springs from barriers located within clients themselves. In those cases, the traditional models for counseling continue to be appropriate and useful. However, exposing students to the alternative role of strengthening the supportiveness of natural systems is apt to prove functional because it becomes increasingly clear that counselors and other professional helpers can't possibly provide all the assistance needed by clients and potential clients. Natural support systems are (for better or worse) involved in the needs and concerns of clients long before we come on the scene; in most cases they will be there after we are gone. The role of strengthening natural systems is a way of spreading counselor impact more widely. In the face of the chronic understaffing found in many counseling operations, imparting the willingness, understanding, and skills required to work with natural support systems is, I believe, a way of contributing to the future relevance and survival of the counselors we prepare.

Conclusion

At the end of this multifocus chapter and the conclusion of the book itself, I find myself asking, "So what's so new about all this?" It's true that most of the specific concepts and applications that have been presented are old wine in new skins. If there is anything that breaks new ground in these discussions, it is, I believe, the integration of material from a wide range of areas and its application to the realities of counseling practice. My intent has not been to displace any existing concepts or to deemphasize current approaches to counseling. Rather, my goal has been to discuss and illustrate how social support—a phenomenon central to human experience—can serve to inform and guide many aspects of counseling practice. The work of the counselor is varied and complex, as is life itself. The more multifaceted our concepts, the more we can discern and understand. The greater our understanding, the broader our base for action will be.

If the foregoing chapters have the effect of broadening and deepening counselors' views and understanding of what they are currently doing, I am pleased. If some practitioners are led to consider a realignment or expansion of their role and activity to place more emphasis on interfacing with clients' natural support systems, I will be deeply gratified.

Appendix A:
Personal Support System
Survey Form

PERSONAL SUPPORT SYSTEM SURVEY

(Adult Form)

Richard E. Pearson, Ph.D.
Syracuse University

This survey is set up so that you start at the back of the booklet and work forward. After you have filled in today's date on this page please turn the pages back until you come to the last page. That page will be numbered "1". When you have finished reading it, turn down the next page, this will be page "2". As you complete each page turn down the next page until you have worked your way back to this page. When you come to this page again, you will have finished the survey.

Name or I.D. (if requested) _____

Date _____ Location _____

General Information

1. Sex: _____ female; _____ male

2. Age _____

3. Parents living? Father: _____ yes; _____ no. Mother: _____ yes; _____ no

4. Number of siblings: _____ sisters _____; _____ brothers

5. Marital status: _____ single; _____ married; _____ divorced; _____ separated; _____ spouse deceased

6. Number of children (if any) _____

7. Highest school grade completed: _____

8. Present (or former if retired) occupation: _____

9. Type of area in which you reside: _____ urban; _____ suburban; _____ small rural town; _____ country

10. How long has your present life situation (e.g., where you live, your work, your family situation) been as it is now?

    _____ years

11. How long has it been since there was an important change in your personal support system (e.g., loss of an important supportor, or a move that separated you from several good friends)?

    _____ years

If you have experienced such a change, would you (in the space below) please describe the nature of the events that affected your system?

9.

How satisfied are you with your support system?

Now that you have described your support system, would you answer the following questions about your satisfaction with it?

A. In general, how satisfied are you with your personal support system

(very satisfied) __ : __ : __ : __ : __ (very dissatisfied)
                     1   2   3   4   5

B. If, to some extent, you are dissatisfied with your system, why? You may check as many of the following as apply to you and add other reasons if you wish.

_____ not enough people
_____ my supportors are too similar, and there are some types of support they can't provide.
_____ I don't see my support persons often enough
_____ though my supportors are sometimes helpful, they sometimes cause difficulty as well
_____ Other (please specify) _____

_____

_____

C. If you are dissatisfied with your support system, do you believe there are things you can do to make it more satisfactory?

_____ yes   _____ no   _____ I don't know

D. If you answered "yes" on item C, what do you think you could do to improve the situation?

_____

_____

_____

E. How satisfied are you with your life situation in general?

(very satisfied) __ : __ : __ : __ : __ (very dissatisfied)
                     1   2   3   4   5

What kind of contact do you have with each person in your system- regular, actual contact, or is this a relationship based primarily upon memory or thought (for example, your relationship with a dead relative, or a distant friend)? Perhaps you've never actually met the person (e.g., an historical figure or well known contemporary person)? but your knowledge of, and thoughts about, them provides you with a a kind of support.

The chart below asks for information about the manner in which your system operates.

How does your system operate?

1. How long has this person been a supporter to you? (give number of years)	2. Do you actually see and talk with this person?		3. If you do have actual contact with this person, how often does it take place?					4. Do you think you are in this person's system?	
	yes	no	daily	weekly	monthly	a few times a year	every few years	yes	no

7.

What types of support do you get from each person you've identified on the previous page? For each person, in the spaces provided, check the type of support (briefly re-defined) that the person provides for you

Types of support you receive from your system

1. Admiration - praise	2. Satisfaction - joy of helping others	3. Love - caring, warmth, affection	4. Physical intimacy - sexuality, intimate contact	5. Companionship - belonging, togetherness	6. Encouragement - boosting, giving confidence	7. Acceptance - respect, confirmation	8. Comfort - reassurance	9. Example - model or example set by another	10. Guidance - advice, direction	11. Help - favors, providing needed resources	12. Knowledge - information, instruction	13. Honesty - candid feedback, opinion	14. Other - (as indicated on page A. 4.)

S .

Your Support System

Who is included in your support system?

First, in column 1, list as many persons as you wish you consider members of your support system. However, please include only those who occupy an important place in the system. Next, in column 2, describe the nature of the relationship these people bear to you. Finally, indicate which other people in your system each person knows.

1. Supporter's name (Use only first names, except in the case of well-known present-day or past figures.)	2. Relationship Who is this person to you? (For example, spouse, friend, mother, well-known person you admire).	3. Who knows whom? List the names of the other persons in the system that each person listed knows.

5.

8. Comfort
the reassurance, comfort you get from those upon whom you can lean.

very important 1 : 2 : 3 : 4 : 5 of no importance

completely satisfied 1 : 2 : 3 : 4 : 5 completely unsatisfied

9. Example
the model or example others provide for you.

very important 1 : 2 : 3 : 4 : 5 of no importance

completely satisfied 1 : 2 : 3 : 4 : 5 completely unsatisfied

10. Guidance
the advice, direction, spiritual assistance others provide.

very important 1 : 2 : 3 : 4 : 5 of no importance

completely satisfied 1 : 2 : 3 : 4 : 5 completely unsatisfied

11. Help
the material assistance received when others do things, or provide needed resources, for you.

very important 1 : 2 : 3 : 4 : 5 of no importance

completely satisfied 1 : 2 : 3 : 4 : 5 completely unsatisfied

12. Knowledge
the intellectual resources, expertise, information you get from others.

very important 1 : 2 : 3 : 4 : 5 of no importance

completely satisfied 1 : 2 : 3 : 4 : 5 completely unsatisfied

13. Honesty
when others honestly tell you about how they, or others, see and feel about you.

very important 1 : 2 : 3 : 4 : 5 of no importance

completely satisfied 1 : 2 : 3 : 4 : 5 completely unsatisfied

14. Other (please describe)
_____
_____
_____

very important 1 : 2 : 3 : 4 : 5 of no importance

completely satisfied 1 : 2 : 3 : 4 : 5 completely unsatisfied

4.

2. Satisfaction
the pleasure you get from being able to help or contribute to others.

very important | 1 : 2 : 3 : 4 : 5 | of no importance

completely satisfied | 1 : 2 : 3 : 4 : 5 | completely unsatisfied

3. Love
the caring, emotional sharing you get from others.

very important | 1 : 2 : 3 : 4 : 5 | of no importance

completely satisfied | 1 : 2 : 3 : 4 : 5 | completely unsatisfied

4. Physical intimacy
the intimate physical contact from others that provides emotional and/or physical satisfaction.

very important | 1 : 2 : 3 : 4 : 5 | of no importance

completely satisfied | 1 : 2 : 3 : 4 : 5 | completely unsatisfied

5. Companionship
the sharing of activities, sense of belongingness, togetherness you get from being with others.

very important | 1 : 2 : 3 : 4 : 5 | of no importance

completely satisfied | 1 : 2 : 3 : 4 : 5 | completely unsatisfied

6. Encouragement
the encouragement, reinforcement, expression of confidence, affirmation you get from others.

very important | 1 : 2 : 3 : 4 : 5 | of no importance

completely satisfied | 1 : 2 : 3 : 4 : 5 | completely unsatisfied

7. Acceptance
the respect, empathy, understanding, trust, or confirmation or affirmation you get from others.

very important | 1 : 2 : 3 : 4 : 5 | of no importance

completely satisfied | 1 : 2 : 3 : 4 : 5 | completely unsatisfied

What are your support needs and how well are they met?

We receive many kinds of support from the persons in our support system. The thirteen types of support that are listed on the next two pages are those most commonly mentioned when persons are asked to tell what it is they receive from their support system.

Each type of support is defined and followed by two rating scales that you are asked to complete:

1) the first rating scale is for you to indicate <u>how important</u> each type of support is to you;
2) the second rating scale is for you to tell <u>how satisfied</u> you are in terms of the amount of this support you receive.

Please complete all of the rating scales by putting a " √ " or a " X " in the space that best describes your judgment. The closer your mark is to the left end of the scale the more importance you attach to, or satisfied you are, concerning the type of support being considered. In contrast, the closer your mark is to the right end of the scale, the less importance you attach to, or satisfied you are, concerning that type of support.

For example, the ratings below indicate that the person attaches a great importance to companionship, but feels that the need for companship is somewhat unsatisfied.

Companionship

(Very important)_√_:__:__:__:__ (no importance)(Completely _:__:__:__√_:__ (Completely
    1   2   3   4   5   satisfied   1   2   3   4   5   unsatisfied)

Importance and Satisfaction Ratings

very   of no   completely
important _:__:__:__:__   importance   satisfied _:__:__:__:__ completely
          1   2   3   4   5   1   2   3   4   5 unsatisfied

1. Admiration
the praise, attention
or interest you get
from others.

2.

INTRODUCTION

Your personal support system - what is it?

Most of us have a number of people who are important to us because they give us various kinds of assistance. In many ways their help makes our lives easier and more satisfying. Their assistance may be of a physical sort, as when someone runs an errand for you or gives you a ride when you have somewhere to go and are without transportation. Also, the help may be emotional in nature as when someone cheers you up when you're feeling sad. Finally, these persons may help by providing information about factual aspects of situations, or information about their opinions or views.

These people may be family, friends, or neighbors whom we see regularly. Also, we may even be helped by people whom we've never actually met. For example, we can be comforted or encouraged by thinking of, or reading about, an inspirational or religious figure.

We may also be helped (in a way) by family or friends whom we no longer see or have direct contact with. Even though we no longer actually come into contact with these people (perhaps because of geographic separation, or their death) they help us because thinking about them brings comfort or satisfaction.

All of these people, both those we actually see and talk to, and those we can only contact in thought and recollection, make up our personal support system. They are the people who support us and make our lives better through the physical, emotional, and informational assistance they give.

This survey was developed as a means of gathering information about the support preferences, needs and resources of people. Some of the questions it poses are:

1) What are your support needs?
2) How well are those support needs being met?
3) Who are the people who make up your support system?
4) How does your system operate (e.g., frequency of contact)?
5) How satisfied are you with your support system?

The rest of this survey is divided into six sections. There is one section for each of the questions just posed. Also, there is a final section that asks for such information as your age, sex, type of area in which you reside.

1.

233

Appendix B:
Rose's Personal Support System
Survey Protocol

PERSONAL SUPPORT SYSTEM SURVEY

(Adult Form)

Richard E. Pearson, Ph.D.
Syracuse University

This survey is set up so that you start at the back of the booklet and work forward. After you have filled in today's date on this page please turn the pages back until you come to the last page. That page will be numbered "1". When you have finished reading it, turn down the next page, this will be page "2". As you complete each page turn down the next page until you have worked your way back to this page. When you come to this page again, you will have finished the survey.

Name or I.D. (if requested) _____Ross_____

Date _____ Location _____

236

General Information

1. Sex: ✓ female; ___ male

2. Age _28_

3. Parents living? Father: ✓ yes; ___ no. Mother: ✓ yes; ___ no

4. Number of siblings: sisters _1_; _2_ brothers

5. Marital status: ✓ single; ___ married; ___ divorced; ___ separated; ___ spouse deceased

6. Number of children (if any) ___

7. Highest school grade completed: _14_

8. Present (or former if retired) occupation: _insurance clerk_

9. Type of area in which you reside: ✓ urban; ___ suburban; ___ small rural town; ___ country

10. How long has your present life situation (e.g., where you live, your work, your family situation) been as it is now?

    _2_ years

11. How long has it been since there was an important change in your personal support system (e.g., loss of an important supportor, or a move that separated you from several good friends)?

    _2_ years

If you have experienced such a change, would you (in the space below) please describe the nature of the events that affected your system?

boyfriend broke off relationship

How satisfied are you with your support system?

Now that you have described your support system, would you answer the following questions about your satisfaction with it?

A. In general, how satisfied are you with your personal support system

(very satisfied) ___ : ___ : ___ : ✓ : ___ (very dissatisfied)
                         1   2   3   4   5

B. If, to some extent, you are dissatisfied with your system, why? You may check as many of the following as apply to you and add other reasons if you wish.

    ___ not enough people
    ✓ my supporters are too similar, and there are some types of support they can't provide.
    ___ I don't see my support persons often enough
    ___ though my supporters are sometimes helpful, they sometimes cause difficulty as well
    ___ Other (please specify) _____

_____

_____

C. If you are dissatisfied with your support system, do you believe there are things you can do to make it more satisfactory?

    ___ yes   ___ no   ✓ I don't know

D. If you answered "yes" on item C, what do you think you could do to improve the situation?

_____

_____

_____

_____

E. How satisfied are you with your life situation in general?

(very satisfied) ___ : ✓ : ___ : ___ : ___ (very dissatisfied)
                         1   2   3   4   5

What kind of contact do you have with each person in your system- regular, actual contact, or is this a relationship based primarily upon memory or thought (for example, your relationship with a dead relative, or a distant friend)? Perhaps you've never actually met the person (e.g., an historical figure or well known contemporary person), but your knowledge of, and thoughts about, them provides you with a kind of support.

The chart below asks for information about the manner in which your system operates.

How does your system operate?

1. How long has this person been a supporter to you? (give number of years)	2. Do you actually see and talk with this person?		3. If you do have actual contact with this person, how often does it take place?					4. Do you think you are in this person's system?	
	yes	no	daily	weekly	monthly	a few times a year	every few years	yes	no
28	✓		✓					✓	
28	✓		✓						?
28	✓			✓				✓	
28	✓				✓			✓	
28	✓			✓					✓
28	✓			✓					✓
17	✓			✓				✓	
28	✓			✓					?
3	✓		✓						?

7.

238

What types of support do you get from each person you've identified on the previous page? For each person, in the spaces provided, check the type of support (briefly re-defined) that the person provides for you

Types of support you receive from your system

1. Admiration - praise	2. Satisfaction - joy of helping others	3. Love - caring, warmth, affection	4. Physical intimacy - sexuality, intimate contact	5. Companionship - belonging, togetherness	6. Encouragement - boosting, giving confidence	7. Acceptance - respect, confirmation	8. Comfort - reassurance	9. Example - model or example set by another	10. Guidance - advice, direction	11. Help - favors, providing needed resources	12. Knowledge - information, instruction	13. Honesty - candid feedback, opinion	14. Other - (as indicated on page A.4.)
✓		✓			✓	✓		✓	✓	✓		✓	
✓		✓			✓				✓				
✓	✓							✓	✓	✓			
		✓		✓		✓							
		✓											
		✓									✓		
		✓		✓	✓	✓						✓	
		✓			✓	✓		✓					
				✓							✓	✓	

6.

Your Support System

Who is included in your support system?

First, in column 1, list as many persons as you wish you consider members of your support system. However, please include only those who occupy an important place in the system. Next, in column 2, describe the nature of the relationship these people bear to you. Finally, indicate which other people in your system each person knows.

1. Supporter's name (Use only first names, except in the case of well-known present-day or past figures.)	2. Relationship Who is this person to you? (For example, spouse, friend, mother, well-known person you admire).	3. Who knows whom? List the names of the other persons in the system that each person listed knows.
Marie	mother	William, Sue, Anne, Walt, Clint, Edna
William	father	Marie, Sue, Anne, Walt, Clint, Edna
Sue	grandfather (mother)	Marie, William, Anne, Walt, Clint, Edna
Anne	sister	Marie, William, Sue, Walt, Clint, Carol, Edna, Ann
Walt	brother	Marie, William, Sue, Anne, Clint, Edna
Clint	brother	Marie, William, Sue, Anne, Walt, Edna
Carol	friend	William, Marie, Anne, Ann
Edna	aunt	Marie, William, Sue, Anne, Walt, Clint
Ann	woman I work with	Anne

8. Comfort
the reassurance, comfort you get from those upon whom you can lean.

very important 1 2 3 4 5 of no importance

completely satisfied 1 2 3 4 5 completely unsatisfied

9. Example
the model or example others provide for you.

very important 1 2 3 4 5 of no importance

completely satisfied 1 2 3 4 5 completely unsatisfied

10. Guidance
the advice, direction, spiritual assistance others provide.

very important 1 2 3 4 5 of no importance

completely satisfied 1 2 3 4 5 completely unsatisfied

11. Help
the material assistance received when others do things, or provide needed resources, for you.

very important 1 2 3 4 5 of no importance

completely satisfied 1 2 3 4 5 completely unsatisfied

12. Knowledge
the intellectual resources, expertise, information you get from others.

very important 1 2 3 4 5 of no importance

completely satisfied 1 2 3 4 5 completely unsatisfied

13. Honesty
when others honestly tell you about how they, or others, see and feel about you.

very important 1 2 3 4 5 of no importance

completely satisfied 1 2 3 4 5 completely unsatisfied

14. Other (please describe)

_____

_____

very important 1 2 3 4 5 of no importance

completely satisfied 1 2 3 4 5 completely unsatisfied

241

2. Satisfaction
the pleasure you get from being able to help or contribute to others.

very important 1 2 3 4 5 of no importance

completely satisfied 1 2 3 4 5 completely unsatisfied

3. Love
the caring, emotional sharing you get from others.

very important 1 2 3 4 5 of no importance

completely satisfied 1 2 3 4 5 completely unsatisfied

4. Physical intimacy
the intimate physical contact from others that provides emotional and/or physical satisfaction.

very important 1 2 3 4 5 of no importance

completely satisfied 1 2 3 4 5 completely unsatisfied

5. Companionship
the sharing of activities, sense of belongingness, togetherness you get from being with others.

very important 1 2 3 4 5 of no importance

completely satisfied 1 2 3 4 5 completely unsatisfied

6. Encouragement
the encouragement, reinforcement, expression of confidence, affirmation you get from others.

very important 1 2 3 4 5 of no importance

completely satisfied 1 2 3 4 5 completely unsatisfied

7. Acceptance
the respect, empathy, understanding, trust, or confirmation or affirmation you get from others.

very important 1 2 3 4 5 of no importance

completely satisfied 1 2 3 4 5 completely unsatisfied

3.

What are your support needs and how well are they met?

We receive many kinds of support from the persons in our support system. The thirteen types of support that are listed on the next two pages are those most commonly mentioned when persons are asked to tell what it is they receive from their support system.

Each type of support is defined and followed by two rating scales that you are asked to complete:

1) the first rating scale is for you to indicate how important each type of support is to you;

2) the second rating scale is for you to tell how satisfied you are in terms of the amount of this support you receive.

Please complete all of the rating scales by putting a " √ " or a " X " in the space that best describes you judgment. The closer your mark is to the left end of the scale the more importance you attach to, or satisfied you are, concerning the type of support being considered. In contrast, the closer your mark is to the right end of the scale, the less importance you attach to, or satisfied you are, concerning that type of support.

For example, the ratings below indicate that the person attaches a great importance to companionship, but feels that the need for companship is somewhat unsatisfied.

Companionship

(Very important) √ _:_ _:_ _:_ _:_ (no importance)
1   2   3   4   5

(Completely satisfied) _:_ _:_ _:_ _√_:_ (Completely unsatisfied)
1   2   3   4   5

Importance and Satisfaction Ratings

very important   _:_√_:_ _:_ _:_   of no importance
1   2   3   4   5

completely satisfied   _:_ _:_√_:_ _:_   completely unsatisfied
1   2   3   4   5

1. Admiration
the praise, attention or interest you get from others.

2.

243

INTRODUCTION

Your personal support system - what is it?

Most of us have a number of people who are important to us because they give us various kinds of assistance. In many ways their help makes our lives easier and more satisfying. Their assistance may be of a physical sort, as when someone runs an errand for you or gives you a ride when you have somewhere to go and are without transportation. Also, the help may be emotional in nature as when someone cheers you up when you're feeling sad. Finally, these persons may help by providing information about factual aspects of situations, or information about their opinions or views.

These people may be family, friends, or neighbors whom we see regularly. Also, we may even be helped by people whom we've never actually met. For example, we can be comforted or encouraged by thinking of, or reading about, an inspirational or religious figure.

We may also be helped (in a way) by family or friends whom we no longer see or have direct contact with. Even though we no longer actually come into contact with these people (perhaps because of geographic separation, or their death) they help us because thinking about them brings comfort or satisfaction.

All of these people, both those we actually see and talk to, and those we can only contact in thought and recollection, make up our <u>personal support system</u>. They are the people who support us and make our lives better through the physical, emotional, and informational assistance they give.

This survey was developed as a means of gathering information about the support preferences, needs and resources of people. Some of the questions it poses are:

1) What are your support needs?
2) How well are those support needs being met?
3) Who are the people who make up your support system?
4) How does your system operate (e.g., frequency of contact)?
5) How satisfied are you with your support system?

The rest of this survey is divided into six sections. There is one section for each of the questions just posed. Also, there is a final section that asks for such information as your age, sex, type of area in which you reside.

1.

244

Appendix C:
Ansel's Personal Support System Survey Protocol

PERSONAL SUPPORT SYSTEM SURVEY

(Adult Form)

Richard E. Pearson, Ph.D.
Syracuse University

This survey is set up so that you start at the back of the booklet and work forward. After you have filled in today's date on this page please turn the pages back until you come to the last page. That page will be numbered "1". When you have finished reading it, turn down the next page, this will be page "2". As you complete each page turn down the next page until you have worked your way back to this page. When you come to this page again, you will have finished the survey.

Name or I.D. (if requested) _____ *Ansel* _____

Date _____ Location _____

General Information

1. Sex: _____ female; _✓_ male

2. Age _22_

3. Parents living? Father: _✓_ yes; _____ no. Mother: _✓_ yes; _____ no

4. Number of siblings: sisters _1_; _1_ brothers

5. Marital status: _✓_ single; _____ married; _____ divorced; _____ separated; _____ spouse deceased

6. Number of children (if any) _1_

7. Highest school grade completed: _12_

8. Present (or former if retired) occupation: _assistant cook_

9. Type of area in which you reside: _✓_ urban; _____ suburban; _____ small rural town; _____ country

10. How long has your present life situation (e.g., where you live, your work, your family situation) been as it is now?

    _6_ years

11. How long has it been since there was an important change in your personal support system (e.g., loss of an important supportor, or a move that separated you from several good friends)?

    _6_ years

    If you have experienced such a change, would you (in the space below) please describe the nature of the events that affected your system?

    parents got divorced

9.

How satisfied are you with your support system?

Now that you have described your support system, would you answer the following questions about your satisfaction with it?

A. In general, how satisfied are you with your personal support system

(very satisfied) $\underline{\quad}$: $\underline{\quad}$: $\underline{\quad}$: $\underline{\quad}$: $\underline{\checkmark}$ (very dissatisfied)
$\qquad 1 \qquad 2 \qquad 3 \qquad 4 \qquad 5$

B. If, to some extent, you are dissatisfied with your system, why? You may check as many of the following as apply to you and add other reasons if you wish.

_____ not enough people
_____ my supportors are too similar, and there are some types of support they can't provide.
_____ I don't see my support persons often enough
_____ though my supportors are sometimes helpful, they sometimes cause difficulty as well
_✓___ Other (please specify) _no friends, no girlfriend_

_____

C. If you are dissatisfied with your support system, do you believe there are things you can do to make it more satisfactory?

_____ yes   _____ no   _✓___ I don't know

D. If you answered "yes" on item C, what do you think you could do to improve the situation?

_____
_____
_____
_____

E. How satisfied are you with your life situation in general?

(very satisfied) $\underline{\quad}$: $\underline{\quad}$: $\underline{\checkmark}$: $\underline{\quad}$ (very dissatisfied)
$\qquad 1 \qquad 2 \qquad 3 \qquad 4 \qquad 5$

What kind of contact do you have with each person in your system- regular, actual contact, or is this a relationship based primarily upon memory or thought (for example, your relationship with a dead relative, or a distant friend)? Perhaps you've never actually met the person (e.g., an historical figure or well known contemporary person), but your knowledge of, and thoughts about, them provides you with a kind of support.

The chart below asks for Information about the manner in which your system operates.

How does your system operate?

1. How long has this person been a supporter to you? (give number of years)	2. Do you actually see and talk with this person?		3. If you do have actual contact with this person, how often does it take place?					4. Do you think you are in this person's system?	
	yes	no	daily	weekly	monthly	a few times a year	every few years	yes	no
22	✓		✓					✓	
22	✓					✓			✓
10		✓							✓
2	✓		✓						✓
2	✓		✓						✓

7.

What types of support do you get from each person you've identified on the previous page?
For each person, in the spaces provided, check the type of support (briefly re-defined)
that the person provides for you

Types of support you receive from your system

1. Admiration - praise	2. Satisfaction - joy of helping others	3. Love - caring, warmth, affection	4. Physical intimacy - sexuality, intimate contact	5. Companionship - belonging, togetherness	6. Encouragement - boosting, giving confidence	7. Acceptance - respect, confirmation	8. Comfort - reassurance	9. Example - model or example set by another	10. Guidance - advice, direction	11. Help - favors, providing needed resources	12. Knowledge - information, instruction	13. Honesty - candid feedback, opinion	14. Other - (as indicated on page A. 4.)
	✓			✓								✓	
				✓				✓					
					✓			✓					

6.

250

Your Support System

Who is included in your support system?

First, in column 1, list as many persons as you wish you consider members of your support system. However, please include only those who occupy an important place in the system. Next, in column 2, describe the nature of the relationship these people bear to you. Finally, indicate which other people in your system each person knows.

1. Supporter's name (Use only first names, except in the case of well-known present-day or past figures.)	2. Relationship Who is this person to you? (For example, spouse, friend, mother, well-known person you admire).	3. Who knows whom? List the names of the other persons in the system that each person listed knows.
Dad	Father	no-one
Mom	Mother	no-one
Bill	friend	no-one
Terry	guy I work with	Gladys
Gladys	woman I work with	Terry

5.

8. Comfort
the reassurance, comfort you get from those upon whom you can lean.

very important 1 2 3 4 5 of no importance

completely satisfied 1 2 3 4 5 completely unsatisfied

9. Example
the model or example others provide for you.

very important 1 2 3 4 5 of no importance

completely satisfied 1 2 3 4 5 completely unsatisfied

10. Guidance
the advice, direction, spiritual assistance others provide.

very important 1 2 3 4 5 of no importance

completely satisfied 1 2 3 4 5 completely unsatisfied

11. Help
the material assistance received when others do things, or provide needed resources, for you.

very important 1 2 3 4 5 of no importance

completely satisfied 1 2 3 4 5 completely unsatisfied

12. Knowledge
the intellectual resources, expertise, information you get from others.

very important 1 2 3 4 5 of no importance

completely satisfied 1 2 3 4 5 completely unsatisfied

13. Honesty
when others honestly tell you about how they, or others, see and feel about you.

very important 1 2 3 4 5 of no importance

completely satisfied 1 2 3 4 5 completely unsatisfied

14. Other (please describe)
_____
_____
_____

very important 1 2 3 4 5 of no importance

completely satisfied 1 2 3 4 5 completely unsatisfied

252

4.

2. Satisfaction

the pleasure you get from being able to help or contribute to others.

very important   1   2   3   4   5   of no importance

completely satisfied   1   2   3   4   5   completely unsatisfied

3. Love

the caring, emotional sharing you get from others.

very important   1   2   3   4   5   of no importance

completely satisfied   1   2   3   4   5   completely unsatisfied

4. Physical Intimacy

the intimate physical contact from others that provides emotional and/or physical satisfaction.

very important   1   2   3   4   5   of no importance

completely satisfied   1   2   3   4   5   completely unsatisfied

5. Companionship

the sharing of activities, sense of belongingness, togetherness you get from being with others.

very important   1   2   3   4   5   of no importance

completely satisfied   1   2   3   4   5   completely unsatisfied

6. Encouragement

the encouragement, reinforcement, expression of confidence, affirmation you get from others.

very important   1   2   3   4   5   of no importance

completely satisfied   1   2   3   4   5   completely unsatisfied

7. Acceptance

the respect, empathy, understanding, trust, or confirmation or affirmation you get from others.

very important   1   2   3   4   5   of no importance

completely satisfied   1   2   3   4   5   completely unsatisfied

3.

What are your support needs and how well are they met?

We receive many kinds of support from the persons in our support system. The thirteen types of support that are listed on the next two pages are those most commonly mentioned when persons are asked to tell what it is they receive from their support system.

Each type of support is defined and followed by two rating scales that you are asked to complete:

1) the first rating scale is for you to indicate <u>how important</u> each type of support is to you;
2) the second rating scale is for you to tell <u>how satisfied</u> you are in terms of the amount of this support you receive.

Please complete all of the rating scales by putting a " √ " or a " X " in the space that best describes you judgment. The closer your mark is to the left end of the scale the more importance you attach to, or satisfied you are, concerning the type of support being considered. In contrast, the closer your mark is to the right end of the scale, the less importance you attach to, or satisfied you are, concerning that type of support.

For example, the ratings below indicate that the person attaches a great importance to companionship, but feels that the need for companship is somewhat unsatisfied.

<u>Companionship</u>

(Very important) √___:___:___:___:___ (no importance)
          1   2   3   4   5

(Completely satisfied)___:___:___:___√_:___ (Completely unsatisfied)
          1   2   3   4   5

Importance and Satisfaction Ratings

1. Admiration
the praise, attention or interest you get from others.

very important ___:___:___:___:___ of no importance
          1   2   3   4   5

completely satisfied ___:___:___:___:___ completely unsatisfied
          1   2   3   4   5

2.

INTRODUCTION

Your personal support system - what is it?

Most of us have a number of people who are important to us because they give us various kinds of assistance. In many ways their help makes our lives easier and more satisfying. Their assistance may be of a physical sort, as when someone runs an errand for you or gives you a ride when you have somewhere to go and are without transportation. Also, the help may be emotional in nature as when someone cheers you up when you're feeling sad. Finally, these persons may help by providing information about factual aspects of situations, or information about their opinions or views.

These people may be family, friends, or neighbors whom we see regularly. Also, we may even be helped by people whom we've never actually met. For example, we can be comforted or encouraged by thinking of, or reading about, an inspirational or religious figure.

We may also be helped (in a way) by family or friends whom we no longer see or have direct contact with. Even though we no longer actually come into contact with these people (perhaps because of geographic separation, or their death) they help us because thinking about them brings comfort or satisfaction.

All of these people, both those we actually see and talk to, and those we can only contact in thought and recollection, make up our personal support system. They are the people who support us and make our lives better through the physical, emotional, and informational assistance they give.

This survey was developed as a means of gathering information about the support preferences, needs and resources of people. Some of the questions it poses are:

1) What are your support needs?
2) How well are those support needs being met?
3) Who are the people who make up your support system?
4) How does your system operate (e.g., frequency of contact)?
5) How satisfied are you with your support system?

The rest of this survey is divided into six sections. There is one section for each of the questions just posed. Also, there is a final section that asks for such information as your age, sex, type of area in which you reside.

1.

255

References

Abramson, S., Seligman, M., & Teasdale, A. (1978). Learned helplessness in human behavior: Critique and reformulation. *Journal of Abnormal Psychology, 87*, 49-74.

Albee, G. W. (1978). *Primary prevention: A fourth mental health revolution.* Philip J. Zlatchin Memorial Award Address, New York University.

Alinsky, S. (1972). *Rules for radicals.* New York: Vintage, Random House.

Allport, G. (1963). *Pattern and growth in personality.* New York: Holt, Rinehart & Winston.

Asher, S. R., & Renshaw, P. D. (1981). Children without friends: Social knowledge and social skill training. In S. R. Asher & J. M. Gottman (Eds.), *The development of children's friendships* (pp. 273-296). New York: Cambridge University Press.

Ashinger, P. (1985). Using social networks in counseling. *Journal of Counseling and Development, 63,* 519-521.

Astin, A. W., & Holland, J. L. (1961). The environmental assessment technique: A way to measure college environments. *Journal of Educational Psychology, 52,* 308-316.

Attneave, C. N. (1969). Therapy in tribal settings and urban network intervention. *Family Process, 8,* 192-210.

Attneave, C. N. (1976). Social networks as the unit of intervention. In P. J. Guerrin (Ed.), *Family therapy: Theory and practice* (pp. 220-232). New York: Gardner.

Bandura, A. (1977). *Social learning theory.* Englewood Cliffs, NJ: Prentice-Hall.

Barkow, J. H. (1977). Human ethology and intra-individual systems. *Social Science Information, 16,* 133-145.

Barnes, J. (1954). Class and communities in a Norwegian island parish. *Human Relations, 7*(1), 39-58.

Beauvais, F. (1977). Counseling psychology in a cross cultural setting. *Counseling Psychologist, 7*(2), 80-82.

Berkman, L. F., & Syme, S. L. (1979). Social networks, host resistance and mortality: A nine-year follow-up study of Alameda County residents. *American Journal of Epidemiology, 109*(2), 186-204.

Blocher, D. H. (1987). *The professional counselor.* New York: Macmillan.

Bogdan, R. C., & Biklen, S. K. (1982). *Qualitative research for education: An introduction to theory and methods.* Boston: Allyn & Bacon.

Bott, E. (1955). Urban families: Conjugal roles and social networks. *Human Relations, 8*(4), 345-384.

Brammer, L. M., & Abregno, P. J. (1981). Intervention strategies for coping with transitions. *Counseling Psychologist, 9*, 19-36.

Braunlich, M. F., Boesharr, D. K., & Esperon, J. P. (1985). *The personal support system survey: Reliability data.* Unpublished Manuscript, Syracuse University, Syracuse, New York.

Brennen, G. (1977). *Work/life segmentation and human service professionals: A social network approach.* Unpublished doctoral dissertation, University of Massachusetts, Amherst.

Brown, B. (1978). Social and psychological correlates of help-seeking behavior among urban adults. *American Journal of Community Psychology, 6*(5), 425-439.

Browne, A. (1982). *High risk lethality factors in abusive relationships.* Paper presented at the annual meetings of the American Psychological Association, Washington, DC.

Bugelski, B. R. (1973). *An introduction to the principles of psychology* (2nd ed.). New York: Bobbs-Merrill.

Burke, R. J., & Weir, T. (1976). Personality characteristics associated with giving and receiving help. *Psychological Reports, 38*, 343-353.

Caplan, G. (1970). *The theory and practice of mental health consultation.* New York: Basic Books.

Caplan, G. (1974). *Support systems and community mental health.* New York: Behavioral Publications.

Carp, F. M. (1975). Lifestyle and location within the city. *The Gerontologist, 15*(1), 27-34.

Cassel, J. (1974). Psychosocial processes and "stress": Theoretical formulations. *International Journal of Health Services, 4*, 471-482.

Chapman, N. J., & Pancoast, D. L. (1985). Working with the informal helping networks of the elderly: The experiences of three programs. *Journal of Social Issues, 41*, 47-64.

Chesler, M. A., & Barbarin, O. A. (1984). Dilemmas of providing help in crisis: The role of friends with parents of children with cancer. *Journal of Social Issues, 40*(4), 113-134.

Christoff, K. A., & Kelly, J. A. (1985). Social skills. In J. L. Matson & S. E. Breuning (Eds.), *Assessing the mentally retarded* (pp. 181-206). New York: Grune & Stratton.

Clark, M. (1983). Recipient-donor relationship and reactions to benefits. In B. M. DePaulo, A. Nadler, & J. D. Fisher (Eds.), *New directions in helping* (Vol. 2). New York: Academic Press.

Claudio, L. C. (1984). The personal support systems of Puerto Rican freshmen college students: Return migrants and nonmigrants (Doctoral dissertation, Syracuse University, 1983). *Dissertation Abstracts International, 44*(07), 2041A.

Cohen, S., & Syme, S. L. (1985). Issues in the study and application of social support. In S. Cohen & S. L. Syme (Eds.), *Social support and health.* Orlando, FL: Academic Press.

Cole, M., & Bruner, J. (1972). Cultural differences and inferences about psychological processes. *American Psychologist, 26,* 867-876.

Combs, A. (1962). *A perceptual view of the adequate personality. Perceiving, behaving, becoming: A new focus for education.* New York: Association for Supervision and Curriculum Development.

Conyne, R. K. (1983). Two critical issues in primary prevention: What it is and how to do it. *Personnel and Guidance Journal, 61,* 331-333.

Conyne, R. K. (1987). *Primary preventive counseling: Empowering people and systems.* Muncie, IN: Accelerated Development.

Corin, E. (1982). Elderly people's social strategies for survival: A dynamic use for social analysis. *Canada's Mental Health, 30*(3), 7-12.

Cormier, W. H., & Cormier, L. S. (1985). *Intervening strategies for helpers: Fundamental skills and cognitive-behavioral interventions.* Monterey, CA: Brooks/Cole.

Cormier, L. S., & Hackney, H. J. (1987). *The professional counselor: A process guide to helping.* Englewood Cliffs, NJ: Prentice-Hall.

Cowan, E. L. (1983). Primary prevention in mental health: Past, present and future. In R. D. Felnes, L. A. Jason, J. N. Moritsugu, & S. S. Farber (Eds.), *Preventive psychology: Theory research and practice* (pp. 11-25). New York: Pergamon.

Cruz-Lopez, M., & Pearson, R. E. (1985). The support needs and resources of Puerto Rican elders. *The Gerontologist, 25,* 483-487.

Danish, S. J., Galambos, N. L., & Laquatra, I. (1983). Life development intervention: Skill training for personal competence. In R. D. Felnes, L. A. Jason, J. N. Moritsugu, & S. Farber (Eds.), *Preventive psychology: Theory, research and practice* (pp. 49-61). New York: Pergamon.

Dodge, K. A. (1983). Behavioral antecedents of peer social rejection and isolation. *Child Development, 54,* 1386-1399.

Dunkel-Schetter, C., & Wortman, C. B. (1981). Dilemmas of social support: Parallels between victimization and aging. In S. B. Kiesler, J. N. Morgan, & V. K. Oppenheimer (Eds.), *Aging: Social change* (pp. 349-381). New York: Academic Press.

Durkheim, E. (1951). *Suicide* (G. Simpson, Trans.). Glencoe, IL: Free Press. (Original work published 1897)

Eaton, W. W. (1978). Life events, social supports, and psychiatric symptoms: A reanalysis of the New Haven data. *Journal of Health and Social Behavior, 14,* 230-234.

Eckenrode, J., & Gore, S. (1981). Stressful events and social support: The significance of context. In B. H. Gottlieb (Ed.), *Social networks and social support* (pp. 43-68). Beverly Hills, CA: Sage.

Edwards, A. L. (1957). *The social desirability variable in personality research.* New York: Dryden.

Eisler, R., & Frederiksen, L. (1980). *Perfecting social skills: A guide to interpersonal behavior development.* New York: Plenum.

Ellis, A. E. (1971). *Rational emotive therapy and its application to emotional education.* New York: Institute for Rational Living.

Erickson, G. D. (1975). The concept of personal network in clinical practice. *Family Process, 14,* 487-498.

Esperon, J. P. (1986). Social support over a life transition: College graduation (Doctoral dissertation, Syracuse University, 1985). *Dissertation Abstracts International, 46*(12), 3601A.

Evans, R. L., & Mobberly, B. D. (1974). Theoretical and empirical assessment of adjustment to civilian living. *Newsletter for Research in Mental Health and Behavioral Sciences, 16*(12), 11-15.

Festinger, L. A., Schachter, S., & Back, K. (1950). *Social pressures in informal groups.* New York: Harper & Row.

Fischer, C. S. (1976). *The urban experience.* New York: Harcourt, Brace, Jovanovitch.

Fisher, J. D., Goff, B. A., Nadler, A., & Chinsky, J. M. (1988). Social psychological influences on help seeking and support from peers. In B. H. Gottlieb (Ed.), *Marshaling social support: Formats, processes, and effects* (pp. 267-304). Newbury Park, CA: Sage.

Frank, J. (1961). *Persuasion and healing: A comparative study of psychotherapy.* Baltimore: Johns Hopkins University Press.

Froland, C., Brodsky, G., Olson, M., & Stewart, L. (1979). Social support and social adjustment: Implications for mental health professionals. *Community Mental Health Journal, 15,* 82-93.

Garrison, J. (1974). Network techniques: Case studies in the screening-linking-planning conference method. *Family Process, 13,* 337-353.

Garrity, T. F. (1973). Vocational adjustment after first myocardial infarction: Comparative assessment of several variables suggested in the literature. *Social Science and Medicine, 7,* 705-717.

Gazda, G. M., Rude, S. S., & Weissberg, M. (Eds.). (1988) Third national conference for counseling psychology: Planning the future. *The Counseling Psychologist, 16*(3).

Gendlin, E. (1962). *Experiencing and the creation of meaning.* New York: Free Press.

Giordano, J. (Ed.). (1976). Community mental health in a pluralistic society [Special issue]. *International Journal of Mental Health, 6.*

Godfried, M. R., & Davison, G. C. (1976). *Clinical behavior therapy.* New York: Holt, Rinehart & Winston.

Goffman, E. (1963). *Stigma: Notes on the management of a spoiled identity.* Englewood Cliffs, NJ: Prentice-Hall.

Golan, N. (1981). *Passing through transitions: A guide for practitioners.* New York: Free Press.

Goldman, W., & Lewis, P. (1977). Beautiful is good: Evidence that the physically attractive are more socially skillful. *Journal of Experimental Social Psychology, 13,* 25-30.

Goldstein, A. P. (1980). Relationship-enhancement methods. In F. H. Kanfer & A. P. Goldstein (Eds.), *Helping people change* (pp. 18-57). New York: Pergamon Press.

Gore, S. (1978). The effect of social support in moderating the health consequences of unemployment. *Journal of Health and Social Behavior, 19,* 157-165.

Gottlieb, B. H., & Schroter, C. (1978). Collaboration and resource exchange between professionals and natural support systems. *Professional Psychology, 9*(4), 614-622.

Gottlieb, B. H., & Todd, D. (1979). Characterizing and promoting social support in natural settings. In R. Munoz, L. Snowden, & J. Kelly (Eds.), *Social and psychological research in community settings* (pp. 184-242). San Francisco: Jossey-Bass.

Gottlieb, B. L. (1978). The development and application of a classification scheme of informal helping others. *Journal of Behavioral Science, 10,* 105-115.

Gottlieb, B. L. (1979). The primary group as supportive milieu: Applications to community psychology. *American Journal of Community Psychology, 7*(5), 469-480.

Gottlieb, B. L. (1981). *Social newtorks and social support.* Beverly Hills, CA: Sage.

Gottlieb, B. L. (1983). *Social support strategies: Strategies for mental health practice.* Beverly Hills, CA: Sage.

Gottlieb, B. L. (1986). Put them together and what have you got? *Journal for Specialists in Group Work, 11*(2), 121-127.

Gottlieb, B. L. (1988). Marshalling social support: The state of the art in research and practice. In B. H. Gottlieb (Ed.), *Marshalling social support: Formats, processes, and effects* (pp. 11-51). Newbury Park, CA: Sage.

Gross, A. E., & Crofton, C. (1977). What is good is beautiful. *Sociometry, 40*, 85-90.

Gross, A. E., Fisher, J. D., Stiglitz, E., & Craig, C. (1979). Initiating contact with a women's counseling service: Some correlates of help utilization. *Journal of Community Psychology, 7,* 42-49.

Gross, A. E., & McMullin, P. A. (1983). Models of the help-seeking process. In B. M. DePaulo, A. Nadler, & J. D. Fisher (Eds.), *New directions in helping (Vol. 2).* New York: Academic Press.

Gurin, G., Veroff, J., & Feld, S. (1960). *Americans view their mental health.* New York: Basic Books.

Hamacheck, D. E. (1965). *The self in growth, teaching, and learning.* Englewood Cliffs, NJ: Prentice-Hall.

Hansell, N. (1970). Decision counseling method: Expanding coping at crisis-in-transit. *Archives of General Psychiatry, 22,* 462-467.

Hansen, F. (1981). Primary prevention and counseling psychology: Rhetoric or reality? *The Counseling Psychologist, 9,* 57-60.

Harker, B. L. (1972). Cancer and communication problems: A personal experience. *Psychiatry in Medicine, 3*(2), 163-171.

Havighurst, R. J. (1972). *Developmental tasks and education* (3rd ed.). New York: David McKay.

Hawley, A. (1973). *Segregation in residential areas: Papers on racial and socioeconomic factors in choice of housing.* Washington, DC: National Academy of Sciences.

Heath, D. (1980). Wanted, a comprehensive model of healthy development. *Personnel and Guidance Journal, 58,* 341-349.

Heitzman, C. A., & Kaplan, R. A. (1983). *Assessment of methods for measuring social support.* Paper presented at the annual meetings of the American Psychological Association, Anaheim, CA.

Heller, K. (1979). The effects of social support: Prevention and treatment implications. In A. P. Goldstein & F. H. Kanfer (Eds.), *Maximizing treatment gains: Transfer enhancement in psychotherapy* (pp. 335-382). New York: Academic Press.

Heller, K., Price, R., Reinharz, S., Riger, S., & Wandersman, L. A. (1984). *Psychology and community change* (2nd ed.). Homewood, IL: Dorsey.

Heller, K., & Swindle, R. W. (1983). Social networks perceived, social support, and coping with stress. In R. D. Felnes, L. A. Jason, J. N. Moritsugu, & S. S. Farber (Eds.), *Preventive psychology: Theory research and practice* (pp. 87-103). New York: Pergamon.

Heubner, L., & Corazzini, J. (1984). Environmental assessment and intervention. In S. Brown & R. Lent (Eds.), *Handbook of counseling psychology.* New York: John Wiley.

Hilberman, E. & Munson, K. (1977-78). *Victimology, 2,* 460-470.

Hinkle, L. E., Jr. (1974). The effect of exposure to culture change, social change, and changes in interpersonal relationships on health. In B. S. Dohrenwend & B. P. Dohrenwend (Eds.), *Stressful life events.* New York: Wiley.

Hirsch, B. J. (1979). Psychological dimensions of social networks: A method of analysis. *American Journal of Community Psychology, 7,* 263-277.

Hirsch, B. J. (1980). Natural support systems and coping with major life changes. *American Journal of Community Psychology, 8,* 159-172.

Hirsch, B. J. (1981). Social networks and the coping process: Creating personal communities. In B. H. Gottlieb (Ed.), *Social networks and social support* (pp. 149-170). Beverly Hills, CA: Sage.

Holohan, C. J. (1982). *Environmental psychology.* New York: Random House.

Hosford, R., & deVisser, L. (1974). *Behavioral approaches to counseling: An introduction.* Washington, DC: American Personnel and Guidance.

Hosford, R., Moss, C., & Morrell, G. (1976). The self-as-a-model technique: Helping prison inmates to change. In J. D. Krumboltz & C. E. Thoreson (Eds.), *Behavioral counseling* (pp. 487-495). New York: Holt, Rinehart & Winston.

House, J. (1981). *Work stress and social support.* Reading, MA: Addison-Wesley.

Hurd, G. S., Pattison, E. M., & Llamas, R. (1981). Models of social network intervention. *International Journal of Family Therapy, 3*(4), 246-257.

Hyman, M. D. (1971). Disability and patients' perceptions of preferential treatment: Some preliminary findings. *Journal of Chronic Diseases, 24,* 329-342.

Ingersoll, B. (1983). *Approaches to combining quantitative and qualitative social support research.* Paper presented at the annual meetings of the American Psychological Association, Anaheim, CA.

Jacobson, E. (1938). *Progressive relaxation.* Chicago: University of Chicago Press.

Jenkins, R., Mann, A., & Belsey, E. (1981). The background description and use of a short interview to assess stress and social support. *Social Science and Medicine, Part E, 10*(4), 404-415.

Jourard, S. (1970). *Personal adjustment.* New York: Macmillan.

Kagan, N. (1964). Three dimensions of cultural encapsulation. *Journal of Counseling Psychology, 11,*(4), 361-365.

Kahn, R. L., & Antonucci, T. (1981). Convoys of socials support: A life course approach. In S. B. Kiesler, J. N. Morgan, & V. K. Oppenheimer (Eds.), *Aging: Social change* (pp. 383-405). New York: Academic Press.

Kanfer, F. H., & Phillips, J. S. (1970). *Learning foundations of behavior therapy.* New York: John Wiley.

Kelly, J. A., (1982), *Social skills training: A practical guide for interventions.* New York: Springer.

Kiecolt-Glaser, J. K., & Greenberg, B. (1984). Social support as a moderator of the after effects of stress in female psychiatric inpatients. *Journal of Abnormal Psychology, 93,* 192-199.

Killilea, M. (1976). Mutual help organizations: Interpretations in the literature. In G. Caplan & M. Killilea (Eds.), *Support systems and mutual help: Multidisciplinary explorations* (pp. 37-93). New York: Grune & Stratton.

Kropotkin, P., (1972), *2.* Boston: Extending Horizons Books.

Kubler-Ross, E. (1969). *On death and dying.* New York: Macmillan.

Ladd, G. W., & Asher, S. R. (1985). Skill training and children's peer relations. In L. L'Abate & M. A. Milan (Eds.), *Handbook of social skills learning and research* (pp. 219-244). New York: John Wiley.

Lakey, B., & Heller, K. (1988). Social support from a friend, perceived support, and social problem solving. *American Journal of Community Psychology, 16*(6), 811-824.

Lanoil, J. (1976). Advocacy and social systems and networks: Continuity of care for adult schizophrenics. *Psychosocial Rehabilitation Journal, 1*(1), 1-6.

Levine, M. (1988). An analysis of mutual assistance. *American Journal of Community Psychology, 16*(2), 167-188.

Lewin, K. (1951). *Field theory in social science.* New York: Harper.

Lewin, K., & Grabbe, P. (1948). Conduct knowledge and the acceptance of new values. In K. Lewin (Ed.), *Resolving social conflicts* (pp. 56-68). New York: Harper.

Lewis, C. E. (1966). Factors influencing the return to work of men with congestive heart failure. *Journal of Chronic Diseases, 19*, 1193-1209.

Lewis, J. A., & Lewis, M. (1983). *Community counseling: A human services approach.* New York: John Wiley.

Lewis, R. A. (1978). Emotional intimacy among men. *Journal of Social Issues, 34*, 108-121.

Liem, G. R., & Liem, J. H. (1978). Social class and mental health reconsidered: The role of economic stress and social support. *Journal of Health and Social Behavior, 19*(2), 139-156.

Likert, R. (1961). *New patterns of management.* New York: McGraw-Hill.

Lin, N., Simeone, R. S., Ensel, W. M., & Kuo, W. (1979). Social support, stressful life events, and illness: A model and an empirical test. *Journal of Health and Social Behavior, 20*(2), 108-119.

Lippitt, R. (1985). Community futuring and planning groups. In R. Coyne (Ed.), *The group workers' handbook: Varieties of group experience* (293-305). Springfield, IL: Charles C Thomas.

Majerovitz, S. D. (1988). Social support for older populations: Let research guide interventions. *Community Psychologist, 22*(1), 7-8.

Maslow, A. (1954). *Motivation and personality.* New York: Harper.

Mayer, P. (1961). *Tribesmen or townspeople: Conservatism and the process of urbanization of a South African city.* Capetown: Oxford University Press.

McClintock, C. C., Brannon, D., & Maynard-Moody, S. (1979). Applying the logic of sample surveys to qualitative case studies: The case clusters method. *Administrative Science Quarterly, 24*, 612-628.

McKinlay, J. (1972). Some approaches and problems in the study and use of services — An overview. *Journal of Health and Social Behavior, 13*(2), 115-152.

McKinlay, J. B. (1973). Social networks, lay consultation and help-seeking behavior. *Social Forces, 51*(3), 275-292.

Mitchell, J. C. (1974). Social networks. *Annual Review of Sociology, 3*, 279-300.

Mitchell, R. E., & Trickett, E. J. (1980). Social networks as mediators of social support: An analysis of the effect and determinants of social networks. *Community Mental Health Journal, 16*(1), 27-44.

Moos, R. H. (1976). *The human context: Environmental determinants of human behavior.* New York: John Wiley.

Moreno, J. L., & Elefthery, D. G. (1975). An introduction to group psychodrama. In G. M. Gazda (Ed.), *Basic approaches to group therapy and group counseling* (2nd ed., pp. 69-100). Springfield, IL: Charles C Thomas.

Mostwin, D. (1972). In search of ethnic identity. *Social Casework, 53*, 307-316.

Michenbaum, D. H. (1971). Examination of model characteristics in reducing avoidance behavior. *Journal of Personality and Social Psychology, 17*, 298-307.

Mitchell, J. C. (1974). Social networks. *Annual Review of Sociology, 3*, 279-300.

Nelson, J. (1980). Support: A necessary condition for change. *Social Work, 25*(5), 388-392.

Neugarten, B. L. (1977). Adaptation and the life cycle. In N. K. Schlossberg & A. D. Entine (Eds.), *Counseling adults.* Monterey, CA: Brooks/Cole.

Pattison, E. M. (1973). Social system psychotherapy. *American Journal of Psychotherapy, 18*, 396-409.

Pearson, R. E. (1979). *The personal support system survey: Network structural and interactive indices data.* Unpublished Manuscript, Syracuse University, Syracuse, New York.

Pearson, R. E. (1982). Support: Exploration of a basic dimension of informal help and counseling. *Personnel and Guidance Journal, 61*(2), 83-87.

Pearson, R. E. (1983). Support groups: A conceptualization. *Personnel and Guidance Journal, 61*(6), 361-364.

Pearson, R. E. (1985). The recognition and use of natural support systems in cross-cultural counseling and therapy. In P. Pedersen (Ed.), *Handbook of crosscultural counseling and therapy* (pp. 299-306). Westport, CT: Greenwood.

Pearson, R. E. (1986). Guest editorial. *Journal of Specialists in Group Work, 11*(2), 65-67.

Pedersen, P. B. (1979). Non-Western psychologies: The search for alternatives. In A. J. Marsella, R. Tharp, & T. Ciborowski (Eds.), *Perspectives on cross cultural psychology* (pp. 77-98). New York: Academic Press.

Pedersen, P. B. (1981). The cultural inclusiveness of counseling. In P. B. Pedersen, J. G. Draguns, W. J. Lonner, J. E. Trimble (Eds.), *Counseling methods* (pp. 3-21). New York: John Wiley & Sons.

Perry, M. A., & Furakawa, M. J. (1980). Modeling methods. In J. D. Krumboltz & C. E. Thoreson (Eds.), *Counseling methods* (pp. 487-495). New York: Holt, Rinehart & Winston.

Phillips, E. L. (1985). Social skills: History and prospect. In L. L'Abate & M. A. Milan (Eds.), *Handbook of social skills learning and research* (pp. 3-21). New York: John Wiley.

Pomerance, B. (1979). *The elephant man: A play.* New York: Grove.

Putallaz, M., & Gottman, J. M. (1982). An interactional model of children's entry into peer groups. *Child Development, 52*, 966-984.

Putney, R. (1981). Impact of marital loss on support systems. *Personnel and Guidance Journal, 6*, 351-354.

Rappaport, J. (1977). *Community psychology: Values, research, and action.* New York: Holt, Rinehart & Winston.

Rathbone-McCuan, E., & Hashimi, J. (1982). *Isolated elders.* Rockville, MD: Aspen.

Riley, M., & Waring, J. (1976). Age and aging. In R. K. Merton & R. Nesbit, (Eds.), *Contemporary social problems* (4th ed.). New York: Harcourt, Brace, Jovanovich.

Rimm, D. C., & Masters, J. C. (1979). *Behavior therapy: Techniques and empirical findings* (2nd ed.). New York: Academic Press.

Rogers, C. R. (1951). *Client centered therapy.* Boston: Houghton Mifflin.

Rogers, C. R. (1962). Toward becoming a fully-functioning person. In A. W. Combs (Ed.), *Perceiving, behaving and becoming.* Washington, DC: Association for Supervision and Curriculum Development.

Rook, K. S., & Dooley, D. (1985). Applying social research: Theoretical problems and future directions. *Journal of Social Issues, 41*(1), 5-28.

Rotter, J. B. (1966). Generalized expectancies for internal versus external control of reinforcement. *Psychological Monograph: General and Applied, 80*(1).

Rueveni, U. (1979). *Networking families in crisis: Intervention strategies with families and social networks.* New York: Human Services.

Sarason, I. G., Sarason, B. R., & Shearin, E. N. (1986). *Journal of Personality and Social Psychology, 50*(4), 845-855.

Sarason, B. R., Sarason, I. G., Hackler, T. A., & Basham, R. B. (1985). Concomitants of social support: Social skills, physical attractiveness and gender. *Journal of Personality and Social Psychology, 49*(2), 469-480.

Sarason, I. G., & Sarason, B. R. (1986). Experimentally provided social support. *Journal of Personality and Social Psychology, 50*, 1222-1225.

Schlossberg, N. (1981). A model for analyzing human adaptation to transition. *Counseling Psychologist, 9*(2), 2-18.

Schutz, W. (1958). *FIRO: A three dimensional theory of interpersonal behavior.* New York: Holt.

Seligman, M. E. (1975). *Helplessness.* San Francisco: Freeman.

Shapiro, E. G. (1983). Embarrassment and help-seeking. In B. M. DePaulo, A. Nadler, & J. D. Fisher (Eds.), *New directions in helping* (Vol. 2). New York: Academic Press.

Shoben, C. (1957). Toward a concept of the normal personality. *American Psychologist, 17*, 183-190.

Shweder, R. A., & Bourne, E. J. (1982). Does the concept of person vary cross-culturally? In A. J. Marsella & C. M. White (Eds.), *Cultural conceptions of mental health and therapy* (pp. 97-137). Dordrecht, Holland: Reidel.

Shumaker, S. A., & Brownell, A. (1985). Introduction: Social support interventions. *Journal of Social Issues, 41*(1), 1-4.

Simos, B. G. (1979). *A time to grieve: Loss as a universal human experience.* New York: Family Service Association of America.

Snygg, D. (1941). *Psychological Review, 48*, 404-424.

Speck, R., & Attneave, C. N. (1973). *Family networks.* New York: Pantheon.

Speck, R., & Rueveni, U. (1969). Network therapy: A developing concept. *Family Process, 8*, 182-191.

Spense, J. (1985). Achievement American style: The rewards and costs of individualism. *American Psychologist, 40*(12), 1285-1295.

Stern, G. C. (1970). *People in context: Measuring person-environment congruence in education and industry.* New York: John Wiley.

Stokes, J. P., & Wilson, D. G. (1983). *The inventory of socially supportive behaviors: Dimensionality, prediction and gender differences.* Paper presented at the meeting of the American Psychological Association, Anaheim, CA.

Stroller, A., & Krupinski, J. (1969). Mental health of immigrants. *Medical Journal of Australia, 2*(7), 365.

Sue, D. W. (1978). World views and counseling. *Personnel and Guidance Journal, 56*(8), 458-463.

Thibault, J. W., & Kelley, H. H. (1959). *The social psychology of groups.* New York: Wiley.

Tolsdorf, C. C. (1976). Social networks, support, and coping: An exploratory study. *Family Process, 15*, 407-418.

Triandis, H. (1985). Some major dimensions of cultural variation in client populations. In P. Pedersen (Ed.), *Handbook of cross-cultural counseling and therapy* (pp. 21-28). Westport, CT: Greenwood.

Trimble, D. W. (1981). Social network intervention with antisocial adolescents. *International Journal of Family Therapy, 3*(4), 268-274.

Turkat, D. (1980). Social networks: Theory and practice. *Journal of Community Psychology, 8*, 99-109.

Unger, D. U., & Powell, D. R. (1980). Supporting families under stress: The role of social networks. *Family Relations, 29*(4), 566-574.

Vaux, A. (1985). Variations in social support associated with gender, ethnicity, and age. *Journal of Social Issues, 41*(1), 89-110.

Velazquez-Acevedo, A. (1983). A study of the relationship between interpersonal support and the incidence of suicidal ideation of Puerto Rican college students (Doctoral dissertation, Syracuse University, 1982). *Dissertation Abstracts International, 44*(07), 2241A.

Walen, S., DiGiuseppe, R., & Wessler, R. (1980). *A practitioner's guide to RET.* New York: Oxford University Press.

Wanlass, R. L., & Prinz, R. J. (1982). Methodologies issues in conceptualizing and treating childhood social isolation. *Psychological Bulletin, 92*, 39-55.

Wilcox, B. L. (1981). Social support in adjusting to marital disruption: A network analysis. In B. H. Gottlieb (Ed.), *Social networks and social support* (pp. 97-115). Beverly Hills, CA: Sage.

Wohl, J. (1981). Intercultural psychotherapy: Issues, questions, and reflections. In P. B. Pedersen, J. G. Draguns, W. J. Lonner, & J. E. Trimble (Eds.), *Counseling across cultures* (revised ed.). Honolulu: University Press of Hawaii.

Wolpe, J. (1982). *The practice of behavior therapy.* New York: Pergamon.

Wolpe, J., & Lazarus, A. A. (1966). *Behavior therapy techniques.* New York: Pergamon.

Yalom, I. D. (1975). *The theory and practice of group psychotherapy* (2nd ed.). New York: Basic Books

Index

Abregno, P., 120
Advocacy, 162, 164, 171
Albee, G., 14
Alinsky, S., 173
Allport, G., 203
Altruism, 31, 70, 202
Antonucci, T., 17
Appraisal support, 96
Asher, S., 90
Ashinger, P., 120
Astin, A., 219
Attneave, C., 19, 153, 154, 157, 159, 160, 163, 164

Back, K., 141
Balance of support to stress, 140, 155
Bandura, A., 114
Barbarin, O., 135
Barkow, J., 202, 213
Barnes, J., 15
Basham, R., 73
Beauvais, F., 213
Belsey, E., 50
Berkman, L., 48
Bicklen, S., 214
Blaming the victim, 143

Blocher, D., 105, 218
Bogdan, R., 214
Bombeck, E., 40
Bott, E., 15
Bourne, E., 213
Brammer, L., 120
Brannon, D., 50
Brennan, G., 120
Brodsky, G., 40, 84, 130, 163, 204
Brown, B., 25
Browne, A., 140
Brownell, A., 143
Bruner, J., 213
Burke, R., 80

Council for the Accreditation of Counseling and Related Programs (CACREP), 217
Caplan, G., 17, 43, 46, 124, 170
Carp, F., 141
Case study material
    Ansel, 76, 82, 177-200
    Arlene, 31-32, 76, 127, 138, 141
    Ben, 29-30, 127
    Carl, 36, 75
    Claudia, 133

Edna, 9-10, 16
Elaine, 33-34, 122
Joan, 28, 126, 141
Rita, 37, 75, 82, 122
Rose, 55, 58-59, 61-65, 67-69
Tammy, 41, 93, 122
Walter, 38, 75
Wilson, 40, 76

Cassel, J., 16, 43, 46
Chapman, N., 103, 126, 148
Chesler, M., 135
Chinsky, J., 39, 41, 61, 69, 75, 78, 79, 80, 82, 86, 104, 134, 205
Christoff, K., 135, 198
Claudio, L., 54
Closed interventions, 152-153, 175
Cohen, S., 49, 50, 71
Cole, M., 213
Combs, A., 36
Community counseling, 20
Community development, 166-167, 171-173
Community psychology, 20
Confrontation of irrational beliefs, 107, 152
Consciousness raising, 169
Consultation with networks, 169-170
Context as a counseling focus, 216-220
Conyne, R., 166, 169, 170, 171, 172, 173, 175, 206, 207, 208
Corazzini, J., 219
Corin, E., 81
Cormier, L., 44
Cormier, W., 44, 97, 108, 110
Counselor activism, 171, 172
Cowen, E., 14, 89
Craig, C., 80
Crofton, C., 92
Cruz-Lopez, M., 54, 64
Cultural encapsulation, 212
Cultural influences on social support, 48

Danish, S., 91
Davison, G., 110
de Visser, L., 114
DiGiuseppe, R., 107
Direct experience, 99
Disengagement from support system, 135
Dodge, K., 75, 76, 88, 89

Dooley, D., 19, 73, 109, 165
Dunkel-Schetter, C., 130
Durkheim, E., 219

Eaton, W., 48
Eckenrode, J., 18, 130, 153, 162, 218
Edwards, A., 71
Effect, law of, 111
Eisler, R., 118
Elders
 abuse of, 140
 rural, 74
Elefthery, D., 102
Ellis, A., 106
Emerson, R., 80
Emotional support, 96
Ensel, W., 48
Erickson, G., 26, 153
Esperon, J., 54, 60, 182
Evans, R., 126
Experience
 corrective, 152
 simulated, 103 vicarious, 101

Factors reducing support availability
 architectural barriers, 141-142
 death of supportor(s), 125
 environmental barriers, 142
 failure to seek or accept support, 80, 205
 lack of transportation, 142
 moving, 125
 oddness, 92
 ostracism, 138
 others' aggression, 140-141
 others' neglect or rejection, 75
 physical attractiveness, 92-93
 prejudice, 123, 128
 resource shortage, 130-132
 social ineptness, 88-89
 social isolation, 76, 82
 shyness, 79
 threat, 120
 withdrawal from others, 77
Family support, 61
Feld, S., 14, 44
Festinger, L., 141
Fischer, C., 14

Fisher, J., 75, 78, 79, 80, 82, 86, 104, 134, 205
Frank, J., 31
Fredericksen, L., 118
Froland, C., 39, 41, 61, 69, 75, 78, 79, 80, 82, 86, 104, 134, 205
Functional measures, 51
Furakowa, M., 114, 116

Galambos, N. L., 91
Garrison, J., 153, 156, 161
Garrity, T., 85
Gatekeeping function, 138, 214
Gazda, G., 217, 219
Giordano, J., 47
Godfried, M., 104
Goff, B., 39, 41, 61, 69, 75, 78, 79, 80, 82, 86, 104, 134, 205
Goffman, E., 78, 104
Golan, N., 14, 44, 125
Goldman, W., 92
Goldstein, A., 118
Gore, S., 18, 29, 130, 153, 162, 218
Gottlieb, B., 17, 30, 34, 62, 65, 77, 107, 116, 117, 120, 127, 140, 146, 147, 155, 174, 212
Gottman, J., 91
Grabbe, P., 103, 216
Greenberg, B., 55
Gross, A., 25, 80, 81, 92
Gurin, G., 14, 44

Hackler, T., 72, 95
Hackney, H., 97, 108, 110
Hansell, N., 156, 170
Hansen, F., 206
Harker, B., 83, 104
Hashimi, J., 39, 68, 81, 142
Havighurst, R., 10
Heath, D., 203
Heitzman, C., 54
Heller, K., 18, 23, 44, 55, 56, 108, 117, 164
Helplessness, 86
Help seeking, 25
Hilberman, E., 140
Hinkle, L., 107
Hirsch, B., 67, 70, 109, 120, 128, 138, 189

Holland, J., 219
Holohan, C., 142
Hosford, R., 115
House, J., 17, 18, 23, 54, 58, 73, 96, 117, 122, 129, 135, 158, 180, 207, 213
Huebner, L., 219
Hurd, G., 158
Hyman, M., 85

Imitation, 114
Immigration, 129
Informational support, 96, 152
Ingersall, B., 52
Interactive measures of support systems, 50, 53, 66-71
  Ansel's system, 187-190
  density, 72, 128, 155, 189
  frequency of contact, 68

Jenkins, R., 50
Jourard, S., 36

Kagan, N., 212
Kahn, R., 17
Kanfer, F., 110
Kaplan, R., 54
Kelley, H., 84
Kelly, J., 135, 197, 198
Kiecolt-Glaser, J., 55
Killilea, M., 12, 13, 42, 208
Kropotkin, P., 12, 213
Krupinski, J., 129
Kubler-Ross, E., 31
Kuo, W., 48

Lakey, B., 55, 56
Lanoil, J., 171
Laquatra, I., 91
Levine, M., 209
Lewin, K., 103, 216, 218, 219
Lewis, C., 85
Lewis, J., 20, 217
Lewis, M., 20, 217
Lewis, P., 92
Lewis, R., 39
Liem, G., 131
Liem, J., 131
Life transitions, 10, 26-28
Lin, N., 48

Lippitt, R., 172
Llamas, R., 158

Majerovitz, S., 68
Mann, A., 50
Maslow, A., 36, 203
Masters, J., 110
Material support, 97
Mayer, P., 15
Maynard-Moody, S., 50
McClintock, C., 52
McKinlay, J., 138, 214
McMullin, P., 25, 81
Mitchell, J., 15, 50, 53
Mitchell, R., 78
Mobberly, B., 126
Moos, R., 219
Moreno, J., 102
Morrell, G., 115
Moss, C., 115
Mostwin, D., 149
Munson, K., 140
Mutual help groups, 13

Nadler, A., 39, 41, 61, 69, 75, 78, 79, 80, 82, 86, 104, 134, 205
Negative network orientation, 77, 80
Nelson, J., 36, 39, 40, 78, 80
Network-focused interventions
  convening, 156
  counselor role, 162
  determining boundaries, 158-159
  difficulties in, 160
  direct and indirect strategies, 148-150
  empowerment, 167-168
  follow through, 164-165
  gaining access, 214
  key figures, 152
  "open" strategy, an example of, 155
  replacement of the system, 146-148
  sessions in the network's setting, 160-161
  skill development, 170
Network map, 159
Neugarten, B., 30
New identities, 138

Olson, M., 40, 41, 44, 84, 130, 163, 204

On time and off time developmental events, 30-31
Operant conditioning, 111

Pancoast, D., 103, 126, 148
Pattison, E., 19, 24, 34, 45, 149, 152, 153, 158, 215
Pearson, R., 46, 54, 131, 148, 209, 210
Pedersen, P., 213, 214, 215
Phillips, E., 10, 110, 116, 117
Pomerance, B., 93
"Poor dear" phenomenon, 81
Powell, D., 163
Price, R., 20
Primary prevention, 171, 206-208
Prinz, R., 89
Professional organizations as vehicles for societal change, 177
Psychobiological theory, 202
Psychodrama, role playing, 102, 162, 198
Psychological health, 203
Putney, R., 29
Putallaz, M., 91

Rappaport, J., 19
Rathbone-McCuan, E., 39, 68, 81, 142
Rational Emotive Therapy (RET), 106-107
Reciprocity of support relationships, 41, 69-70, 87, 88, 205
Reinharz, S., 18
Renshaw, P., 90
Retribalization, 161
Riger, S., 20
Riley, M., 29
Rimm, D., 110
Rogers, C., 195, 203
Role playing, 103
Rook, K., 19, 73, 109, 165
Rotter, J., 169
Rude, S., 217, 219
Rueveni, U., 19, 34, 149, 153, 156, 158, 160, 161, 164

Sarason, B., 55, 73, 74, 95
Sarason, I., 55, 73, 74, 95
Sarason, S., 14, 124
Schachter, S., 141
Schlossberg, N., 26, 31, 10

Schroter, C., 148, 174
Schumaker, S., 143
Secondary prevention, 89
Self-esteem, 79
Self-sufficiency, 80, 203
Seligman, M., 86
Separation from supporters, 67
Shaping of behavior, 112
Shapiro, E., 78
Shearin, E., 74, 95
Shoben, E., 203
Shutz, W., 40
Shweder, R., 213
Simeone, R., 48
Simos, B., 10
Skill training, 116-117, 152
    conversational, 198
    nonverbal self-presentation, 198
    steps in, 118
    support-focused, 119-121
Skinner, B., 111
Snygg, D., 57
Social embeddness, 48
Social learning, 114
Social skill deficit, 10
Social support
    behavioral science perspectives, 12-13
    cultural influences on, 48
    elders and, 39, 71
    effects of, 16-18, 45, 207
    historical perspectives, 11, 13
    individual/environmental variable
        and, 73, 143
    interdisciplinary construct and, 15
    negative effect of, 45
    phenomenological perspectives on,
        56-57
    primary prevention and, 14
    rural elders and, 39
    vicarious, 67
Speck, R., 19, 34, 153
Spense, J., 81
Spousal abuse, 140
Stern, G., 219
Stewart, L., 40, 41, 44, 84, 130, 163, 204
Stiglitz, E., 80
Stokes, J., 71
Strategies contrasted to interventions, 97
Stroller, A., 129

Structural aspects of support systems, 49,
    53, 59
Structural measures of support systems,
    59-65
    composition percentages, 62
    size, 60
    stability, 63-64
Structured Learning Therapy (SLT), 118
Sue, D., 213, 214, 216
Support groups as surrogate support sys-
    tems, 209-210
Support system analysis, 120-121
Swindle, R., 108
Syme, S., 48, 49, 50, 71
System burnout, 134, 204
Systematic desensitization, 110

Thibault, J., 84
Todd, D., 120
Tolsdorf, C., 77, 79, 80, 94, 120, 146
Tocqueville, A., 80
Transitions, 69
Triandis, H., 213
Trickett, E., 78
Trimble, D., 159, 161
Turkat, D., 40, 134

Unger, D., 163
Uniquely preferred supporter, 126-127

Vaux, A., 130, 131, 185
Veroff, G., 14, 44
Vulnerability hypothesis, 79

Walan, S., 107
Wandersman, L., 20
Wanglass, R., 89
Waring, J., 29
Weir, T., 80
Weissberg, M., 217, 219
Wessler, R., 107
Wilcox, B., 62, 67, 128, 155
Wilson, D., 71
Wohl, J., 212
Wolpe, J., 110, 117
Work isolation, 129
Wortman, C., 130
Wren, G., 212

Yalom, I., 209

About the Author

Richard E. Pearson, Ph.D., is Associate Professor of Counselor Education at Syracuse University. He received his doctoral degree in Educational Psychology from the University of Illinois. Among Dr. Pearson's publications are numerous journal articles and chapters focused on such counseling-related topics as group work, life transitions, support groups, cross-cultural variation in natural support systems, and counseling in rural settings. He is a member of the American Association for Counseling and Development, and the American Psychological Association. He has participated in the divisional and regional programs of those associations, serving as the president of the North Atlantic Regional Association for Counselor Education and Supervision, and on the editorial board of the *Journal for Specialists in Group Work*. Dr. Pearson is a recipient of the 1985 Excellence in Publication Award of the National Association for Group Work.